Register for Free Membership to

solutions@syngress.com

Over the last few years, Syngress has published many best-selling and critically acclaimed books, including Tom Shinder's *Configuring ISA Server 2004*, Brian Caswell and Jay Beale's *Snort 2.1 Intrusion Detection*, and Angela Orebaugh and Gilbert Ramirez's *Ethereal Packet Sniffing*. One of the reasons for the success of these books has been our unique **solutions@syngress.com** program. Through this site, we've been able to provide readers a real time extension to the printed book.

As a registered owner of this book, you will qualify for free access to our members-only solutions@syngress.com program. Once you have registered, you will enjoy several benefits, including:

- Four downloadable e-booklets on topics related to the book. Each booklet is approximately 20-30 pages in Adobe PDF format. They have been selected by our editors from other best-selling Syngress books as providing topic coverage that is directly related to the coverage in this book.

- A comprehensive FAQ page that consolidates all of the key points of this book into an easy-to-search web page, providing you with the concise, easy-to-access data you need to perform your job.

- A "From the Author" Forum that allows the authors of this book to post timely updates and links to related sites, or additional topic coverage that may have been requested by readers.

Just visit us at **www.syngress.com/solutions** and follow the simple registration process. You will need to have this book with you when you register.

Thank you for giving us the opportunity to serve your needs. And be sure to let us know if there is anything else we can do to make your job easier.

SYNGRESS®

SYNGRESS®

Software
Piracy
Exposed

Paul Craig
Ron Honick
Mark Burnett   Technical Editor

KEY	SERIAL NUMBER
001	HJIRTCV764
002	PO9873D5FG
003	829KM8NJH2
004	RPZ367DXRP
005	CVPLQ6WQ23
006	VBP965T5T5
007	HJJJ863WD3E
008	2987GVTWMK
009	629MP5SDJT
010	IMWQ295T6T

PUBLISHED BY
Syngress Publishing, Inc.
800 Hingham Street
Rockland, MA 02370

Software Piracy Exposed

Transferred to Digital Printing 2008
ISBN: 1-93226-698-4

Publisher: Andrew Williams
Acquisitions Editor: Jaime Quigley
Technical Editor: Mark Burnett
Cover Designer: Michael Kavish

Page Layout and Art: Patricia Lupien
Copy Editor: Judy Eby
Indexer: Nara Wood

Distributed by O'Reilly Media, Inc. in the United States and Canada.
For information on rights and translations, contact Matt Pedersen, Director of Sales and Rights, at Syngress Publishing; email matt@syngress.com or fax to 781-681-3585.

Acknowledgments

We would like to acknowledge the following people for their kindness and support in making this book possible.

Syngress books are now distributed in the United States and Canada by O'Reilly Media, Inc. The enthusiasm and work ethic at O'Reilly is incredible and we would like to thank everyone there for their time and efforts to bring Syngress books to market: Tim O'Reilly, Laura Baldwin, Mark Brokering, Mike Leonard, Donna Selenko, Bonnie Sheehan, Cindy Davis, Grant Kikkert, Opol Matsutaro, Steve Hazelwood, Mark Wilson, Rick Brown, Leslie Becker, Jill Lothrop, Tim Hinton, Kyle Hart, Sara Winge, C. J. Rayhill, Peter Pardo, Leslie Crandell, Valerie Dow, Regina Aggio, Pascal Honscher, Preston Paull, Susan Thompson, Bruce Stewart, Laura Schmier, Sue Willing, Mark Jacobsen, Betsy Waliszewski, Dawn Mann, Kathryn Barrett, John Chodacki, and Rob Bullington.

The incredibly hard working team at Elsevier Science, including Jonathan Bunkell, Ian Seager, Duncan Enright, David Burton, Rosanna Ramacciotti, Robert Fairbrother, Miguel Sanchez, Klaus Beran, Emma Wyatt, Rosie Moss, Chris Hossack, Mark Hunt, and Krista Leppiko, for making certain that our vision remains worldwide in scope.

David Buckland, Marie Chieng, Lucy Chong, Leslie Lim, Audrey Gan, Pang Ai Hua, and Joseph Chan of STP Distributors for the enthusiasm with which they receive our books.

Kwon Sung June at Acorn Publishing for his support.

David Scott, Tricia Wilden, Marilla Burgess, Annette Scott, Andrew Swaffer, Stephen O'Donoghue, Bec Lowe, and Mark Langley of Woodslane for distributing our books throughout Australia, New Zealand, Papua New Guinea, Fiji Tonga, Solomon Islands, and the Cook Islands.

Winston Lim of Global Publishing for his help and support with distribution of Syngress books in the Philippines.

Author

Paul Craig is currently working in New Zealand for a major television broadcaster, and is also the lead security consultant at security company Pimp Industries. Paul specializes in reverse engineering technologies and cutting edge application auditing practices. Paul has contributed to many books including the first and second editions of *Stealing the Network* (Syngress, ISBN: 1-931836-87-6 and 1-931836-05-1). None of this would be possible without the love and support from his fiancé, Kim Meyer. If you would like to contact Paul for any reason, e-mail: headpimp@pimp-industries.com.
Paul wrote Chapters 2 through 11.

Technical Editor and Contributing Author

Mark Burnett is an independent researcher, consultant, and writer specializing in Windows security. Mark is author of *Hacking the Code: ASP.NET Web Application Security* (Syngress Publishing, ISBN: 1-932266-65-8), co-author of *Microsoft Log Parser Toolkit* (Syngress Publishing, ISBN: 1-932266-52-6), co-author of *Maximum Windows 2000 Security*, and co-author of *Stealing The Network: How to Own the Box* (Syngress Publishing, ISBN: 1-931836-87-6). He is a contributor and technical editor for Syngress Publishing's *Special Ops: Host and Network Security for Microsoft, UNIX, and Oracle* (ISBN: 1-931836-69-8). Mark speaks at various security conferences and has published articles in *Windows IT Pro* (formerly *Windows & .NET*), *WindowsSecrets.com* newsletter, *Redmond Magazine*, *Security Administrator*, *SecurityFocus.com*, and various other print and online publications. Mark is a Microsoft Windows Server Most Valued Professional (MVP) for Internet Information Services (IIS).
Mark wrote Chapter 1.

Contributing Author

Ron Honick has been an electronics engineer for over 30 years, with a career spanning electronic hardware design, research and development, engineering management, and running his own small telecommunications company. A relentless inventor, he holds two patents.

Ron wrote Appendices A through D.

Contents

Foreword
By Mark Burnett

In the last two decades, much of our world has undergone a major transformation. It started slow, switching from rotary to touchtone phones, TV knobs to digital remotes, and vinyl records to digital CD's. Then it rapidly picked up speed as home computers became a standard household appliance and Internet service became a typical monthly utility bill.

At one time the home computer was a tool for students, hobbyists, and businesses. We used our computers to accomplish some specific task, such as balancing our checkbooks or keeping track of our schedules. Now the computer is a content delivery tool serving up communications, entertainment, education and other content. Our lives are now flooded with content. Weekly HTML newsletters in our inboxes link to blogs that link to clips from *The Daily Show*, or highlighting clips from 24-hour network news programs that we already keep up with via RSS feeds. We watch movie segments in games and game segments in movies. There's always more content and there's always another link to follow.

Sometimes the content is the highest quality, and sometimes it just plain sucks. If anything, this cultural transformation has changed how we perceive the value of content. Most often, we see it as something we should get for free—as if being in this modern world entitles us to an unlimited content license. With so much out there free for the taking, a fixed price tag somehow seems out of place. The result? An epidemic of global piracy.

We got a small glimpse of this world back in the eighties. It wasn't uncommon to see someone's family room shelves full of video tapes with hand-written labels of all the latest movies they had recorded. It didn't seem illegal to make a mix tape of your favorite songs for some friends. Into the nineties, even computer stores loaded your PC up with the latest piracy-aiding software when you bought a computer from them.

But that pales in comparison to piracy in this century. Once a couple casual copies are now a couple thousand casual copies. Even beginners are able to locate and download just about any song, movie, game, book, or software application they want. It's so easy to just take what you want.

Piracy, and more specifically, software piracy, is not just about casual copying. To some it is a business. To others it's a contest. Sometimes it's simply belonging to a community. And to some it's an addiction. Piracy invades so many aspects of this modern world, it's impossible to avoid contact with it. This has caused much panic for the content owners. And although they sometimes react with every legal weapon in their arsenal, they have done little to stop the explosive growth of piracy.

This book dives into the unique world of software piracy. It explores the personalities and motivations of those behind much of the illegal software distribution on the Internet. Paul's aggressive investigation and reporting of this world allowed him to explore the inner depths of the software piracy scene and gained him exclusive interviews with some of the most notorious individuals in the scene. Throughout the course of his year-long investigation, Paul sought out the individuals behind this highly organized collection of individuals who somehow flew under most of the public's radar. Everyone seems to know about P2P networks, but few are familiar with top sites, couriers, and other aspects of the software piracy scene.

This book is the result of Paul's extensive investigation. Here, he tells all. This is software piracy.

Chapter 1

Inside
Software Piracy

A Glimpse into
the World of Piracy

Even before researching this book, I had disdain for the
aggressive legal tactics used by the software, music, and
movie industries. The big guys with lots of money are suing
the little guys for making copies of some of their songs. It is
not like these companies are being deprived of anything;
they still own the songs, which they can sell.

Our research into the *piracy underground* opened our
eyes to an entirely new world of *suppliers*, *crackers*, *couriers*,
and *counterfeiters*. We never imagined the immensity of the
warez (exaggerated plural derivative of software) community, or that it pervaded so many aspects of the modern
entertainment culture.

Warez refers to the copyrighted packages distributed by software pirates (or *release groups*). These release groups are exceptionally well organized yet loosely connected associations of members, defined by nothing more than the boundary of the chat rooms they visit.

Although warez is only one small aspect of piracy, the warez scene is vitally important because it is the model for everything. Most every aspect of piracy (movies, MP3s, ISOs, street vendors, and person-to-person [P2P] networks) is joined together by a common interest: the warez scene.

A simple principle drives the warez scene: everyone wants something and the only way to get it is if you have something that someone wants. Crackers have skills that release groups want and release groups have *0-day releases* that *topsites* and *dump sites* want. These sites have enormous hard drives and bandwidth for couriers to distribute the software from one site to the next. Put all of these things together and you have a self-propagating phenomenon that rivals nearly all other organizations.

Terms such as topsites and couriers only hint at the secret but organized world of software piracy. The only way to comprehend it is to become immersed in the warez society, to get inside the scene and reveal its story.

Our approach was simple: we worked our way into a warez group and documented the scene from the inside. We saw first-hand the dizzying hubris that at first disgusted us yet sometimes intrigued us. We experienced the intoxicating excitement, power, and eliteness of being a part of this scene. We understand what it feels like to be a pirate, yet we also see the devastating effects of an activity that its participants presumptuously propagate under the guise of being moral and accomplishing something for the greater good.

This book is the story of a scene that few know of; a scene that exists not only on Russian streets and in Hong Kong markets, but everywhere. A scene where an 18-year-old from New Jersey works alongside a 40-year-old government network administrator in Budapest, uploading software to a site run by a kid in the Netherlands. Some people are allowed entry into the scene because of their skills, while others buy their way in with expensive computer hardware.

This book takes you inside the world of *software piracy*.

Copyright Pirates

Piracy is robbery, an infringement of a copyright. Therefore, anything that is copyrighted can be pirated, and almost anything worth copyrighting is worth pirating.

For many people, small-time infringement is so commonplace— taping a television show, photocopying sheet music, or recording music for a friend—that it is hard to imagine that it hurts anyone. Downloading an MP3 or making a copy of a shareware application does not seem much worse. Many people grew up casually copying files off the Internet, but things have changed in our modern digital world: digital copies do not degrade in quality. One digital copy can quickly become ten, then a thousand, and then a million digital copies. Digital piracy can do real damage. These works are no longer replicas or forgeries of the originals; they *are* the originals.

Copyright owners believe that if you copy something without paying for it, you are stealing. Aggressive media campaigns by the entertainment industry have tried to portray piracy as a crime equivalent to stealing a car or robbing someone. They would have you think that their employees are losing their jobs because you robbed them of their salaries.

Pirates do not believe it is theft, because they are not depriving the owner of their property; theft is *taking* something, and piracy is *copying* something. Pirates argue that they are only depriving the owner of potential revenue, the value of which is debatable because they cannot predict how many people would purchase the work.

"I'd never, ever pay for the 3D graphics apps I pirate that sometimes cost up to ten grand," one pirate who called himself ^Evil told me. "So if I'd never buy it anyway, how can they say that's a loss that I'm using it? At least I'm learning how to use their software and recommending it to others. They don't lose a sale but stand to gain a few more."

He added, "We're not stealing copyrights, we're *infringing* copyrights. If I photocopied someone else's book and gave it away for free, I wouldn't go to jail. Sued maybe, but not put in jail."

^Evil went on to explain more of his philosophy (see the sidebar), making me wonder where he draws the line between motivation and justification.

---

^ Evil's Economy of Piracy

Me: Tell me what you think about piracy.

^Evil: Piracy can be good for software. Okay, we shouldn't steal stuff, duh... we know that. Everyone knows that. But the fact is I'm not going to buy most of that crap anyway. If I bought some of the crap I get I'd be pissed. Piracy keeps the whole thing fair. It's really not any different than capitalism in the sense that consumers control prices and consumers decide who gets rich. Piracy does what competition can't in the software business.

Me: What do you mean by that?

^Evil: Take Windows for example; there are competing OS's but there are no competing Windows. Microsoft is the only company that can make Windows; therefore, they have a monopoly on Windows. In that sense they have no competition and we know that's bad. So, guess what? Piracy is now their competition. That keeps it all fair and that's the way it should work.

Me: So you condone piracy for everyone?

^Evil: We shouldn't condone piracy; we pay for stuff we know we should buy. That's how we reward the good companies. If I get some crap piece of software, I shouldn't have to pay for it. This way I pay only after I'm satisfied. Okay, some people will never pay and some people can't pay. But if you have good product, you'll always make the money. Don't worry so much about the pirates. If we like your stuff, we want you to do well. I'd argue that sometimes the stuff in an *.nfo* file can result in just as many sales as an ad campaign. An ad campaign costs money, but these people just can't stand seeing their stuff copied, even if it does get them more sales.

Me: What do you recommend these companies do?

^Evil: What it comes down to is that people will pirate no matter how much effort is spent trying to stop it. Stop wasting money on

Continued

---

that and spend the money on improving your product. Even us criminals know when a company deserves money for their product. If you do anything to stop piracy, don't worry about us, worry about the people selling the stuff for a profit. We don't make any money at all here. Ever.

Copyright infringement is practiced by people from all walks of life, from organized criminals to educated professionals. There is no age limit. What vary are the motivations to pirate, which may be for financial gain, because some people are too cheap to pay, or because some people love the thrill of the crime. For some, piracy is a consumer voice in price and quality control; to others it actually helps companies by creating a market for their work.

Copyrights are exclusive legal rights granted by a governing entity to the creators of various works. These works must exist in a tangible and fixed form, and can include any expression including creative or intellectual works. Copyrights do not cover ideas or concepts, only the presentation. For example, you cannot copy and sell a software company's application, but you can develop your own application that accomplishes the same purpose. Copyrights protect owners' right to copy and sell their work, import or export their work, copy and sell derivative works, publicly display their work, and assign, sell, or license these rights to others. Copyrights should motivate people to produce works by allowing them to solely profit from those works.

The United States Constitution, Article 1, Section 8 grants the U.S. Congress the right to "promote the progress of science and useful arts, by securing for limited times to authors and inventors the exclusive right to their respective writings and discoveries." It is important to note that it specifies that copyrights exist only for a limited time, meaning that they will eventually expire and that the work will become public domain.

Although the U.S. copyright office accepted the registration of computer programs as early as 1964, computer software was not recognized as intellectual property until the Computer Software Copyright Act of 1980 was passed, which defined compiled applications as copyrightable. Before 1980, a developer could copyright the source code of a computer program but not the compiled application, because only the source code was readable.

Shortly before the Computer Software Copyright Act, Bill Gates passionately demonstrated this point in an interview taped by Dennis Bathory-Kitsz (see *www.thesync.com/geeks/gates1980.html*). During the interview, Gates stated, "There's nobody getting rich writing software that I know of. There are people who would like to stay in business and earn a salary writing packages for these low-cost computers."

In 1976, Gates wrote an open letter to hobbyists in which he stated that less than 10 percent of Altair owners never paid for their copy of BASIC. Gates complained that his royalties on Altair BASIC made the time they spent developing it worth less than $2 an hour. In this letter, he said that he "…would appreciate letters from anyone who wants to pay up… Nothing would please me more than being able to hire ten programmers and deluge the hobby market with good software."

The Computer Software Copyright Act was the beginning of a series of legislation that afforded software developers the same rights as authors of other works, and made software development a profitable industry.

Nevertheless, even after this legislation passed, legal authorities were hesitant to pass or enforce laws addressing copyright infringement that did not involve making a profit. Consequently, computer hobbyists felt comfortable trading software without fear of retribution.

By this time, the social aspect of piracy began to grow. Hordes of Amiga, BASIC, and C64 enthusiasts frequently gathered in large numbers, holding weekly computer *meets* in local town halls and universities. Intent on sharing tips, giving advice, and trading pirated software among themselves, this was the original manifestation of the modern day P2P environment—socially fueled and uncontrolled by any legal authority. Piracy became an access key to an underground world of like-minded people and drew much popularity with computer enthusiasts. That underground world continues to grow, so much so that entire online communities have formed around piracy.

First Contact

Our trip into the world of software piracy began last summer on the last day of DefCon. Our first contact, referred to as "Rodan," was in a chat room talking about DefCon. I began to chat with him, telling him I was at DefCon, too, and he described himself to me. "I have long black hair and I'm wearing a black t-shirt, black jeans, and black leather boots." Of course, anyone who has ever been to DefCon would realize that description hardly distinguishes him from any of more than two thousand other attendees. "My t-shirt says pr0n star," he added. Surprisingly enough, we ran into him in less than an hour.

In the months we spent preparing this book, we made sure our Internet Relay Chat (IRC) clients were constantly connected to various piracy-related IRC channels. The more we learned about the scene, the more we were able to locate the secret IRC channels. We conversed just enough so that people would get used to seeing us around. Eventually, everyone just assumed we belonged there.

The channel where we met Rodan was one of the first channels we entered that was operated by a release group. IRC is a crucial element of the software piracy scene. In fact, it is so important that some of the larger release groups operate their own private IRC networks complete with Secure Sockets Layer (SSL) encryption and public key certificates. Their channel, or *chan*, is what makes a group a group.

Many groups originated from early computer enthusiasts who met at local computer clubs by connecting via the bulletin board system (BBS) world. These systems were used exclusively by pirates to discuss new techniques being used to defeat software protections, and to maintain the complex roles each member plays in the group. With the growth of the Internet, IRC became the place to connect.

It's their office, but it's also their help desk, break room, bar, and sometimes confessional. Even if the channel doesn't have much chatter, just being connected with friends keeps the piracy groups together.

Although the security measures of each group vary, most have at least a couple of *bots* (scripts that respond to certain actions or commands entered in the channel) to maintain access and prevent attacks. For example, a bot can automatically ban certain users and automatically give operator status to others upon entering. The bots prevent attackers from taking over a channel, and attempt to protect those users in the channel. Some groups write sophisticated scripts to relay chats across different networks or to look up information about software releases or File Transfer Protocol (FTP) sites. The first thing that happens when you officially join a group is that someone adds you to the group's bot.

It was midday in the middle of a Las Vegas summer. We had just sat down at a table in the shade when Rodan walked past us. He looked just like everyone else, but his t-shirt had the words "pr0n star" in thick white letters.

Rodan, tall and thin, walked by with small dark glasses, a tight black long-sleeved t-shirt, black jeans, and long black leather boots. He looked somewhat Asian, and his long thin black hair hung over his shoulders.

"Rodan!" I called out.

He glanced towards me and acknowledged me by slightly nodding his head upward.

He walked around the pool then along the backside of a row of lounge chairs, and finally sat down across from us at the table. "You that guy I was chatting with earlier?" he asked in a soft, intellectual voice that hardly matched his appearance.

"Mhmm," I answered

We spoke for a few moments but he seemed too distracted to carry on much of a conversation. Shortly, a friend of his approached and they began talking among themselves. They got up and left the table. I felt pretty lame and somewhat disappointed because I knew he had many contacts in the software piracy scene.

Later that afternoon we passed again, and once again he acknowledged me by slightly nodding his head upward.

Later that night I saw a completely different side of him. I was walking into the Hard Rock casino to meet some friends and I heard a voice calling me: "Dude!"

"Dude!" he repeated.

I glanced over and saw Rodan waving me to come over to the bar where he was sitting with some friends, some of whom turned out to be members of the same release group as him. I walked over and he began talking to me as if I we had known each other for years. He introduced me to his friends by my IRC nickname, prompting a couple of familiar "ohs" from those who had seen me in their channel. The rest of the night we talked about warez.

The Scene People

Piracy's increased popularity has given birth to underground piracy groups and the existence of the *scene*. This scene is a collection of piracy enthusiasts from all groups and lifestyles. Scene activity and piracy group hierarchy are a large part of what this book focuses on. For many, the scene is their life. Whether from Hungary, Canada, or Sweden, they all spend a part of their life in the scene.

During that one night at the bar, I gained more insight into the scene than I had from reading the hundreds of text files and other documents I found on the Internet. In my mind, the scene evolved from a bunch of anonymous thieves to real people with real lives. I realized that there was so much more to piracy than free software or financial gain, at least on the level that these guys operated at. Each of them had complex reasons for taking the risks they do and continue to do daily, mostly without any financial compensation. Something motivated these guys, but it certainly wasn't money.

"Rodan"

I got a chance that night to speak with Rodan. I found out he operated an FTP dumpsite for the group. A dumpsite is a second-level distribution site, rivaled in size and importance only by several dozen topsites worldwide. "The releases get to my site minutes after hitting any topsite," he told me.

"I see gigabytes of traffic a day leaving my network," he added, "I just upgraded my storage to three terabytes."

They say you can't understand someone until you have walked a mile in his shoes. But, after just a few minutes with Rodan his motivation was clear: he was a collector. He obviously would never use or even open the tens of thousands of software applications stored on his servers, he just loved the idea of having them. Our short conversation was filled with *gigabits of traffic, terabytes of storage,* and *hundreds of ISO's*. He could just as easily have been talking about his vintage wine or his AOL CD collections. And, despite how much he already had, he always wanted more.

I was intrigued so far, but I still had a lot of unanswered questions. For example, why would one spend so much time and risk just to collect stuff? How do you stop someone like this? Threaten more criminal punishment or civil retribution? No.

"Fre0n"

That night I also got a chance to meet another group member named "Fre0n." He looked like the typical American college-aged male. He was athletic, had short blonde hair, and a trace of a tan. Once we started talking, however, it became clear that his outward appearance was a cover for the true geek that he was.

Fre0n was a cracker. He first learned to crack when he was 14 and has been through several large cracking groups. One thing was clear: he did not crack to show off his skills or gain respect from others. He cracked because he loved it. In fact, he was obsessed. I saw it manifested through his rapid foot tapping and tick-like blinking. I could have talked with him all night about cracking, and he would never have considered sleep, food, or anything else. Even as we spoke, he was completely unaware of what was happening around him or that all of his friends had already left. Perhaps the only thing he was aware of was that he was *not* cracking at that moment.

We talked for several hours, but he kept my interest the entire time. We talked about key file protection, dongles cracking application program interface (API) hooking, in-memory patching, FlexLM, IDA Pro, and just about anything else related to cracking.

By the time we finished, it seemed like the whole scene revolved around crackers. In fact, the way Fre0n explained it, the entire software industry revolved around crackers. Of course, he was egotistical, but I couldn't help but admire his passion for cracking.

We finally parted ways and returned to our hotels. Despite just a few hours sleep, the next morning I was back on IRC and to my surprise, so was everyone else. That morning the bot sent me an invitation to join the group's other channel—their private channel.

"kEM0"

Over the next few months, I had a chance to speak to many others in this and other groups. It was clear that there was no such thing as a *typical* pirate. Sure, free software is a common thread, but each had their unique reasons for being there.

"It's my rebellion. Some guys ride Harley's, I pirate software," a 40-year-old who went by the pseudonym "kEM0" told me, "I have spent more than twenty years disciplined in military service. The crew here is my connection to the civilian world; it's the only exposure I have to life on the other side."

As I spoke with him, kEM0 told me that he held a sensitive position with North Atlantic Treaty Organization (NATO). Despite the risks involved, he still participated.

"If I ever got found out, my life would be over," he told me, "jail instantly, pension gone."

kEM0 has been a programmer since he was 17. He graduated from school two years early and immediately went into the military. "I spent seven years carrying a rifle, going to all the shit holes of the world," he explained. "Then I decided I wanted to fly instead."

"When I was being cleared for this job, I dropped out 'til the checks on me were done. I have friends that work in military intel, and they let me know when the screening was done. A couple of them are the worst MP3 and movie hounds you have ever seen."

After he was cleared for his job, he was right back into the scene.

"I've been sucked into the vacuum; I can't get out," he confessed.

For kEM0, it was all about friends and loyalty. He explained to me, "Now, I have known a lot of these guys for so many years, I even send them stuff for Christmas. If they ever needed it, I would help some of these guys out in real life. They are friends. Not online only, but real friends from many different countries around the world."

"Recreant"

While talking to people in the scene, we repeatedly heard the same stories: everyone was risking something to be a part of the scene, but the risk was worth it. People don't take these risks for money alone. They usually gain something deeper, something that feeds their basic human needs. Sometimes it's not just their own needs they seek to satisfy, but also the needs of society as a whole.

I spoke to "Recreant," the leader of a medium-sized utility group. They had their glory days once but are now smaller and focus more on the quality of their releases. They often release expensive CAD/CAM or other specialty software that many people in many countries cannot afford.

These people who once felt shame and regret for what happened to their country were now free but unable to compete in the world economy. They finally broke from the structure of socialism where prices are fixed by the government, to a world where prices are based on the U.S. cost of living. How do you explain to them that they will have to work 15 weeks just to buy their copy of Microsoft Office? Obviously, you can't; therefore, this country has one of the highest piracy rates in the world.

For Recreant, it's the political cause that keeps him going. He is leveling the playing ground for his own community. Not only is he helping people, he's helping *his* people. Recreant explained his point of view with one simple sentence: "It's all a conspiracy. I'm just part of it. Maybe God heads it all."

Social and personal needs fuel piracy, not greed. (See the sidebar *0xDEADBEEF: An Interview* later in this chapter).

Figure 1.1 shows a group application for Razor 1911, a piracy group formed in 1985. Compare that to one from a decade later (see Figure 1.2) and you can see that the tone is still the same: joining the ranks of the elite. More recently, Razor 1911 *.nfo* files make no mention of becoming a member. It is so elite that you don't ask them to join; they will find you if you have the proper skills.

Figure 1.1 Razor 1911 Piracy Group Application Form

```
        Razor 1911 : Application to Become a Razor 1911 Courier
Don't fill this out unless you are able (and intend) to call out three
or more hours a day to elite systems to trade the newest in IBM games.

Don't fill this out if you're not prepared to give 110% every day, to
make 'elite' synonymous with 'Razor Courier.'

Don't fill this out if you're not ready to meet the challenge of being
a part of the oldest and most respected cracking brotherhood on IBM.

... and don't fill this out if you call out on less than two modems.
```

Figure 1.2 Razor 1911 Piracy Group 1996 Application Form

```
        So, you're interested in becoming a Razor 1911 Courier.
Razor 1911 is always on the lookout for talented new couriers.  If you
think you are good enough to join the ranks of the elite, leave us a
mail of your voice information and what you're capable of doing.  If
you do not leave us your voice info, you will not be contacted at all!
        For a BBS courier position email xxxxxxxxxxxxxxxxxxxxxx
        For a NET courier position email xxxxxxxxxxxxxxxxxxxxx
```

The following interview describes how much more secret the scene has become over the years. On the other hand, this secrecy and eliteness adds to the appeal for those who seek this.

0xDEADBEEF: An Interview

Me: How would you describe your role in your group?
0xDEADBEE7: "Elder Statesman" LOL.
Me: How long have you been in your group?
0xDEADBEE7: Must be 6+ years now, I think. Time is so malleable when you're having fun. I used to work on my own outside the...ahem "scene." I crack what I like to crack. The cool thing about this group is there is no juvenile rush to put out loads of crap: we do (mostly) the apps we like.
Me: How and why did you learn to crack?
0xDEADBEE7: Well, I'm a programmer. I learned FORTRAN 77 way back when the applications you paid for came with source code. I came to cracking through the rise of binary-only programs and "Intellectual-Property" restrictive licenses. I think a binary-only program is by definition unfit for the purpose for which it is intended, and the people who sell them would be prosecuted under trade-descriptions legislation, if there was any justice in this world.
Me: When you run into a difficult crack, do you try to finish it or move on to get more releases?
0xDEADBEE7: I continue 'till I'm out of ideas, then move on. I am not concerned one iota with releases. I often return to old targets if I get a brainwave.
Me: So, you'd rather finish something you started than crack more software?
0xDEADBEE7: I spent 8 months on and off getting one product the first time. Well I've been beaten many times, but I learned something new from nearly all of them.
Me: Are you ever afraid of the risks you take?
0xDEADBEE7: There isn't really a brief answer to that, but I'll try: I'm as capable of denial as anyone else, so I can put any fears I have out of my mind. That being said, if I ask myself the question: "Am I really afraid that I might have my life ruined by some thieving, corrupt collection of multinationals in cahoots with a bought and paid for state

Continued

apparatus?" then the answer is no. I'm old enough to have had some real troubles in my life, including nearly being killed on a couple of occasions, so a lame prison sentence or fine wouldn't really bother me too much.

Me: Do you ever feel any guilt or remorse for what you do?

0xDEADBEE7: Of course; I suffer the same self-doubt as anyone else, and in the event that my fundamental philosophy is totally wrong, then I might've hurt some people unnecessarily. An example to illustrate: a database app I cracked. Back in the early days of that product, I released full versions of the software by decrypting the ZIP archives it was released in. I was approached by the author, who made a good case that I was hurting his business, so I stopped. Not necessarily out of guilt per se, but because he was so civil and polite and logical about it. He felt I was hurting his business, so I gave him the benefit of the doubt. He made it clear that anyone who asked could have a full version for development and evaluation purposes, so I thought that was very reasonable.

Me: If one of these companies hired you to protect their software, would you take the job?

0xDEADBEE7: No.

Me: Will you ever stop cracking, quit the scene?

0xDEADBEE7: I don't feel I would ever have to quit the scene, because I don't feel I'm part of it. Here we have a few friends that get together on the 'net, have some fun, and talk a load of old bollocks. Nothing more, nothing less.

Me: What motivates you to crack software?

0xDEADBEE7: Its difficult to summarize my motivation for cracking, there are many reasons. First, I'm not much into this ultra-capitalist thing. I think that intellectual property laws are ripping (PPL) off left, right, and center. There is no such thing as intellectual property in the sense that PPL talks about it nowadays.

Me: You say people are being ripped off so you are helping people who can't afford the software?

0xDEADBEE7: No. I think you slightly misunderstood. It's not the price of software per se that rips people off, it's the fact that I think they're only being sold half a product. The beginning and end of protection for software is copyright law; not patents, not "Intellectual

Continued

Property." My basic motivation is political, I suppose. The intellectual challenge is a bonus, as is the thrill/fear factor. But I can't, of course, answer for other crackers.

Me: Okay, so this is a form of protest?

0xDEADBEE7: A protest? I wouldn't give myself that much credit. "Doing my bit" would be more accurate. The commonality of man is at least equal to the individuality of man. It's complicated, but let's just say I have problems living in a world where everything is a product to be exploited and sold.

Me: So, what do you think about pirates who profit?

0xDEADBEE7: Just another corporation.

Me: Are you saying that software should be free?

0xDEADBEE7: No. Listen, I think that people should be able to live off their labors. That doesn't mean I think people should be able to live off other people's labors. I'm a professional musician. That's the only other thing that I do apart from sit around with my philosophical friends drinking coffee and talking shit. I do programming on the side.

Me: Your career is being a musician and your hobby is programming?

0xDEADBEE7: One of my first jobs after leaving college was in the military processing meteorological data about gas dispersion that only later I realized could be used to facilitate more effective biological weapons.

Me: So, what happened?

0xDEADBEE7: So I quit and became a street musician. The best time of my life was in the summer of 1988, when I had only the clothes I wore and a mandolin.

As I spoke to various people in the scene, I saw certain themes emerge. Everyone's motivations are different on the surface but have some common elements.

"It's the only way I feel like I'm accomplishing something, managing the group; I'm addicted," one young group leader told me.

"It's being part of something so exclusive that I can't give it up. People would kill to get access to the sites I get and know the people I know," another long-time scene junkie told me.

I heard these words repeatedly; words like junkie, obsessed, loyal, fascinated, devoted, and passionate. These aren't the words of criminals; they are the words of addicts. They may be addicted to the challenge of cracking, the race for the release, the status of being elite, or the flood of technology. These are human people feeding human needs. Piracy isn't their hobby; it's the core of their human relationship. And that's not something you can easily take away from people.

Chapter 2

The History of Software Piracy

Humble Beginnings

Piracy and counterfeiting has been widespread since the dawn of artistic expression. In medieval times, counts and kings demanded paintings from high-class painters, but often received forgeries or low-quality replicas. So began the idea of a replica—a copy that impersonates the real McCoy.

Digital piracy is much younger. When personal computers first came on the public market in the late 70s, the notion of what role software would play was very different from what it is today. Until the Computer Software Copyright Act of 1980, software was not recognized as intellectual property, so there were no laws against theft or reproduction. When the Computer Software Copyright Act was implemented, software was defined as "literary work," thereby making programmers the equivalent of modern day literary authors.

In late 1989, the U.S Patent Office began to issue patents to software developers, giving birth to the notion that all digital media is the intellectual property of the author; therefore, the author owned the rights to the compiled program and the underlying source code.

Software piracy's origins are very innocent in nature. Before pirated material became hot property, before the widespread use of the Internet, and even before laptops and CDs, there were computer geeks.

Computer geeks are universal and are the forefathers of software piracy. Piracy began in the 1980s when computer technology was still new. Computer software was either for extreme hobbyists or large corporations. The few computer geeks lucky enough to have their own computers at home were few and far between.

Computer geeks loved their computers and were proud to own such a marvelous piece of technology. Owning a computer meant you had the ability to solve complex mathematical equations at home, or run one of some 20 available commercial software packages at any time.

Computer geeks flocked to local universities, which held monthly computer clubs where computer geeks met to share ideas and talk about their computers. At this point in time, few very people even knew what a computer was, let alone held a conversation about one, so, meeting another computer geek was a real treat. These computer clubs offered a way for club members to share the software that they had written with other members. Some of the first games ever developed were first shown off in computer clubs.

PIRACY FACT...

Computer club members designed many software firsts. Most note-worthy is the first application designed to play a piece of music from a computer by using the in-built 8-bit "beep" speaker.

It was in the social computer club environment that piracy first appeared. Although computer geeks had already invested a substantial amount of money in their home computers, most computer owners were not wealthy. In many cases, commercially available software designed to run on these computers was more expensive than the computer itself. After all, computers and software were designed for large corporations with large technology budgets.

The first act of piracy was probably something like this:

```
Geek 1:Man, I wish I had a compiler, I would love to make my own
applications, I want to make something I call a "Spreadsheet", so I can
do my accounts with, I think it will be really handy.
Geek 2:My company just bought a copy of that compiler, ill copy the disk
and bring it next month for you.
Geek 1:Oh wow man thanks, I have a copy of Edit the editor v1, ill swap
you if you like.
Geek 2: Wicked, I need an editor, its a deal!
```

Computer clubs soon became "swap meets" where computer geeks could share applications that they had obtained from other computer clubs. Computer geeks were curious about what their computers could do. Without piracy, they could never have experimented with technology and never written their own applications. It is important to note that many of these early software pirates went on to start some of the most successful game development companies in the world. Experimentation with software and the availability of software piracy was essential to the success of computers and software.

Computers and software grew in popularity. By the late 80s, there were hundreds of home computers. Although still not mainstream, computer technology was having a profound effect. Computer clubs were now relatively common. Groups posted advertisements in newspapers looking for new members and computer geeks everywhere began joining.

Around this time, a new era of computer club called Bulletin Board Systems (BBS') was almost entirely digital, and its members could be physically located anywhere. A BBS was a computer that everyone could dial into using their phone line and modem. Users could connect a modem and soon have access to a text-based, menu-driven interface. Message boards, online chat, file archives, games—BBS' were what computer users had dreamed of for years. Now they could socialize with other computer geeks from home. (See Figure 2.1.)

Figure 2.1 Textual Interface of a BBS System

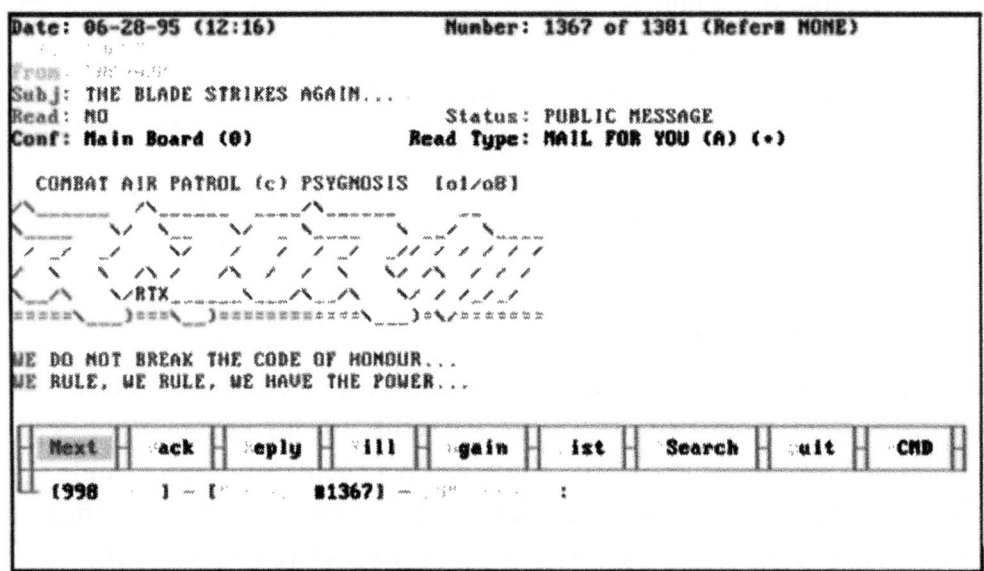

PIRACY FACT...

In every modern day piracy group, you can still see remnants from the BBS era. The American Standard Code for Information Interchange (ASCII) played a huge role in BBS', since the menu interface was entirely text driven. ASCII was used to design pictures and logos from printable characters. Complicated and colorful pictures could be created that were small in size and high in detail. ASCII is still used today; the use of ASCII has not changed in more than 20 years. (See Figure 2.2.)

Figure 2.2 God's Realm: DrinkOrDie

With time, both BBS' and piracy grew drastically. BBS' spawned the first piracy groups; groups that would race to crack and upload the latest software to their affiliated BBS'. Although the piracy scene was miniscule in size, it was growing at a rapid rate thanks to technology. Soon, 5- and 10-node BBS' began appearing, some capable of speeds as much as 9600 baud.

PIRACY FACT...

A node is an available phone line and modem. Five nodes allow five users to simultaneously login, which is useful for chatting with other group members. A connection speed of 9600 baud means that the connection is capable of 9600 bits per second (bps).

Modern modems are capable of connecting at 56,600 bps and can transfer a CD worth of data in under a week. A 9600 modem would take a month and a half to transfer a CD worth of data.

Pirates loved the 9600 bps speed. Original BBS' were only capable of 300 bps, therefore, it would take over three years to transfer a CD worth of data.

BBS' began to bulk up in size, some containing more than a gigabyte (GB) of online storage. Games and applications were often only a few floppy disks in size. A GB could hold over 700 floppy disks worth of information, roughly 250 applications or games.

BBS' were very popular; pirates from all over the world wanted to call them to access their often massive repositories of data. A BBS in Sweden may have users from Australia, Russia, and America. Although many do not know this, the popularity and growth in the hobby phone "phreaking" was greatly fueled by BBS' and piracy.

PIRACY FACT...

Phone phreaking involves hacking the phone system, sending specialized tones or carrier signals in order to fool the phone exchange into giving you a free long-distance call.

Pirates needed to be skilled phone phreakers in order to access BBS' out of their local calling range. Although phone phreakers originally developed the system and tools, pirates were by far the largest users of the phreaking devices.

Piracy groups continued to grow in size. There was not an excess of software produced, but pirates managed to crack and release almost everything created. For the first time, the software industry began to feel the burn of piracy.

A text published by the Independent Association of Atari Developers (IAAD) states the dissatisfaction and level of frustration held by early software developers, many of whom were going bankrupt because of piracy. (See Figure 2.3.)

Figure 2.3 Angry Atari Software Developers

A good example of the speed at which pirates can destroy the
sales potential of a new release is shown by the upload date on
this entry found on the Rats Nest (the notation "Off" indicates
that this file has been removed, probably when a later version
superceded it

336 | Warp9370.Zip   --Off-- 09-13-92 Warp 9 v. 3.70 - Glendale Release

CodeHead released this version on Saturday, September 12, 1992 at
the Glendale AtariFaire. By Sunday, before the second day of the
show was even over, it was already in distribution by pirates.

The BBS referred to here, "The Rats Nest," was located in Loma Alta, California, and in its day, was one of the largest Atari pirate BBS' on the west coast.

Although software developers were angry, there was little law enforcement could do. Computer forensics was unheard of and most law enforcement agencies still did not have computers. Organizations such as the Software Publisher's Association (SPA), the Canadian Alliance Against Software Theft (CAAST), the Florida Alliance of Assistive Services & Technology (FAAST), and the Business Software Alliance (BSA) were created in an attempt to stem the popularity in trading copyrighted information. These organizations offered rewards for information leading to the arrest of a software pirate. However, little could be done against the piracy epidemic; by 1994, there were over 10,000 active BBS' in the United States alone, and law enforcement agencies only arrested a handful of BBS owners each year.

Law enforcement relied on anonymous tips for information, but the suspected culprit was often a teenager or youngster who had little or no money. Computer cases were costly to try in court, requiring lawyers specializing in digital copyright infringement and a high technology crime expert. There was no point in suing if financial retribution was impossible; therefore, there were very few court cases.

PIRACY FACT...

One of the largest BBS raids occurred in 1993. The "Fear and Loathing in Las Vegas," BBS, located in Birmingham, Alabama, was raided by the local Federal Bureau of Investigation (FBI) and the local police. The owner, the "Doctor," a local general practitioner, was targeted because he charged users an access fee to access his BBS, effectively charging users for access to pirated software, an action sure to bring attention to the FBI.

When the FBI raided the Doctor's home, they found 7GB worth of pirated software running from a 7-node BBS on 16.8k modems, a setup worth over $15,000 at the time.

The news shocked the piracy world, because the Doctor's BBS was a central meeting place for many groups and pirates alike. By this stage, the police were becoming more vigilant in catching anyone trying to make money from piracy, because they were easy targets in court and required less technical expertise in order to prosecute.

PIRACY FACT...

Officially, the first patent issued for a piece of software was in 1983. Only after this point was software recognized as a trademark or product. Legally, this was very important, because only after this point could acts of copyright infringement be tried in court.

Pirates knew they had little to fear. They were bold and flamboyant, actively flaunting their presence everywhere they went. Evidence of this fearless attitude can be seen in the publication of BBS phone numbers within group Info File (NFO) files. Modern day piracy groups are too scared to give out the names of group members, never mind the details of their own private phone numbers. (See Figure 2.4.)

Figure 2.4 The Humble Guys (THG) BBS List From Their Release of "Bards Tale 3"

```
³Plato's Place        ³ (618) 25▓▓▓▓3 ³ Mr. Plato      ³
³Iron Fortress        ³ (508) 798-▓▓63 ³ Predator        ³
³SpamLand             ³ (508) 831-▓1▓1 ³ Eddie Haskel    ³
³Final Frontier       ³ (602) 491-▓▓▓▓ ³ Barimor         ³
```

The early days of piracy were carefree and pirates were only at risk from their phone phreaking activities. Phreaking was easier to prosecute in court than piracy, and still carried a substantial fine.

In 1992, piracy changed forever. Until this point, the warez scene had been based primarily on BBS'. Release groups first uploaded their releases to BBS'. Although the Internet was available, BBS' were still preferred.

However, in 1992, many Internet service providers in America and Canada began to offer ISDN and dual ISDN Internet connections. Universities and large corporations were eager to get "online" and the first warez sites soon began to appear.

PIRACY FACT...

One of the first warez sites online was called Sentinel. Hosted on an Integrated Services Digital Network (ISDN) connection, Sentinel was PWA's (Pirates with Attitude) legendary site, which was later infiltrated by the FBI in 1999.

Internet sites, unlike BBS', were not limited by nodes or connections. A single ISDN connection could accept as much as 100 users simultaneously. Piracy began to shift, and release groups began uploading new releases to both Internet sites and BBS'.

Internet technology was faster than BBS', and over the years, release groups began to phase out BBS' completely, choosing to become early adopters of the Internet.

ISDN connections were the fastest thing available in the early 90s when Internet technology was still new. Pirates began to move online, BBS' were left behind, and the online community began to form. Internet technology turned piracy from a small-scale hobby to an epidemic. Pirates from any country in the world could now unite. Previously, pirates were limited by geography, and long–distance communication was hard. Internet technology made it easy; you could simply e-mail another member in Russia, or hold a massive conference chat on a server with members from every corner of the earth.

Groups grew from 5 or 10 members to 100. DOD, PWA, RAZOR1911, SODOM, HYBRID, PRESTIGE, and CLASS were all created by the Internet. With resources and connectivity at their fingertips, piracy seemed unstoppable. Fiber-optics soon became available and 1 and 2 megabit (Mb) sites began appearing.

Technology progressed, and what had once been computer geeks trading software had become a large-scale epidemic—a world-wide piracy movement.

In the beginning, piracy was used to make software available to others. Piracy soon evolved and pirates no longer copied software with the sole purpose of helping someone else. Most did not care if anyone actually used the software. Pirates were addicted to beating the system; addicted to cracking, releasing, and racing other pirates. It did not matter what the release was, it did not matter if one person used it or 1000. Winning was everything and speed was the name of the game, all made possible by Internet technology.

The .com age of the late 90s spawned millions of failed software companies and a massive flood of technology and failed software applications. Pirates took every piece of software created and broke its copy protection in half, zipping the software and releasing it on the Internet. Piracy was growing at a rapid rate, the number of piracy groups grew from 10 to over 60 releases per day. New groups were appearing daily, with more people becoming hooked on the rush of piracy. Fiber-optic connections only increased in speed. After two years, 10MB connections were beginning to surface, with 100MB connections just around the corner.

With increased speed and storage readily available, the BBS scene was completely dead. No one bothered with phone lines and nodes anymore. The Internet had completely taken over.

For the first time in the history of piracy other types of media also began to be pirated. Early films shot with portable hand cameras were compressed to under 100MB and released, giving birth to the now fledgling video piracy scene. Music piracy also flourished during this time. Warez pirates joined MP3 groups, showing them how to establish their own sites and share access to group resources.

Piracy was unstoppable and millions were now hooked on the rush of the warez scene. Many of these original pirates only quit the piracy game when the FBI came knocking.

PV27

www.syngress.com

Chapter 3

The Suppliers

Racing Against Time

"W00t, I got the gold RTM, two weeks pre-ship," ^Evil typed into the group channel. "It needs a license key to install. Can someone look at it?"

"We have two weeks until others get a shot at it," he added.

Gold RTM and two weeks pre-ship. At first confused, I suddenly realized what ^Evil meant: this was the final product released to manufacturing, and it would be another two weeks before it was shipped to the stores.

I hesitated for a moment, but could not help but ask, "How'd you hook up with that?"

"How?" he asked, "I'm a *supplier*, that's how."

Less than an hour later ^Evil typed, "I've got another one. This one's going out tomorrow so we need to get right on it."

During my time inside the piracy underworld, it amazed me at how resourceful and hard working suppliers are, all in the name of releasing final product before it hits the stores. They will not sleep until a new release is cracked, packed, and released. They do not do it for financial gain—they do it to be first.

How many project planners, PowerPoint presentations, and meetings do corporations require in order to do as much work as a *warez* (exaggerated plural derivative of software) group? The effort is staggering; a group of loosely connected people, often led by a high school or college student, taking on the largest software corporations in the world, and winning.

I began to understand the efficiency of piracy, seeing warez groups as elite business units instead of groups of mislead troublemakers.

How do these groups acquire the software that they release every month (hundreds of thousands of dollars worth)? How do they obtain the software before it hits the stores? It was clear that this was not just a casual group of anonymous thieves; there were also insiders at the software companies.

An entire subculture of suppliers exists to forward the software to the release groups. In most cases, suppliers are highly regarded as the bread and butter of the groups and are treated with respect. Without dedicated, quality suppliers, the group has little chance of succeeding.

The riskiest part of the piracy process—supplying software—has grown into a highly demanding and creative hobby. Suppliers are quick thinkers, resourceful, and entrepreneurial in their quest for a final build of the latest and greatest software. Quality must be assured; if any betas, alphas, or pre-release copies are released, a supplier can lose his or her role in the group; the release must be final and complete.

How ^Evil finds this endless supply of software is confusing, especially because he supplies at least one RTM CD per week (up to five or six in a good week). Even by extreme piracy standards, this is a significant amount of software. ^Evil is the group's top supplier, bringing in the majority of the releases. He is given anything he wants that will keep him active and happy.

^Evil supplies the most software (titles this month include fluid dynamic simulators, controlling software for sign printers, and Hebrew language translators). Where this myriad of software comes from is anyone's guess.

^Evil is a typical supplier. He maintains accounts on every group site and wants a share of any hardware given to the group. In return, he uploads complete CD images of new applications to crack and release.

The world of supplying intrigued me and I began talking to ^Evil on a regular basis. I discovered how supplying works and soon found myself completely immersed in the world of supplying releases.

Why Be a Supplier?

As I talked to suppliers, I began to understand the attitude and motivation that drives this niche subculture of pirates. Supplying media to warez groups is risky; if caught, the punishment is strict and carries a long jail sentence.

Supplying is one of the most exciting and exhilarating roles, which can turn the average Joe into a large-scale crook over night. A day in the life of a supplier may include stealing software from their employer, ordering software with a stolen credit card, and hacking software development companies for the latest final build.

This is the world of supplying. The goal? Acquire and supply the latest copyrighted works at any cost or risk, only the release matters.

Suppliers risk their freedom daily (all in the name of software piracy) so that others can enjoy digital media for free. It is a hard, grueling job that many undertake with little or no financial gain. "No one is in the scene to make money," one supplier told me. "I am sure I could make some dollars if I wanted to, but it is not about the money." How many readers would undertake a risky part-time job without financial gain?

I befriended and interviewed every warez supplier I met, asking questions such as "Why do you do this?" and "Are you worried about being caught?" The results shocked me; the majority of suppliers do not believe that what they are doing is illegal, perhaps immoral, but definitely not illegal. Simply put, suppliers lack any association with breaking the law and supplying groups with new, unreleased games or applications. It is a game to them, a race between suppliers and warez groups, nothing more. "My goal this year was to supply the new Battlefield 1942 Vietnam final to my group," said one games supplier. "I felt terrible for days after I was beat out on that one. I really love BF1942 and wanted to be the supplier behind it. I hated RAZOR1911 for beating me," he added.

Although there is little monetary reward in supplying, there are substantial social and emotional rewards. Groups with active suppliers work hard to keep them content and satisfied.

Piracy Fact...

Groups value suppliers so much that they often reward them with substantial gifts.

The legendary group, Pirates with Attitude (PWA), had five members who worked for Intel and supplied the group with hardware and complete top-of-the-line desktops. Each month, PWA's top supplier and top cracker is rewarded with a piece of Intel hardware or a complete machine shipped directly to their door.

This lavish and frequent breach of Intel policy eventually led to the group's demise, when in late 1999, FBI agents raided the group's leaders and arrested the majority of its members.

Groups know that if a supplier is unhappy, any number of other groups will happily take them aboard. Suppliers are desirable and wanted by every group in the scene. You cannot get enough suppliers; groups will do just about anything to get them.

This is a major reason why people want to become warez suppliers; although the work is hard and the risks are high, it is all worth it to be accepted, wanted, and desired by your peers.

The majority of suppliers I interviewed said they loved the attention and praise they get from warez groups. "I got a Christmas card from ＊＊＊＊＊＊ this year," said [xyx]. Thanks for the great work this year," it read. "It was the only Christmas card I got that year. I can't tell you how much it made my day. My wife thinks I am nuts, but I put that card on the mantle piece!"

Everyone likes to be popular and everyone wants to make new friends; therefore, it is easy to understand why popularity can be more of an incentive than money. Working is easy if you work for your friends. Suppliers find it easy to be complacent about risk and danger if it is in the name of friendship or family.

Relationships with suppliers are often intimate; groups depend on them to survive. Therefore, suppliers are made to feel like a valued member of the online family.

Several European warez groups with members local to each other have yearly parties where the entire group gets together and talks about the online world they share. The motivation that drives suppliers soon becomes clear to me; these are not co-workers engaged in corporate battle, but rather friends working together, having fun, and playing a game.

Supplying Guidelines

There are strict rules that suppliers must follow. Failure to meet any of the rules will cause sites to decline the release, therefore invalidating the groups' work and emphasizing their lack of professionalism. Piracy is a serious game and amateurs are not welcome. Rules must be obeyed. No exceptions.

There are seven major rules that suppliers must obey:

- **Final Release** Each supplied release must be final (no beta, alpha, build, or technology preview, and the release cannot be different from the retail version).

- **Virus- and Spyware-free** Real warez scene sites are 100 per-cent virus free; each archive is virus-scanned upon upload. If a release contains a virus, it is not accepted.

- **Complete** A release cannot be missing any vital parts needed for installation, and it must be true to form (e.g., if a release is labeled a CD image it must be a complete CD image).

- **Not Free** The golden rule of piracy: you have to pirate some-thing copyrighted. Each release must have a retail value.

- **Useable** The release must be useable by any member of the general public. It cannot require additional hardware and must work the first time after installation. Games such as Everquest, which require an online account, technically are not useable by anyone who downloads them, and thus are not pirated.

- **Latest Version** The release must be the latest version available; there is no point in releasing Photoshop v6 if Photoshop v7 is in the stores.

- **Not a Minor Upgrade (MU)** Minor upgrade (MU) ensures that groups do not continuously release each new minor version of an application.

For example:

```
01/04/05 SuperZipper v1.0.0.2.1
01/05/05 SuperZipper v1.0.0.2.2
01/06/05 SuperZipper v1.0.0.2.3
```

Although each version is different, the changes are miniscule; the group releasing this is simply trying to increase their number of releases per week. Users do not need all three versions of SuperZipper in one week. The last two releases would not be accepted by any of the sites.

Scene rules for suppliers are simple and relatively straightforward, and are created to ensure that the quality of pirated goods is kept high. A common stereotype is that warez material is *dodgy* and likely to contain backdoors, Trojans, or viruses.

Professional pirates take their job very seriously. All releases are scrutinized by competing groups and sites. A release containing a virus is not acceptable. The majority of scene sites will ban a certain group if their standard of quality does not meet expectations.

Supplying in Motion

How would you get a $5,000 graphic design application for free, or obtain the latest First Person Shooter (FPS) directly from the software developer two weeks before it goes on sale?

Most people would resort to piracy as a way of getting what they want for free. But where do the pirates go when they need something that is not yet pirated? Software suppliers are keen, intelligent, and sharp-witted people who focus on any way possible to get software for free.

Through talking to ^Evil and his fellow suppliers, I learned the basic tricks used to supply software. Ranging from the outrageously extreme to the deviously discreet, every supplier has a favorite method they like to use. I have categorized these methods into the following common groups:

- Physical Insiders
- Credit Card Fraud
- File Transfer Protocol (FTP) Snooping
- Social Engineering
- Demo CDs
- Legitimate Retail

Each method targets a different genre of software and carries a different level of risk if the supplier is caught.

Suppliers usually have a preferred method; however, the more resourceful suppliers have multiple scams running at any given time, thereby increasing the amount of software they receive.

Physical Insiders

Perhaps you work at a company that prints or packages software CDs or DVDs, or maybe you work for a large software company such as Microsoft. Being an insider is a clear advantage in the race for software; warez groups constantly seek insiders. The trick is simple. Sit at work all day and keep your eyes and ears open for any news of a possible release. Internally developed products, any products the company bought for its own use, or anything that looks interesting is copied and uploaded.

Whether you work for Microsoft or Adobe, your valuable services are greatly appreciated by any warez group; insiders are usually rewarded handsomely for their hard work.

Microsoft software is available for free to all Microsoft employees, usually well before either MSDN (Microsoft Developer Network) or retail copies are released. Helpdesk staff is also involved in the scene. They are given copies of the company's software to familiarize themselves with, weeks before the product officially goes on sale.

Being an insider may sound easy, but it is not without peril. Insiders face huge risks because they are closely linked to the product they supply. Insiders risk everything in the name of piracy.

Many products can be clearly spotted as originating from insiders. The most obvious trait is when software is released weeks before the official release date, or is released with an internal CD key or serial number that is not usually given out. Companies are usually quick to respond if they think their products are being leaked; it is not uncommon for large-scale internal investigations to be launched.

PIRACY FACT...

You may already know the story of Michael S. Lewis (a.k.a. Grazer) from the Paradigm warez group of 1999. Paradigm specialized in cracking and releasing PC games; ironically, Michael had recently finished an internship at Electronic Arts, a large entertainment software development house.

Michael gave the group an amazing head start by having access to finished software titles and additional insider knowledge of how

Electronic Arts protects their games from copy theft. Receiving copies of the games the second they were completed and clear instructions on how to defeat the copy protection, Paradigm soon became infamous for releasing all Electronic Arts titles weeks before they appeared in stores.

It did not take Electronic Arts long to realize someone inside the company was leaking their games. Within a few months, Grazer and the majority of Paradigm were caught and arrested.

Modern day warez groups have become increasingly careful, if not extremely paranoid. Frequently, groups obtain copies of games much earlier than the expected release date; however, they wait until the precise moment the product hits the stores before they release their own cracked copy. Safety, security, and anonymity are primary objectives for anyone in the scene; releasing software before its official release date is asking for trouble.

Another common source of insiders is the low paid *packers* at media packaging warehouses. Being paid $7.50 an hour to shove a CD and manual into a box is not an incentive to remain loyal to your employer. Often, employees pocket CDs for themselves, giving the supplier an endless source of releases and a relatively discreet and safe method of supplying to the group. Tracking down a leak to a single person in a packaging plant is close to impossible, since warehouses usually have many people employed on a shift basis, all doing the same job.

The thought of having a new CD image to crack and release daily makes a warez group's mouth water. It is not unheard of for groups to offer employee's of CD manufacturing companies a cash incentive to stay in their mundane job and supply the group with new releases.

PIRACY FACT...

November 9, 2004, was a date Microsoft wanted everyone to remember. Dubbed the official "Sick Day" of the gaming community, Microsoft and Bungie software were set to release the Xbox game, Halo 2, to the public, and were expecting a massive onslaught of fans to skip work to play.

Over a million people pre-ordered the game and the hype was almost unbearable. That was until someone leaked a DVD image of the Xbox game on October 14, 2004, almost a month before pre-ordered copies were to be shipped. DiFFUSiON claimed responsibility for the leak, with their NFO file showing just how happy they were with themselves: "0wnag3? Yeah, think so...," it read.

Although the release was multilingual, the game ran in French by default, with English subtitles.

It was suspected that an insider at a French CD manufacturing plant was responsible for the leak, which was estimated to have cost Microsoft hundreds of thousands of sales.

Microsoft has vowed to "aggressively pursue" whoever leaked the game," said a Microsoft spokesperson. "Microsoft takes the integrity of its intellectual property extremely seriously, and we are aggressively pursuing the source of this illegal act. We consider downloading this code or making it available for others to download, as theft. "

Courier drivers and mail workers are encouraged by warez groups to "lose" packages that may contain software or that originate from a publishing house. Like an addict, groups will do anything to obtain a release. One member of a warez group told me that he would quit his high paying legal job if he could work as a cleaner at AutoDesk, a Computer-aided Design (CAD) software company. "I would spend all night stealing CD's from people's desks. I don't care about the pay. I could get so many releases; it would be leet."

I managed to talk to one insider who works at a well-known software company that manufactures document-processing software. For the last few years, he has been smuggling software out of the company and leaking it to a well-known warez group, thereby costing the software company millions in lost revenue. Below is a brief discussion I had with him about what he does for the company and how he feels about his actions. We call this insider "X" to retain his privacy.

INTERVIEW WITH AN INSIDER...

Me: How long have you worked at ****** and what do you do there?

X: About three years or so. I started as a junior sysadmin running the dev servers, but recently moved into programming and implementing new product features in some of our smaller products.

Me: How many releases have you smuggled out of **** and how?

X: I would say maybe 15, mostly the enterprise versions. I try to be discreet and usually just copy the contents of the CD to a small USB 1GB thumb drive; everyone uses them around here so it doesn't raise any eyebrows.

Me: Has anyone at **** ever noticed that their software was pirated? What did they say?

X: Yeah, they had this big meeting to discuss 'product security.' We were told never to lend copies of CD's to anyone. I think they suspect it is someone inside the company, but it is a big place.

Me: Do you sleep at night? Ever had any regrets or remorse about what you are doing?

X: In the beginning I wondered if I would get caught, but after the fifth or so time I relaxed. I sleep just fine; the software is over priced and the company sucks. I am hardly robbing the blind.

Me: Do you enjoy being an insider?

X: Yeah, very much. It is nice to feel like you really have something to offer. I am valued in the scene and people know me as "That guy who gets all the OCR stuff.

Me: Do you have any plans to stop leaking intellectual property to piracy groups?

X: You make it sound so official. No, I am here to stay. I would stay in this job just to remain "The OCR guy." I love it. The scene gives me everything I need (movies, MP3s, games). All I have to do is share what I get. It's actually really worth my time. Ever since I began supplying I haven't bought a single game. I am given accounts on amazing sites and spend all day downloading whatever I want.

Continued

> **Me: :** You know that what you are doing is illegal and you will go to jail if caught. That doesn't bother you?
>
> **X:** Yes, but I try not to think of it like that. To me it is just a game; find and release as many applications as I can. To be honest, though, if I had to choose between jail time and stopping, I would stop.

Every warez release group has at least one active insider; others insiders are sought after by different release groups. Frequently released NFO files contain an open offer to anyone who works at a software developer or a publishing house to join the group's ranks (see Figure 3.1).

Figure 3.1 A Quote from *DEViANCE's* NFO File

```
You think you can contribute to the scene too?
You have even just one of the following talents in:


- supplying new unreleased games (maybe you work at a game/util magazine,
courier delivery firm, newspaper, game press/marketing company,
distributor, publisher, duplicator, tv/radio show, shop, warehouse, design
firm, language translation company, packing companystore etc).
```

Insiders are constant suppliers to the piracy market. It is ironic that those most involved in piracy are often within a company's own walls.

FTP Snooping

The majority of warez releases come directly from a company's FTP site. Most companies have CD images of retail software (and sometimes source code) sitting on their publicly accessible FTP sites. This information is uploaded by an employee or client and used by developers to send new software releases to remote locations.

FTP snooping is commonplace. Monitoring known directories on FTP servers allows FTP snoopers to pick up releases before their retail release date. (It is a well-known fact that applications can be found on a company's FTP site along with license files, confidential company information, sales reports, and program source code.)

Most Internet users will not check a company's FTP site unless a Web site mentions or links to a FTP site (out of site, out of mind). People generally only use the Internet for e-mail and the Web.

FTP snooping takes up a large part of a supplier's day. FTP snoopers study 10 to 20 different FTP sites each day, rechecking each of them twice or three times.

PIRACY FACT...

Small, inexperienced companies are not the only ones exposing their software. Several large companies have directories full of employees' personal information, accounts, records, and retail zip files of the software they have produced.

Installation software developer, Install Shield, was one of these companies. Although Install Shield has since closed their FTP server, it used to be home to many interesting zip files harvested by warez groups.

Officially, the public directory /incoming was used by clients to post information to Install Shield, and to post information regarding broken scripts, logs, error dialogs, and so forth. The directory /outgoing was used by the company to pass information back to the clients and between employees, including retail versions of their software and sometimes confidential documents.

Install Shield applications were always released a few hours after they were found, and at least a week before they were officially available to customers.

Many internal applications were developed by warez groups to aid FTP snooping. Homemade "scripted snoopers" are used greatly by warez groups. These automated applications scan hundreds of FTP servers hourly, looking for new files and reporting any changes that may point to a possible new release being uploaded.

Automated checkers function more efficiently than individuals. Because files containing final versions of a company's flagship product usually do not remain on their FTP site for long, it is important to quickly establish a release the second it is uploaded. A press release announcing the immediate availability of a new release version is a signal to begin watching a company's FTP site. Three to four different groups can watch a FTP site at any given time. Following is a list of the most common directories to watch on an FTP site:

- */support*
- */outgoing*
- */private*
- */users*
- */tmp*

The */support* and */outgoing* directories are used by the software support team to send files or information to customers and clients. Often riddled with new builds, final release versions and other miscellaneous files such as contracts and e-mails, these directories are a good place to start watching.

Directories such as */private* and */users* should be well protected on any FTP site because they usually contain personal information that could be damning to a company's reputation. Although the majority of companies account for security, problems can arise (e.g., permissions on the private directory may change when the FTP server is moved or when a backup is restored that did not store the file permissions).

More often than not, companies withhold security, thereby allowing the public to have full access to large amounts of intellectual property (including source code and personal files).

PIRACY FACT...

To give you an idea of how personal some information can be, one company employee kept several password-protected zip files containing pictures from a digital camera, inside his personal directory on his company's FTP site.

A curious supplier mistook the files for software and downloaded them. After finding out that they contained pictures, the supplier became more curious and began trying to break the zip file password.

After a few days of brute force, the password was discovered revealing photographic proof of a romantic getaway the employee recently went on. Obviously, the personal directories were designed to be readable only by that particular user; however, somewhere along the line the permissions were changed, allowing full access to everyone.

From a security point of view, temporary directories such as */tmp* and */temp* are often overlooked. Employees use these temporary directories to store files for a short amount of time. They are also used to give a file to a customer or co-worker who does not have access into the internal company network).

The file is saved and then retrieved by the intended recipient; however, sometimes it is not removed from the FTP server until several days later, thereby leaving a wide window of opportunity for a snooper to watch the directories on a FTP server.

PIRACY FACT...

I was told that finding source code on FTP servers is not out of the ordinary, but I did not believe it until I saw it for myself.

One afternoon, I received a message from my new friend, ^Evil. "Hey dude, check this out." I was then given an FTP address.

The FTP server belonged to a Computer-aided Design and Computer-aided Milling (CAD/CAM) software company that produced some of the most expensive and elaborate software I have ever seen. With a single-user license costing over $20,000, you would expect them to guard the source code carefully.

Inside the publicly accessible anonymous FTP server, hidden under a maze of 14 directories, were two zip files:

- Release-16.zip, 280meg in size)
- Release16src.zip, 350meg in size.

^ Evil asked me, "Do you see it? That's v16 of ****. We don't even have to worry about the copy protection, because we have the source code too!"

Having the source code made defeating the copy protection trivial because their crackers could now use the source code to recompile the application with the "copy" protection commented out.

By using an FTP client alone, we effectively stole and cracked one of the most expensive CAD software applications on the market. I was beginning to see just how easy piracy can be.

Credit Card Fraud

Credit card fraud is big in the warez group scene. If you are a supplier in a large warez group and have a quota to meet (e.g., you have to supply at least one new release to the group every month or risk being extricated), you have the choice of using either the more strenuous methods of supplying software or buying it with a stolen credit card. Most people would probably choose the stolen credit card; a credit card fraud can supply hundreds of thousands of dollars worth of software in a single night.

Carding is frowned upon because it draws unwanted attention from legal authorities such as the FBI, especially when *carders* go on expensive, noticeable shopping sprees.

The process of carding is relatively simple, First, a carder must be affiliated with, or have links to, hacking groups that collect credit cards. Or, perhaps the carder is a hacker and can therefore supply his or her own credit cards.

Next, the carder finds some form of anonymous, untraceable Internet access (important because the ordering process is the only tangible evidence tying the perpetrator to the act of fraud). Using your own Internet Service Provider (ISP) to order goods with a stolen credit card is asking for serious trouble.

PIRACY FACT...

Carders use every form of anonymous Internet access when shopping; Internet café's, open unencrypted wireless access points, even insecure SOCKS proxy servers. The aim is to hide the Internet Protocol (IP) address from the remote Web server logs.

Modern day software vendors use the Internet for software delivery using a process known as Electronic Software Delivery (ESD). Once the software is ordered and the credit card transaction accepted, customers are e-mailed a link where they can directly download the complete CD. No more waiting around for packages to arrive—the user can have the software running hours after buying it.

ESD has made obtaining legitimate purchases easy, and has also made carding software so easy that anyone can perform online fraud. Before ESD was popular, a carder had to find a *drop site* that would accept the packaged software.

PIRACY FACT...

A drop site is a location that receives packages. Carders use many different drop sites, which usually fall into two distinct categories: *busy industrial* and *empty residential*.

Busy industrial sends the package via a busy mailroom in a large corporation. Packages are addressed to fictitious employees and discreetly picked up by the carder employed there.

A large corporation (2000+ employees) has hundreds of packages sent out and delivered daily, an enormous amount of mail for mailroom staff to keep up with. Aside from allowing the carder to smoothly slip between the cracks, this process has the added benefit of a legitimate company being the receiver, thereby increasing the legitimacy of the order.

The empty residential approach uses abandoned or empty "houses for sale" as the drop site.

First, the carder cases out the house for at least two weeks to be sure it is empty. They remove any "For Sale" signs and regularly empty the mailbox, making the home look quiet, but not empty. Next, a note is placed on the doorstep reading something like this:

"To couriers: Gone out to do some shopping. Please leave package under bushes by the doorstep. – Joe"

Legally, couriers must obtain a signature for all packages they deliver, to track the delivery process and hold the recipient accountable if there are any problems.

The carder returns to the house daily (usually at night), empties the mailbox, and picks up any packages that were delivered.

The majority of carders prefer the residential method because it offers the most anonymous and untraceable way of receiving the stolen goods.

Thanks to Electronic Software Distribution (ESD), a carder only needs an e-mail address to receive software (preferably not hotmail or any other free e-mail provider).

Once the software is ordered, the carder receives an e-mail similar to the one shown in Figure 3.2.

Figure 3.2 ESD Software Receipt

```
Dear Jim Bob

Thanks for ordering Snippet v1.1 from SnipSoftware
To download your version, please go to
http://www.snipitsoft.com/registered/download.htm
When prompted for a username and password, please enter
User:Jim_bob_1
Pass:ja538fje!


Please keep this username and password and use it when updating further
versions of Snippet.


After downloading snippet you will require a registration key to fully
enable the registered user features.
Your key is:

08123-19836514183-GEIX-1238712-APQM
```

Even though the registered key is noted in the e-mail, the software can still be released. Untraceable and fully anonymous purchases are now possible thanks to the Internet.

If a credit card victim calls their bank to refuse to pay a credit card bill, the bank must accept any fraudulent charges, and the credit card supplier (e.g., VISA) must issue a charge-back to the card for the amount spent. This charge-back goes directly to the software vendor (*snipitsoft.com*); the software company will not receive any money for the product and will usually face a $10.00 to $20.00 surcharge incurred from the charge-back process.

PIRACY FACT...

The easiest way to tell if a group has carded software is by the registration key. If the registered user looks legitimate (e.g., James Macarthur – *jmcur@myemail.com*), chances are very good that the software has been carded. No one would risk releasing an application using a real registered user name. Warez groups often attempt to hide the fact that they carded software, by placing the username and registration key inside a registry (*.reg*) file that automatically registers the software.

Hardware and software are the most commonly carded items; however, hardware requires more effort because the order must be received and signed by someone. Additionally, the billing address on a credit card must be similar to the delivery address of the goods (e.g., if the credit card belongs to the "German Investment Company," sending laptops to a residential address in Utah will look highly suspicious). Credit cards must be from the same country (and preferably state) as the delivery address, which means the carder needs a wide range of cards at his or her disposal.

PIRACY FACT...

One of the best jobs for harvesting credit cards for carding is working as a pizza delivery person. The job is easy to get (all you need is a car) and you can take copies of any phone orders paid for with a credit card.

Additionally, since you drive around many different neighborhoods, you can look for potential locations that can be used as drop sites. Delivering pizzas allows a carder to obtain credit cards that belong to someone else, making the credit card order look legitimate.

Carded hardware is often given to group sites or as a reward for the top cracker or top supplier of the group each month. Commonly carded hardware includes laptops, hard disks and graphic cards; anything that comes in a relatively small box so it can be left "under the bushes."

Hacking

Although hacking exists in the warez group scene, it is by no means a common or popular method of supplying releases to groups. In fact, hackers are relatively uncommon in the scene, with only a few groups using hacking as a method of obtaining releases. Hacking for releases is relatively straightforward. First, a hacker finds out when a software company is about to launch a new product, usually from a press release or news bulletin on the company's Web site. Next, the hacker breaks into the company with one objective; steal the final version of the latest software, possibly stealing the source code in the process.

PIRACY FACT...

Software development companies place a lot emphasis on copy protection technology; however, if a hacker obtains the source code to a piece of software, that technology becomes worthless. Reading source code allows anyone to learn exactly how copy protection technology functions and which part of the application uses it. If a group obtains a copy of the source code, they can crack the copy protection in a matter of minutes, thereby greatly reducing the required time and effort.

Hacking with direction and focus removes many of the elements that help catch hackers. The majority of hackers are not caught when trying to break into a system, because preemptive security measures such as Intrusion Detection Systems (IDS') are relatively rare on networks. Hackers are usually caught when they become either bored or too curious, which is when they begin wandering around the network, using servers for their own means. At this point, system administrators usually take notice and realize they have been hacked.

If a hack is focused, directed, and completed within 8 hours, the chance that someone will notice the hacker is low. By nature, human beings only notice things out of the ordinary; as long as a hacker is discreet, there is no reason to think that the system has been hacked. Unlike hackers who deface Web sites with their own slogans, software companies have little idea if someone has copied software from their development server.

Hacked software is often highly valuable. Some of the most news-worthy releases have come directly from hackers. Most recently, a hacker penetrated Valve Software's corporate network and stole a copy of the source code for Half Life 2, possibly the most anticipated game of the year. The source code was given to a friend of the hacker who was an active pirate in the scene, who promised to release it.

A few hours later, the source code was packaged and uploaded to a few sites. Scattering millions of dollars worth of intellectual property across the Internet, the release took a matter of minutes to spread around the world.

In 1998, third animation software company, Caligari (manufacturer of real-time graphic design software) was hacked. Although the hack did not make the news, pirates from a group named REVOLT released the source code of the company's flagship product, True Space (see Figure 3.3).

Figure 3.3 True Space 4 Source Code NFO File

```
For all you developers out there,  how would you like to
have the SOURCE for TRUESPACE4.0? This is the source code
made by Caligari! YES this IS the REAL SOURCE!! All of it!

All of the trueSpace4 source code has been made in MSVS97
I'm pretty sure it will work with MSVS98, although if you
don't have VS9X I would suggest getting it if you would like
to use this code..
```

Contained inside the release was the full source code that could be used by anyone to recompile the application and make his or her own version of TrueSpace.

Hackers have a distinct advantage over other suppliers; they are *insiders* themselves, floating between companies. Hackers can pick up releases from any company they previously compromised; software companies often deploy substandard levels of security.

Although hackers exist in the scene, the majority of releases stem from other supplying methods; hacking is not a preferred tactic. Suppliers have said that they never heard of another supplier hacking software companies to obtain releases. They suggested that it would be hard to navigate an internal software company without prior interior knowledge.

"I work at xxxxx," said one supplier. "We have about 1000 unofficial builds to every official product release. A hacker would either have to know the exact build number of the final version, or the software company would have to have clearly labeled it as a final build. It would be easy for a hacker to pick up a beta or near-final build of the product and think it is the final. We run out so many last minute builds just before a product release. It would be hard work for anyone who hacked us to find the final version," he added.

Social Engineering

Suppliers will do just about anything to obtain a release. Desiring status, accomplishment, and credit, or perhaps just to be accepted, suppliers never stop developing creative methods of bringing new releases to the table.

One of the most creative methods used is the "fake magazine" scam, a mixture of social engineering and plain old hard work. During this con, game publishers are convinced to send advanced copies of upcoming titles to an online Web site that reviews games.

Game publishers usually send press organizations copies of games a few weeks before the official retail release date, thereby allowing the magazine to write a review and hopefully increase sales of the product when it becomes available. It did not take long for pirates to figure this out, and soon many suppliers were creating their own online game magazines, hoping to attract attention from game publishers and be sent advanced copies of all upcoming titles.

The suppliers worked hard to create a semi-legitimate looking magazine; if the magazine looked shabby or suspicious, game publishers would not want to work with them. Legitimate-looking Web sites and legitimate reviews were written regularly; hours of work are invested into creating Web sites whose only purpose is to get more releases for the warez group.

Prepaid cell phones and post office boxes were used to call game publishers and to receive product. The trick was to not be too obvious; the best fake magazines were the ones that did not release every single game they were sent. A supplier should only release one or two games per month, while still writing full reviews for each game so as to continue looking legitimate. Those who were greedy and showed no restraint when using this scam were soon caught. Game publishers began to notice that the same warez group was pirating their games before their official release date.

PIRACY FACT...

Game publishers would find out about fake magazines when they sent watermarked marked copies of each game to the press organizations.

Although the games sent were the correct retail versions, they also contained a marker showing the original ship to address, thus finding the leak when the group released the game. This scam is used to crack and release games.

Groups aim to have at least one fake magazine set up in each of the three major game producing countries: the United Kingdom, the USA, and the European Union. Each magazine would specialize in obtaining titles from the closest publisher, thereby reducing delays and ensuring that the group had the maxim amount of time to crack the title.

Publishers are more at ease sending advanced copies to local countries; remote online magazines out of Russia or Serbia make publishers skeptical of their legitimacy.

Fake magazines reportedly are still used by many warez groups, but the majority of game publishers now only send beta copies of games to magazines for review.

Demo CD

A license is often the only difference between a retail product and a demo or evaluation copy. If a product is installed with a demo or trail license key, it acts and functions like a demo. However, if the product were reinstalled with a retail key, the installed product would function in full retail mode.

Commercial license managers are popular with software developers because they give them the ability to distribute an application while limiting its usability with a license code or file. A company can send out 1000 demo CDs to potential buyers; the demo licensees included would function for 30 days and then expire.

If a customer wants to purchase a copy of the product or wants to extend the demo trail period by another 30 days, they only need a new license file, not a new CD. Any company employee can generate a new license for a customer. When a product is purchased, the customer is sent a retail license file that ensures that the application never expires.

Pirates love demo CDs; once they figure out the license scheme and have a retail license generated by a group cracker, the group has a functioning retail product that is ready for release.

Obtaining a demo CD is relatively easy, although it does require some social engineering. The following is a "sample" attempt to obtain a demo of an enterprise copy of a costly animation tool.

THE DEMO CD SCAM...

Pirate: Hi there, can I speak to someone in your sales department please? (Sales people are always looking for new sales. Most work on commission so they are usually the best place to start.)

Company: One moment please.

Company: Transfer.

Company: Hi there, Jack Altern speaking. How can I help you today sir?

Pirate: Hi Jack, my name is Frank Journ and I work at an animation company called Digital Realize. I was very curious about your Pro-Designer product and was trying to get a hold of an evaluation copy. I would very much like to get our 500 animators on it.

At $1,000 per license, Jack should be drooling and willing to do anything to close the sale.

Company: Okay, I think that can be arranged. Where are you based? I could drive out and give you a demonstration. We don't give out demo CDs unless we have to.

Okay, the company is a little wiser than expected and wants to give a personal demo. They must have had problems with pirates getting their hands on the demo CD.

Pirate: We are based out of Japan. It would be a long drive.

Company: That's a good point. Why don't you tell me a little more about what you do and I'll find out which product version suits you. I am sure we can get a CD out to you.

He wants the sale and will trust me, but first I must assure him that I am legitimate.

Continued

> **Pirate:** I am the CTO of Digital Realize. It is a new company and we are doing a lot of work on Japanese TV commercials and small films. We have just over 500 animators and are looking at using Pro Designer for all of our character designs and physics.
>
> *By reading the company's Web site, I found out that the Enterprise version is the only version that includes the "physics" plug-in; all other versions such as Professional and Standard lacked physics. He should send me the Enterprise version.*
>
> **Company:** Okay, sounds like you need the Enterprise version.
>
> *Yes. I could work at this company.*
>
> **Company:** I'll tell you what, I'll send you a copy of the Enterprise product, but I'll e-mail you through a demo license file. It should give you access to all of the plug-ins (including the physics plug-in) for 30 days after you install it. How does that sound?
>
> **Pirate:** Perfect. I really look forward to having a play; you can send it to: En passant 4-4-10, Nippombashi, Naniwa-ku, Osaka-shi, Osaka, Japan. My personal e-mail address is *Fjourn5@hotmail.com*, which is the best way to get me while I'm on the road.
>
> *This is the address of my cracker's post office box in Japan. It will be faster if I have the CDs sent directly there. Giving a personal e-mail address is a nice touch that shows that I take the product seriously and want to maintain direct contact with him.*
>
> **Company:** Okay then, I'll send the CD out tomorrow and e-mail you the license file today. I look forward to hearing back from you.

Once the product arrives, you will notice that it looks completely authentic. There is no obvious "DEMO" printed on the box and it appears to be a complete retail copy. The sales agent has sent us a retail copy of the Enterprise version of the company's flagship product; however, the attached license file contains information indicating that it is a trial version and will expire in 30 days (See Figure 3.4).

Figure 3.4 The Demo License File

```
FEATURE Prodesigner_Enterprise prodesign 14 01-jan-2005 30 \
        5DD00E49759D5D354243 SN=DEMO
FEATURE Physics_plugin prodesign 14 01-jan-2005 30 DD209E39A409649F3746 \
SN=DEMO
```

This license file is from the Flexible License Manager (FlexLM). This license allows you to install the product and have it function for no more than 30 days after January 1st. After 30 days, the product refuses to load and a new license file must be obtained.

PIRACY FACT...

FlexLM is very common in the warez group scene. Here's what one cracker thinks about FlexLM technology:

"It's just not viable to have a commercial protection system such as FlexLM. I have cracked at least 20 Flex applications in a day, because once you do one, you've done them all. It is the same protection routine for all of these applications."

After the software passes through the hands of the cracker, a new license is generated with more features (see Figure 3.5).

Figure 3.5 The Retail License File

```
FEATURE Prodesigner_Enterprise prodesign 14 permanent uncounted \
        ED62F3B310B5 HOSTID=ANY
FEATURE Physics_plugin permanent 14 permanent uncounted
8374FA83DE09647E189A \ HOSTID=ANY
```

This retail license file lacks the "01-jan-2005 30" section, indicating that the license will expire 30 days after January 1st. Instead, the license file contains "permanent uncounted," representing that the license is a full permanent retail license.

With a little social engineering and some handiwork, we were able to obtain a retail copy of a company's flagship product that was ready for release. It cost nothing and there was relatively no risk. After 30 days, a supplier would e-mail the sales representative and tell him that the product did not meet their expectations. In a few months or when a new version was released, the supplier would e-mail the sales representative again, asking for another trial CD in the hope that this version fixed some problems that the previous version had (another release in the making).

I am amazed at how many times this scam is used in the scene. It is by far one of the most popular methods for obtaining new, expensive applications. Because of this widespread abuse, many companies refuse to send out demo CDs unless you are willing to pay a fee or meet with a sales representative in person.

Legitimate Retail

Legitimate retail-supplying methods (known as *store pickups*) are one of the oldest and most widely used forms of supplying games to warez groups. Suppliers use this method to watch product Web sites and to find out exact release dates, which countries receive the product first, and which stores are most likely to put the game on a shelf first.

The goal is to buy the software first, and then get the copy cracked and released, all while racing two or three other groups that are trying to do the same. Monday morning at 8:30 a.m., the store supplier will be the first one into the software store to purchase a copy of the latest released title.

PIRACY FACT…

Money is not an issue with store suppliers, since the majority of warez groups refund the purchased price of any software they release. A hobby turned addiction; warez groups put their money where their mouth is and are usually willing to pay anything to get a release out first.

Next, the supplier makes a complete image of the CD and sends it to the cracker as soon as possible. Speed is key; successful store suppliers usually have at least 100MB of Internet connectivity at their disposal.

Finally, the release is uploaded to a group dumpsite and the cracker is notified. The supplier's job is done and he or she waits for another release.

PIRACY FACT...

It is not uncommon for a store supplier to drive to a local cracker's house with an original CD; many infamous relationships have formed between store suppliers and local crackers. Speed is always the key; in many cases, driving to a cracker's house can be faster than uploading a DVD image even when using a 100MB connection.

Store suppliers constantly fight the clock; a new retail title is usually cracked and released within six hours of being placed on a store shelf. Store suppliers have one of the most demanding and time-consuming roles in the scene; stopping for coffee can mean the difference between winning and losing.

If a supplier buys a title but is not the first to release it, warez groups will not refund the supplier for the purchase, leaving the supplier out of pocket and stuck with a title they cannot use. What does a supplier do with leftover software?

Product returns are a sore point with software retailers. Due to customers abusing returns, the majority of stores will not accept a returned product unless it is still in its shrink-wrap (so it can be resold).

Recently, the software chain Electronic Boutique offered a "money back guarantee," even on opened products. However, the majority of software stores refuse any opened products. In such circumstances, supplier's re-shrink-wrap the product so that it can be returned to any store. For approximately $20.00 a supplier can buy a home "shrink wrap kit," including the plastic bags to wrap the products in. With some practice and a powerful hair dryer, any box can be re-shrink-wrapped to its original pristine condition. Patience is key; the process of shrink-wrapping is an art form and it can take many attempts to create a product that looks like the original.

What if you worked at a software store and a customer returned one product a week, still in its shrink-wrap. You would probably become slightly suspicious of the customer. Although re-wrapping the box is a viable method, it is not sustainable; suppliers can only return one or two products per month.

Another popular method of store supplying is pre-ordering the product online.

Pre-orders are often shipped a few days before a product goes on sale in stores, allowing a warez group to get a head start and potentially beat any other groups trying to get the title from the store.

Suppliers will do anything to win on a release. ^Evil once told me that the feeling of winning on a highly anticipated title is "better than any drug, a true emotional high. You feel like you just won the Nobel Prize. It is such a great feeling." Supplying is a game to people in the scene; little thought goes into the financial and emotional harm piracy causes software developers.

Chapter 4

Crackers

Digital Pissing Contest

One of the first things FreOn said to me was, "It's just a pissing contest. We're all thrill seekers. All crackers want to crack the hardcore games before anyone else can. You can almost taste the respect and prestige you get from releasing a respected crack," he said.

A pissing contest—digital thrill seekers addicted to their own egos.

I could tell that FreOn had more fun cracking games than playing them. He was born a *cracker*, and his job is to defeat all copy protection programs that are developed.

Every application and game on the market contains some type of copy protection (e.g., the application/game may not run from a copied version of the CD, it may require a CD key or license code for installation, or a hardware dongle may have been plugged into the computer while the software was running). This technology (designed to stop pirates from distributing licensed software on the Internet) is the latest initiative that software developers are using in order to increase sales. New copy protection techniques are constantly being developed. Anti-piracy technology has grown so much that commercial anti-piracy solutions are now a multi-million dollar industry.

Despite all of the time and money invested in copy protection techniques, crackers can still defeat the most elaborate and complex copy protection technology, often hours before it is placed on a store shelf. Crackers are the brains behind releases and the *warez* group scene. Piracy would not exist without input from a cracker. It is a mental competition: software developers create a lock and crackers digitally pick it as fast as possible.

The cracker's job is the most mentally challenging. They are required to break cutting-edge technology (designed specifically to stop them) within a tight deadline. When a cracker receives a new game that requires the original CD, they have 6 to 12 hours to fully understand and defeat the technology. Reading the code, they must identify logic and code flaws, exploit those flaws, and then copy the CD to be played freely, all while racing against other crackers trying to do the same thing. The adrenaline rush from *thrill seeking* is incentive enough to motivate a cracker for hours, even days.

Cracking is a tough job and is not meant for everyone. Successful crackers possess a common *semi-autistic* personality. The process of cracking involves thinking in a highly illogical, almost backward manner. The process is so confusing that even the most experienced computer programmer can fail to understand the principles. You must be born a cracker; it is impossible to be trained to think like one.

Very few highly skilled crackers exist in the scene; however, the existing talent is outstanding. Consider this: in his spare time, a 19-year-old defeats a copy protection routine developed by a team of highly experienced programmers. This is not uncommon. Many skilled crackers are in their late teens and early twenties. Younger minds seem to find cracking easier than others.

Crackers tend to come from strong programming backgrounds with vast knowledge of low-level operations such as programming hardware and kernel-level programming. Cracking techniques are not easy. Years of training and experience are required before a cracker feels comfortable.

Why would someone spend time undertaking such a mentally challenging and mind-bending hobby? For many, it is the challenge of the game; trying to defeat technology designed specifically to stop them. For others, there is a significant financial incentive involved. Many black market counterfeiting operations employ crackers to remove copy protection from software titles, thereby allowing the material to be copied and sold.

Cracking is taken very seriously, and is the most respected role in the warez group scene.

Fre0n

Fre0n was the first cracker I ever met, a tall, athletic kid. I never would have picked him for a cracker; however, looks are deceiving.

"I judge new people based on how they present themselves and how they respond to me. With this information, I can usually figure out their level of intelligence, what their main interests are, and how to talk to them."

Fre0n shocked me. He was in his early twenties and lacked any formal education (he was a high school dropout), even though at 15 years old, he was in accelerated classes and was invited to join MENSA, an organization comprised of people with genius IQs. I did not expect him to be overly intelligent. He was a quiet, reserved person who hardly spoke in public.

Fre0n and I began having conversations on the Internet Relay Chat (IRC), at first talking about weather and politics, and then moving on to business, stocks, finances, and technology. Even though Fre0n was unemployed, he had a good knowledge of programming and could easily have obtained a job at a development company. However, he had no ambition to work for a corporation. "Me in a tie? You're kidding, right? Nah; I like sitting at home, plus I get to work on fun stuff," he told me.

"Fun stuff?" I asked.

It turns out Fre0n is an avid day trader on the NASDAQ and DOW JONES, a hobby well beyond the scope of his peers. Fre0n was making a fortune on the stock market and was using the profit to buy new technology and gadgets. He did not work because he did not need to.

Fre0n used his programming skills to write automated stock trading applications (i.e., robots that invest money across a broad stock portfolio and then quickly sell each stock after it rises to the desired amount). "It works well," he said modestly.

Fre0n became my new pet project. His mind was amazing; even though he was a high school dropout, he was one of the brightest people I ever met. We often had lengthy conversations where Fre0n made me think about ideas that I had never considered. He was a genius by any modern standard and definitely not what I expected.

He lived at home with his parents, so he did not need much money to live on. He started developing a commercial Content Management System (CMS) in his spare time and eventually sold the CMS rights and source code to another development company for $120,000. He then moved out on his own, and has been cracking and coding ever since.

Fre0n's group recently defeated a copy protection routine thought to be uncrackable. FreOn invested 6 days of continuous cracking into this protection, sleeping an hour here and an hour there. He was beyond focused; he lived for the scene and for cracking."

"Screw 'em all," was Fre0n's catch phrase. "'I'll crack any code people think is secure. I will always win at cracking." I do not know why FreOn was so driven or why he wasted so much time in the scene. Everyone in the scene is motivated for different reasons; you must be passionate and focused.

So, what drove FreOn? Why did he invest so much time and effort into this?

"Cracking is like boxing; two people enter the ring to test their skills against each other. Crackers compete directly against other programmers, including PhD's in software development, people who write their own encryption algorithms, and just plain geniuses," Fre0n said. "Sometimes it takes a day, sometimes it takes a month, and some routines have taken many months, but they always break in the end, it's just a matter of when," he added.

I began to see why Fre0n enjoyed the challenge: he was a mental athlete who could focus his skills on any topic that appealed to him. Directed, focused, enthralled in the sport of outwitting others, FreOn wanted to fight and win. "I get really annoyed when coders write shoddy protection programs that takes 5 minutes to break. It's not fun. I mean, why bother? I like busting out my ninja skills and cracking the stuff no one else can."

PIRACY FACT...

If caught by authorities, crackers in the warez group scene tend to face a lesser charge than others. Recently arrested crackers were sentenced on "conspiring to violate the criminal copyright laws," a lesser crime than its counterpart, "violating the copyright law," which carries a steeper sentence.

In late 2001, warez group DrinkOrDie (DOD) was busted in an FBI sting known as "Operation Buccaneer." Buj, a cracker in the DOD group and a friend of FreOn, was one of those arrested.

FreOn often raced Buj to crack new CAD applications; however, DOD was a formidable force to compete against. FreOn felt sorry for Buj because, although they competed against each other, FreOn knew that cracking was not worth jail time. "I almost cried the day DOD was busted. I knew a lot of those guys. They were good guys; they didn't deserve that," FreOn told me.

The following is the official United States Department of Justice (DOJ) statement regarding Buj's conviction.

"United States Attorney Paul J. McNulty announced today that Sabuj Pattanayek, age 21, of Nashville, Tennessee, was sentenced to 41 months in federal prison by the Honorable T.S. Ellis III, United States District Judge, for conspiring to violate the criminal copyright laws as a member of one of the oldest and largest international software piracy rings on the Internet.

Sabuj Pattanayek, a student at Duke University known by his screen nickname 'Buj,' was a council member and a highly skilled 'cracker' for the online software piracy group DOD. DOD was a well-organized, security-conscious, Internet software piracy group that specialized in acquiring new software, 'cracking' it (i.e., stripping or circumventing its copyright protections), and releasing the software over the Internet. DOD consisted of approximately 65 group members from more than 12 countries, including the United Kingdom, Australia, Sweden, Norway, and Finland. Sabuj Pattanayek participated in virtually every aspect of the group's 'release' work.

This sentence should serve as a wake up call to every young person who is tempted to squander the privilege of education and a promising future on the short-term notoriety of crime," said U.S. Attorney Paul McNulty.

Fre0n often told me about the current programs he was cracking and the applications that the group released. He was also a cracker in another group that released games.

"Cracking games is much harder than applications. You need serious skills to crack them. Most applications take a few hours to crack and, on average, games take a day and sometimes two or three. It's a real buzz when you finally get it, though."

The reference to "ninja skills" perplexed me, so one day I asked Fre0n, "Are you a code ninja or something? What do you mean you have ninja skills?"

"Every cracker approaches a target in a different manner," he said. "There are many different ways to crack a program and cracker's are usually skilled in one particular technique. The level of ninja skills a cracker possesses determines how effective and efficient the crack will be (e.g., does the cracker patch every binary or create a smooth keygen?). Even when a cracker has serious ninja ability, they don't always use it," Fre0n said. "I have seen crackers defeat programs in *Zen*, a method that doesn't use a disassembler or a debugger. Some of the stuff they do is impressive. True Zen crackers are rare, though, and most just do it for kicks."

FreOn never questioned my constant probing for information. In a way I felt like I was cracking FreOn, studying and detailing his every action. I used the same mindset on him that he used when cracking.

One day FreOn made me an offer I could not refuse. "Dude, I got some spare time. Do you want me to show you how to crack the easiest game I have ever seen?"

A mentoring offer from an experienced cracker; how could I refuse?

Cracking with FreOn

Freon: You will need a disassembler to crack this. It will show the assembler code that your CPU runs when you run the executable. There are a few applications that do this, but *w32dasm* is the easiest for newbie's to pick up. Get it from *http://hjem.get2net.dk/T-Stick/cracking/w32dasm.zip.* *(I downloaded the application and FreOn sent me the executable file from the game I was going to crack.)*

Freon: The game has a CD check and will only run if the *.exe* is run from a CD-ROM drive. If you copy the *.exe* to your hard disk and run it, it will say, *Please insert the CD.* Lame protection, but lots of people still use it. Now open the *.exe* in *w32dism* and tell me when it's finished loading.

Me: Okay, it's finished."

CRACKING FACT...

Inside the .exe there were 21,464 pages of Assembler Source Language (ASM), PUSH, MOV, and INC code. These were the RAW instructions my CPU would run. All compilers compile code to ASM, C, C++, and VB; however, in the end it has to be ASM in order for the CPU to run.

Freon: Okay, press **Goto** and enter page 18,147. You should see an entry labeled "GetDriveTypeA." (See Figure 4.1.)

Me: I'm there.

Figure 4.1 GetDriveTypeA

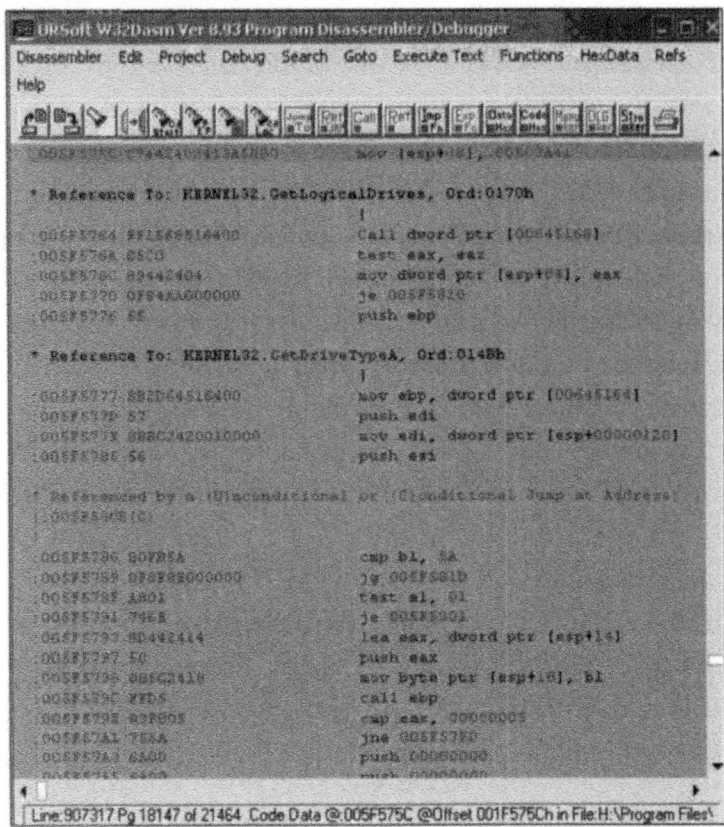

Freon: Do you see that entry? GetDriveTypeA queries the operating system as to what type of drive the *.exe* is currently running from. The function returns seven possible values, depending on if it's a CD-ROM, a hard disk, etc. (See Figure 4.2.)

Figure 4.2 GetDriveTypeA Returns

Value	Meaning
0	Error; drive type cannot be determined
1	Disk has been removed or cannot be accessed
2	Removable drive
3	Hard drive
4	Remote Network drive
5	CD/DVD Drive
6	Ram Disk

Freon: Basically what happens is the application asks the operating system, "What am I running from?" It then compares this value (005F579E "cmp eax, 00000005)" to 0000005. If it is not equal, it jumps to the line below (JNE 005F57FD). The code looks like this:

App: Operating system, what media is this *.exe* running from?

Operating System: We are running from 00000003 (hard disk).

App: Compare 00000003 to 00000005. If they are not the same, jump to the "Please insert CD-ROM" message, otherwise, continue.

Fre0n: Get it? If you change the 00000005 to 00000003, it will only work if you run it from the hard disk. If you changed it to 00000004 it would only run from a remote network drive.

Me: Whoa, yeah, I understand. That's it, and its cracked?

Freon: Ha-ha, don't think all games are like this; however, in theory, this is what every crack is like. A bunch of functions that return values, and a few conditional jumps that act on those returned values.

Me: So, if I wanted to change this *.exe*, how would I do it?

Fre0n: The best way is to change the Jump If Not Equal (JNE) jump (conditional jump) to be an unconditional Jump (JMP), and then run it from any media. But if you want to change the 00000005 to 00000003 so that it works from a hard disk, you would first load the *.exe* into a hex editor and search for "83 F8 05 75 5A," which is the hex for lines "CMP EAX, 000000005 and JNE 005F57FD." (See Figure 4.3.) You want to change bytes "83 F8 05" to "83 F8 03," which will make the corresponding ASM "CMP EAX, 00000003." If you wanted to make the JNE a JMP you would change "75 5A" to "EB 5A," 75 = JNE and EB=JMP. Get it? (See Figure 4.3.)

Figure 4.3 Altering the .exe

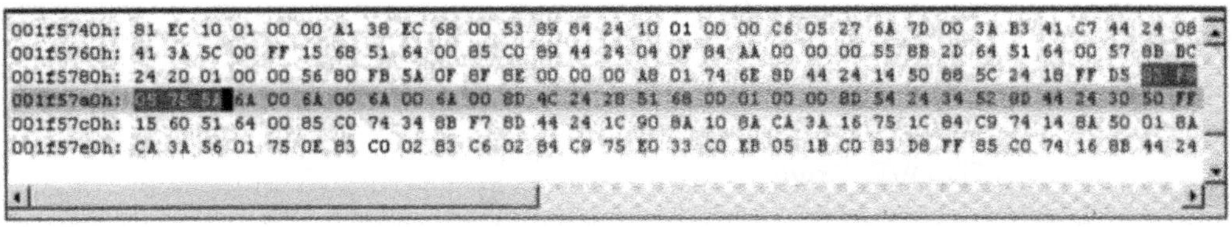

```
001f5740h: 81 EC 10 01 00 00 A1 38 EC 68 00 53 89 64 24 10 01 00 00 C6 05 27 6A 7D 00 3A B3 41 C7 44 24 08
001f5760h: 41 3A 5C 00 FF 15 68 51 64 00 85 C0 89 44 24 04 0F 84 AA 00 00 00 55 8B 2D 64 51 64 00 57 8B BC
001f5780h: 24 20 01 00 00 56 80 FB 5A 0F 8F 8E 00 00 00 A8 01 74 6E 8D 44 24 14 50 68 5C 24 18 FF D5
001f57a0h: 6A 00 6A 00 6A 00 6A 00 8D 4C 24 28 51 68 00 01 00 00 8D 54 24 34 52 8D 44 24 30 50 FF
001f57c0h: 15 60 51 64 00 85 C0 74 34 8B F7 8D 44 24 1C 90 8A 10 8A CA 3A 16 75 1C 84 C9 74 14 8A 50 01 8A
001f57e0h: CA 3A 56 01 75 0E 83 C0 02 83 C6 02 84 C9 75 E0 33 C0 EB 05 1B C0 83 D8 FF 85 C0 74 16 8B 44 24
```

It seemed easy enough. I made the changes and saved the file *.exe* to disk.

Now when I ran the *.exe*, I was prompted with an error saying critical game files were missing, understandable since I was only given one file. However, previously when I ran the file, a large intrusive message would appear telling me to insert the correct CD-ROM.

To my shock, I had become a cracker, an incredibly inexperienced cracker, but I still defeated a piece of copy protection. The rush was amazing.

Fre0n: Welcome to the world of cracking.

Varying Cracking Methods

Each cracker's "ninja skills" is very different; therefore, each method of copy protection is best defeated in a different manner. With this in mind, certain crackers are more suited toward a certain protection routine. For example, some cracks are based purely on mathematical principles, which require the cracker to have advanced mathematical training, while other technology requires an in-depth knowledge of hardware registers and interrupts. A successful cracker must adapt his cracking style to accommodate any new technology.

This section looks at the most common methods used to both defend and attack copy protection from the point of view of the developer (the defender) and the attacker (the cracker). First, you will see what mindset is required from these mental gladiators. Remember, in the end, cracking is a battle between two minds. Both the defender and the attacker lay their ninja skills on the line and do battle in a virtual arena.

Serial Numbers and CD Keys

Serial numbers and CD keys are synonymous with copy protection. Serial numbers offer a unique method of mapping a piece of information (e.g., a name or e-mail address) to an unrecognizable string of numbers and letters.

Unreadable to the naked eye, serial numbers contain a wealth of information. They act as watermarks that can be used to identify license owners and the types of licenses they own.

Serial numbers first became widely used in the mid 1990s during the dawn of shareware (share at will) applications. Shareware was designed to be freely available to all. However, after a pre-determined amount of time, shareware applications prompted users' to purchase the software, or forced them to discontinue using it. If a user decided to purchase the application, and after paying the license fee, they were sent a serial number matching their real name or e-mail address.

For example, when Jim Bob/29123908129 was entered into a shareware application, it unlocked the application and turned it into the "complete" version (only for the name "Jim Bob"). This was done to stop Jim from distributing his serial number to others, because the serial number directly correlated to the name "Jim Bob," which would allow the serial number to be traced back to him.

Serial number algorithms have progressed greatly since the early 1990s, and the technology has grown to be very intricate. Because of the growth in popularity, almost every retail application installed today has some form of a serial number or CD key.

Following is a breakdown of the different types of serial numbers and the logic behind each of them.

Statically Encoded Serial Numbers

Defender

In this situation, the *serial number* is constructed entirely from a "Registered User" field or another static text field. Serial numbers are encoded versions of a piece of physically binding information. A serial number that is given out over the Internet or being used by pirates can be directly linked to the license owner. Static encoding is the simplest and most common form of serial number technology used, giving developers an easy method of tracking the source of the serial number.

Methods used to encode a serial number algorithm range from simple to complex, but the ideology does not vary. Developers do not want anyone to guess a serial number that corresponds to a username, so the code is often long, containing a mixture of letters and numbers (e.g., Joe Bob/98234983-AEA-8923487234-XWZ).

PIRACY FACT…

An example of a static serial number encoding routine may look like this:

If the username is over six characters in length, take each letter and assign it an incremental value (e.g., A = 1, B = 2, C = 3 and so forth). Then take each letter's value and multiply it by the next value in the sequence to produce a longer value (e.g., Jimbo = 10(J) 9(i) 13(m) 2(b) 15(o) 10 9 13 2 15 = 35100)

The resulting value is further lengthened by multiplying it with the incremental values of the username from the first step. When 10913215is multiplied with 35100 it produces the final serial number (i.e., 35100 10913215 = 273921696500).

When Jimbo/273921696500 is entered into an application, the "Thanks for supporting our software" message appears." However, if you try to enter the same serial number with the username "Ralf," the message "Invalid serial number" appears.

Encoding static information is a good way to track a license code to a license holder. Real names, phone numbers, and e-mail addresses are commonly used in this method. Companies often refuse sales that originate from free disposable e-mail addresses (e.g., hotmail) because they require personal information. Accountability is required; however, even though a hotmail account is legitimate, it is not physically binding to the license holder.

When the application is cracked and a license belonging to "Evil Cracker" is distributed in the release, what options does the developer have? Obviously, the license is not legitimate and cannot be used to trace the license owner, so what can be done?

Developers cannot do anything until a new major version comes out, thus allowing the pirates to continue using the product. Alternatively, developers can blacklist the serial number within the application, explicitly prohibiting the username "Evil Cracker" from registering the software.

Piracy Fact…

"Blacklisting" is the process of banning known pirated serial numbers or usernames within an application. When software is cracked and a serial number is distributed on the Internet, developers' hardcode known pirated user names and serial numbers inside the application, thereby inhibiting pirates from using the cracked license key with further versions. Software developers protect their software by not requiring that a licensing routine be rewritten and sending every legitimate customer a new license key.

Developers are also known for employing other tactics to inhibit pirates, including using malicious code inside applications that is triggered when a user attempts to register the software with known pirated information. Malicious software will attempt to delete critical windows files or send e-mails to the software developer with personal information. Developers do not take kindly to theft and often seek revenge on those who crack their software or use pirated licenses.

Attacker

Connecting license codes with real names and e-mail addresses is a good way to keep track of legitimate licenses; however, the licenses are not always legitimate to begin with. Crackers often find ways of generating their own serial numbers, which they then register to "Evil cracker" or another cracker handle. Creating an untraceable license number carries no apparent risk to the cracker and gives the end user a fully working application.

Cracking serial numbers is done using one of two different methods. One method allows a cracker to patch an application to allow all serial numbers to work (much like the example FreOn showed with the CD check). By manipulating an application's machine code, it is possible to change conditions, thus allowing any serial number entered to appear legitimate. (See Figure 4.4.)

Figure 4.4 Changing ASM to Defeat a Serial Number Check

```
CMP EAX, ECX
JE 000012345
PUSH "License problem"
PUSH "Sorry, that serial is not valid"
CALL MESSAGEBOXA
```

This ASM reads something like the following:

- Compare the EAX and ECX registers (EAX contains the serial number entered; ECX contains the correct serial number).

- If equal (meaning the serial number is correct), go to another block of code and thank the user for buying the software.

- If they are not equal, the serial number is incorrect; continue with the next line of the ASM.

- Push the "License problem" and "Sorry, that serial is not valid" strings to the stack and call them *messagebox*.

Entering an invalid serial number produces a messagebox named "License problem" with the text, "Sorry, that serial number is not valid." Changing one byte can defeat this protection. In this case, Jump Equal (JE) to JNE will reverse the logic of the serial number check. If the serial number entered is legitimate, the user sees the "License problem" messagebox; however, if the license number entered is invalid, the application thanks the user for purchasing the software.

To make the distribution process easier, pirates often include a small *patch* application in the release. This patch will automatically modify the needed binaries, without having to include the entire cracked executable.

PIRACY FACT...

A patch is a small program that modifies another program's machine code.

Because a patch is small in size (<5K), a cracker does not have to include a large executable (e.g., 10+MB) if there are only a few byte changes.

The second, preferred method for defeating a serial number code is for a cracker to generate a new, legitimate license key. This method is more easily distributed with the release, because it does not require changes to the binary. Obtaining a valid serial number has the added benefit of allowing you to work with later versions of software that uses the same license routine.

In order for a cracker to generate his own license, he or she must first understand exactly how the key generation routine works. Line-by-line, every precise detail must be accounted for and then replicated.

"Sometimes a good serial number generation routine might be 200 to 500 lines of ASM. It can take hours to fully understand what it's doing," FreOn told me.

A cracker's best tool for this task is a memory debugger. A good memory debugger is essential for understanding machine code; cracking would be impossible without using one.

Debuggers allow crackers to view each line of ASM that the CPU is currently executing (a CPU runs billions of lines of machine code every day). Using a memory debugger allows a cracker to watch each instruction execute in real time, while at the same time study the effect they have on the environment. Six hours with a debugger can give a cracker a complete low-level blueprint of how an application is behaving.

If a cracker spends enough time studying an application licensing system, they will eventually replicate the entire process and create their own license code generator. Key generators (keygen) are handmade license generators commonly distributed with pirated releases, which offer users' the ability to generate legitimate licenses in their own name (most end users prefer to license software to their own names).

Although useful, not all crackers want to invest time writing a keygen for every $10.00 shareware application created. This process can be staggering, and therefore, many crackers opt to find only one working name/registration key combination.

Also, when using a memory debugger, a cracker does not have to know how a key was generated, only what the correct key is for a particular user name. Many shareware applications can be cracked in under a minute, greatly decreasing the time involved. (See Figure 4.4.)

The first line in the "CMP EAX, ECX" example is the only instruction a cracker needs to worry about. A quick investigation into the values for EAX and ECX shows why:

```
EAX = 123456789
ECX = 931622512
```

EAX is the serial number entered (i.e., 123456789). This value is then compared to 931622512, the correct serial number code for the user name.

When username "Evil Cracker" and serial number key "931622512" are entered, the "Thanks for registering" messagebox appears.

This process is commonly known as *fishing*, because the cracker effectively fishes the serial number out of the application's memory.

Conclusion

Although static key encoding works, it does not provide adequate protection against a really determined cracker. What protection it does provide inhibits those who purchase legitimate licenses. Keys are only bound to names or e-mail addresses, not to volume or independent machines. Furthermore, static key encoding offers no fail-safe method of tracking cracked licenses such as those generated by crackers. Possibly the earliest form of license protection, these keys are often the first to fall into the hands of a pirate, with keygens and cracked serial numbers quickly distributed over the Internet.

Node-locked Keys

Node-locked keys are an evolutionary step forward from statically encoded keys. They offer better protection against crackers and, using simple techniques, can make an application significantly harder to crack.

Defender

Keys in this situation are not bound to just usernames or e-mail addresses, but also to unique information that is relative to the host computer. Creating a unique binding to each specific computer, node-locked keys were the first license protection method to offer a way to control the number of instances that an application could be installed within a company, without needing a physical security device (e.g., a dongle).

Node-locked keys also inhibit pirates from distributing an application with just one license key. Each key works on only one machine; therefore, if a license is distributed on the Internet, it will be rendered useless. (See Figure 4.5.)

Figure 4.5 Node-locked Keys

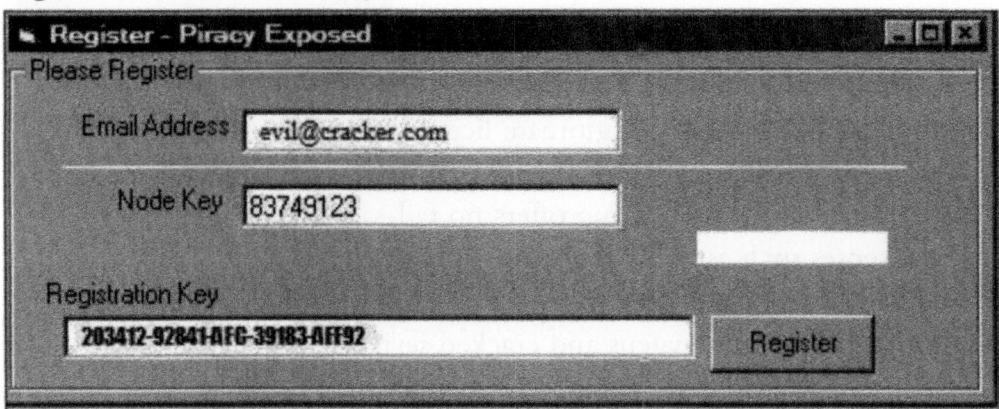

The registration key is only valid for node key "83749123" and the sample e-mail address, "*evil@cracker.com*." If either value changes, the resulting registration key also changes.

If this application were installed on another computer, the node key would change. In this case, the node key came from the Media Access Control (MAC) address of the network card (each network card has a unique MAC address). In this case, licenses are bound to each unique physical installation of the software, allowing for restrictions on the amount of installations that can occur within an environment.

After software is purchased, the user is prompted to contact the software company and receive the registration key that matches their specific node key. Applications usually do this automatically by interfacing with a license or registration Web server. This method is the most popular method, with everyone from Microsoft, Citrix, Symantec, and Autodesk using it.

Attacker

Defeating a node-based license is significantly harder than defeating a statically encoded key. Crackers can only obtain one key, because every software user requires a different key. The cracker has to either create a keygen (designed to generate keys unique to each node), or they have to create a patch for the application that will disable the checks completely.

Keygen creation is more involved than other methods, because the cracker must understand how the node key is generated. Node-based keys are the best method of licensing and, if implemented correctly, can slow an attacker down considerably. If enough energy is invested in researching a node key generation routine, creating a keygen will still be possible.

Algorithmic CD Key

Next to node-based keys, algorithmic *CD keys* have become the most accepted form of license protection, with a majority of software developers shipping applications with a CD key stamped on the jewel case. Unlike static- and node-based keys, algorithmic keys are based solely on algorithms and are best explained as mathematical patterns or formulas that contain a wealth of knowledge.

Defender

Although each key looks random and unpredictable, they are actually the result of an equation with an incrementing factor and many embedded values. Embedded values identify the type of product, where it was purchased, and the sequential sales number it corresponds to. (See Figure 4.6.)

Figure 4.6 Algorithmic CD Key

CD key 00193-0391-75463 (found on a product jewel case) could represent the following information when broken down.

Product Type	Vendor	Number of Licenses	Checksum
001	93	0391	75463

```
00193-0391-75463
001 = Professional version
93 = Bought online from the companies official store
0391 = the 391'th copy sold
75463 = the result of the first two fields when multiplied together (193
391)
```

A clear formula for the CD key is visible, and each incrementing key will be unique while also being linked to every other key in the series, carrying its own unique information. Applying this formula to further sequential keys would generate a series like this:

```
00193-0391-75463
00193-0392-75656
00193-0393-75849
```

CD keys are not usually used as a form of strong copy protection, but more as a way of tracking registered users. Services such as updates to products and access to knowledge bases often require validating the CD key online, or the key is used to obtain technical support. Recently, however, CD keys have been tied into node-based serial numbers, with a CD key replacing the username or e-mail address that would have otherwise been used.

PIRACY FACT...

CD keys have recently become a very effective tool in limiting the playability of pirated copies of online games.

Electronic Arts have made the *dual algorithmic* CD key process highly popular. Dual algorithmic keys have two embedded sequences: the most common sequence allows the game to be installed locally, and the other sequence checks only when online play is attempted.

Key 001-002-00000011 may work flawlessly during the installation process, but online servers will reject it, thus giving an "Invalid CDKEY" message and forcing pirates to only play local games.

Such CD keys also inhibit the ability of a cracker to debug or reverse engineer a protection routine, since an online CD key is checked by a remote server and not locally.

Although keygens are commonly released for pirated games, none of the generated keys will function online; the game can only be installed locally.

Attacker

CD keys are not a fail-safe method of copy protection, because they are completely mathematically based and lack any binding or physical information. CD keys are commonly attacked in two fashions.

First, the target is reverse-engineered and the algorithm is learned. As with other protection methods, if there is a mathematical calculation, the cracker will break it down and duplicate it. Mathematics used in CD keys often break down into a simple number series.

Once two or three keys are discovered, a cracker can usually guess the next keys. The most common attack method is attacking the key space inside the CD key itself. Say you have 10 million copies of a product that you want to sell, each with a unique CD key printed on the jewel case. Key space is often overlooked when designing a protection routine, and in a case where 10 million possible keys exist, guessing becomes increasingly difficult. The method of guessing keys is known as *brute force*. Crackers develop their own applications to test thousands of possible keys against a program until a working key is found.

Piracy Fact...

External libraries are often used to check the validity of a CD key within an application. Such functions can be exploited with a little crafty programming. For example:

Keycheck.dll – with an exported function called "ValidateCD key." When passed a string, this function returns a *1* if the key is valid or a *0* if the key is invalid.

During the installation process, *keycheck.dll* is called and given the CD key you have supplied. If the returned value is *1*, you can continue; if it's *0*, you are prompted with an "Invalid CD key" error.

In this case, the cracker sequentially tests CD keys until a legitimate key is found:

- ValidateCDKey("0000000001")
- ValidateCDKey("0000000002")

This is done until the returned value equals *1*. If the key space is large and there are millions of possible key combinations, it may only take a cracker a few minutes to find the first key in the sequence. Crackers use this method when the logic behind a key is too complex to reverse-engineer.

CD-ROM Protection Methods

Floppy disks are no longer the main media used for transporting software. Physically, it is not feasible to put a game or application on 100 different disks; if one of those disks became corrupt it would cause immense problems.

Defender

Growing media demands and the growing size of applications has moved software distribution to CD-ROMs, although they are slowly being replaced by DVDs.

Software technology has changed little; many of the protection methods used for CD-ROM copy protections are almost identical to those used for floppy disk protections. The copy protection that was used on floppy disks was either unreadable or contained invalid sectors designed to stop pirates from copying the media.

The application verifies the bytes that cannot be copied. If the bytes exist, the application will run from legitimate media. If they are missing, someone has tried to copy the disk. Allowing applications to validate their own source media, this method is still used greatly in CD-ROM protection routines.

One of the first types of CD-ROM protection methods used was a corrupted or invalid Table of Contents (TOC). CD's are often printed with invalid details inside the TOC (e.g., the lengths of tracks are too long or they start in an invalid position within the disk). Using an invalid TOC is a simple and effective way to make CD-ROMs impossible to copy.

PIRACY FACT...

The TOC is a record that identifies the start position and the length of the tracks on a CD-ROM. TOC's are present on all CDs. If they are missing, the disk will be unreadable in any player. CD recorders write the TOC as part of the "finalizing" stage.

If a TOC is invalidated, the CD-ROM cannot be copied; however, it would still be fully readable.

Attacker

In mid-2001, CD-ROM protection changed greatly when the ability to copy CDs in RAW (unprocessed data) mode was made available to the public.

RAW mode enabled CD writers to clone a CD based on the raw bytes of each track; it did not care if the byte was damaged, unreadable, or looked strange. If you cloned a damaged CD with a RAW mode copier, the resulting CD would be damaged in the same exact sectors.

Although the RAW writing technology was a powerful tool for end users, it was bad news for the game industry. A majority of copy protection systems rely on the operating system's help. Operating systems determine if a file or track should be copied. RAW copiers, however, never see files or file systems; consequently the majority of protection methods are avoidable by using a copier in RAW mode. An entire 1:1 replica takes less than 10 minutes to produce complete with unreadable bytes, invalid blocks, and invalid tracks.

Recently, the technology used to combat RAW mode copiers changed to allow for monitoring the finite hardware that is used to write CDs. Each CD has a unique fingerprint. Such finite details can be used to determine if a CD was written in a standard CDR, or in the correct machine language designed to master the originals.

By reading the density of sectors on a CD and timing the seek response time between sectors on the disc, copy protections can determine which writer was used to create the CD-ROM. Average home CD writers use standard hardware, with a predictable sector density. If a protector identifies that a home user's CDR (compact disk recordable drive) wrote the media it is running from, the copy is obviously pirated.

Commercial Game Protectors

Commercial CD copy protections such as SafeCast, Securom, SafeDisc and Starforce, are found on most PC games released today. These commercial protectors position themselves in the executable files within a game, to constantly check and re-check the validity of the source media. These protectors offer an easy method of securing a game against piracy.

Defender

The key to a commercial protector's success is its ability to be symbiotic with the game itself, often replacing exported code functions with its own interim functions, thereby making their presence essential in order for the game to operate. If the protection exists, the game will not run from copied media; however, if a cracker manages to remove the protection, the game will not function and will crash unexpectedly, because it requires protections for call libraries.

With Starforce, developers do not apply the protection themselves. Instead, they send the core executable of the game to the Starforce developers, who then send back a secure, copy-protected version of the file, ensuring that the copy protection is implemented correctly while keeping the technology itself hidden and unknown to crackers.

Starforce spells trouble for crackers; it is the hardest, most challenging commercial protector on the market. Virtual CPU technology is used within Starforce; therefore, any Starforce-protected executable will run inside a virtual environment inside an operating system. Such an obfuscated method makes debugging impossible. When a single ASM instruction is passed through Starforce, the virtual memory (VM) turns into over 300 lines of instructions for the CPU to run.

A call to GETDRIVETYPEA was under 10 lines of ASM. However, if the application were running Starforce's protector, it would grow to over 2.3 million lines of code.

"Starforce? Oh yeah," said FreOn. "That protection is tough. I can do most protections, but Starforce really takes it out of you. It's so intricate that it becomes a part of the executable in more ways than one. It takes weeks to fully crack it. Some guys in the scene are really pumped about it, and can crack/remove it in under a week. A week of cracking Starforce? No way dude."

The technology used in anti-piracy measures is amazing and shows how much thought goes into commercial copy protection methods. After all, the copy protection industry is now a multi-million dollar business.

Attacker

CDR copying technology has ways to copy commercial protectors. Applications such as Alcohol 120% and CloneCD can make working replicas of most copy protection methods by emulating the protection routine internally, and using a specialized writing method for each protector. This software allows the user to reproduce the CD as long as they have the required hardware. Usually, only the high-end CD writers can write the specialized copy protection information back to the CD; lower-end models tend to lack this advanced functionality. (See Figure 4.7.)

Figure 4.7 Replication Made Easy

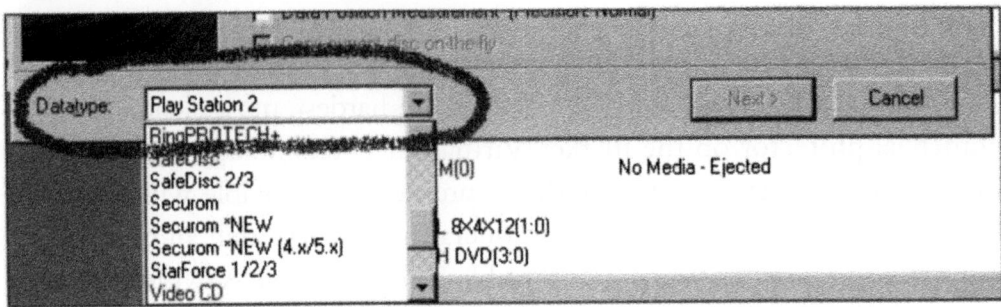

Not surprisingly, game companies hate both CloneCD and Alcohol 120%. After copyright infringement allegations were brought against them, CloneCD was forced to abandon its product line.

Also, many games will not install if CloneCD, Alcohol 120%, or any other copy protection emulation applications are present on the system.

PIRACY FACT...

One example is "The Sims 2," by Electronic Arts. A sequel to the hit people simulator, "The Sims," The Sims 2 will not install if any CD emulation programs are found on the computer.

These applications include CloneCD and Nero, which are often pre-installed by the computer manufacturer before purchase. "My version of Clone CD is so old that it doesn't do any emulation, probably wouldn't beat any modern copy protection," writes one disgruntled SlashDot (*www.slashdot.org*) reader who could not install the game he purchased.

When you clone a CD, you are only bypassing the copy protection; you have not defeated it. Warez group scene rules state that copy protection must be removed; bypassing it is not acceptable.

PIRACY FACT...

The day "Doom 3" was officially released, cloned CD images were being traded on peer-to-peer (P2P) networks.

These images did not come from the professional crackers who were working on the game's copy protection, they came from end users who were able to make a transferable, working image of the CD.

Doom 3's copy protection was a custom version of SafeDisc 3, which was proving hard to remove. However, if the CD were copied in its entirety, the protection would also be copied and would still function.

Although the cloned CD image worked, the protection routine was still present, which meant that the user still had to insert the CD in order to play the game.

Two days later, a working cracked version was released with the main executable rebuilt. Lacking any traces of SafeDisc, this new version would run even if the CD was not present.

Because not all CD writers can reproduce clone images, crackers still work with the commercial protectors to give everyone the ability to write the CDs. The copy protection must be removed, stripped clean, and the executable left in a virgin state.

When new versions of Starforce, SafeDisc, or the like are released, scene groups panic. Is this the version that will defeat us? What happens if we can't crack it? Countless crackers take the challenge; the protector is put through its paces night and day, as crackers look for ways to remove or disable it.

PIRACY FACT...

Some of the crackers that specialize in cracking commercial game protectors are developers of competing copy protection software. They study their competition's work night and day. It is their life, not just a hobby.

It took just over three months to find a method that could beat Starforce 2. However, some Starforce 2 protected titles remain uncracked because it is so complex it would take too long to remove it.

Commercial copy protection, especially in games, is the hardest and most complex protection method used today. These software companies offer a ridiculously hard challenge to any cracker who wants to make an attempt.

Size

One of the most creative copy protection methods used in early CD-ROM protection was sheer size. When computers still had small hard disks with only a few gigabytes of storage, and the majority of Internet connectivity was 56k or slower, size and the overhead of the data pirated were valued. When CD-ROMs first started emerging, very few pirates had the time to upload and download a complete CD image worth of data. CD writers were also expensive, and many pirates still transferred the CD-ROM games onto floppy disks, which were smaller and easier to transfer via modem.

The process of putting a CD-ROM image onto a floppy disk is known as *ripping*. Ripping is relatively simple and involves taking out, or compressing, various content of an application or game to make it smaller.

For example: Jack bought a new game called "Horror 3D," which comes on one CD and is 100MB in size, much too big to put on floppy disks. After some investigation, Jack discovered that the majority of the CD was composed of background music; in fact, 85MB were *wave* files. Jack replaced each wave file with a blank, 0-second sample, cutting the size of the CD-ROM game down from 100MB to 15MB. It will now easily fit on 11 disks and can be quickly uploaded to Bulletin Board System (BBS) or Internet site.

Developers knew that pirates were removing content from their games in order to replicate them. They also knew that if their game was too big and content could not be removed, pirates would not bother with it. This idea spawned many CD-ROM games to contain "junk files." Junk files are large, unnecessary files located on the CD-ROM that act as copy protection.

When the game was first loaded, copy protection checked the presence of the junk file and its contents. If the file was not present or the size was incorrect, the game would refuse to load. Copying the CD is easy if you have the money and resources. Uploading the complete CD image to another BBS or Internet site would be almost impossible. Even if you managed to upload 650MB at 56 KBs, the majority of BBS' only have a few gigabytes of online storage. BBS owners were not willing to sacrifice so much storage for one game. This simple method saved many games from piracy, although the more determined professional crackers soon found ways to defeat the technology.

PIRACY FACT...

One of the most memorable games that, which used its size to its advantage was "Diablo 1" from Blizzard Software. When Diablo was released in 1997, some Internet users were starting to get faster connections and move away from dial-up technology. However, the majority of users were still stuck on dial-up.

Diablo's directory structure was composed of only a few files, with the majority size being in several large *.mpq* files located on the CD-ROM. These files contained all of the game content, from the background music to the speech and in-game video, totaling 506MB of the CD-ROM. Additionally, the .mpq files were compressed, encrypted, and obfuscated with propriety technology. No one could decompress the mammoth game files. Blizzard almost beat the crackers.

Blizzard knew that no one would download a complete CD image over a dial-up; it was not practical. However, there was one person who managed to break the protection.

Cyber from the group HYBRID, and a developer for a leading games production company, was able to reverse engineer the *.mpq* files without any additional information about its format. The process was very complex; however, the original game size of 550MB was shrunk to a mere 144MB when he was finished. Although it was a huge download for modem users, 144MB was seen as a radical improvement over the 550MB CD image.

The HYBRID "rip" of Diablo was missing very little. Background music, some speech, and the in-game videos were removed, but the game was still intact and fun to play.

Modern day technology has removed this completely.

Dongles

In the late 1980s, dongles made a big splash in the computer world when software publisher Ocean announced "Robocop 3" featuring a new "uncrackable" protection system—a dongle.

Figure 4.8 Robocop 3, Halt Citizen, Please Insert the Dongle

Ocean released a press announcement about their new dongle technology. The small device would plug into an unused joystick port; without the dongle the game would not function. This was the supposed piracy killer; no one would be able to copy the dongle, so the game would remain uncrackable. However, it took just under 30 minutes for a warez scene group to obtain a copy of the game and defeat the dongle checks, thereby making the game fully functional.

Modern day dongles no longer appear in game copy protection systems, but instead are synonymous with high-end graphic design and engineering applications such as those used in the film and graphic design industry.

Figure 4.9 A Parallel Port Dongle

The growth in dongle software technology requires cracker's to specialize in cracking them in order to break the more advanced targets. Only a limited number of people are capable of cracking the "hardcore" secure dongles.

 **PIRACY FACT...**

One such specialized cracker is an ex-employee of Aladdin, makers of the HASP dongles.

With internal knowledge of Aladdin's protection system, he can break the secure products they create. Technology is becoming increasingly difficult to combat. Dongles have evolved along way and they are now some of the hardest protections in the world when implemented properly.

Many different types of dongles exist, each with varying strengths and success in the real world. The simplest of dongle technology is called the *unlock key* or the *product serial number device*.

Unlocked Key Dongle

Unlocked key dongles possess a small ROM chip that contains no more than 10 or 20 stored bytes. ROMs contain a serial number or passkey that the host application will use as a license, much like a serial number or license code, only held on an external device.

Periodically, programs will question the dongle for its validity and for the contents of its ROM. Dongle passkeys or serial numbers commonly show the license purchased for the application (whether a single user, a network only, or the enterprise version should be running.

Internal dongle checks will fail if the dongle is removed, or if its license expires, which will cause the software to either exit or prompt the user with a license warning.

For example, an application may check to see if a dongle is connected to the system and whether the ROM of the dongle contains the string "Apples4Me." If the string is located on the dongle, its validity is proven. If the dongle contains a different value or there is no dongle attached, the license check fails.

Encryption methods are also common in dongles. These methods are seen when the key or serial number contained in the dongle is an actual encryption key or a password used to unlock missing information within an application. Without the dongle present, the information will not decrypt, and without a copy of the legitimate dongle, a cracker has no chance of defeating it.

PIRACY FACT...

Think of encrypted unlock keys much like a zip password for a *WinZip* zip file.

Even if you make WinZip think you entered the correct password, when incorrect the archive will not decompress because the decryption will fail. Only the password contained on the dongle will let the archive unzip; it cannot be bypassed.

Encryption key dongles are becoming increasingly popular, because they offer an easily implemented solution that achieves a high level of security. Encryption methods require crackers to obtain a copy of the software and a legitimate *dongle-dump* if they wish to defeat it.

PIRACY FACT...

Dongle dumps are copies of an original dongle's contents. They contain the necessary information to unlock the application, such as the key or serial number code. Crackers must find a way to hard-code this information back into the application so that it is still decrypted when the dongle is not present.

Another popular dongle protection method is *enveloping,* which is similar to an unlock key dongle, only it works in reverse.

Dongle Envelopes

Think of a dongle envelope as a small deciphering machine. Applications send themselves to deciphering machines for decoding; the application will not function without this process.

Envelope dongles work much like an unlock key dongle, only the unlocking routine is performed by the dongle without a key or code.

Enveloped dongles are one of the most formidable forms of dongle security, thus making reverse engineering much harder. Security levels are much greater because no one really knows what the dongle is doing; they only know that they need it. The technology used in enveloped dongles is black box (unpublished trade secrets). Very few people have the ability to reverse engineer their protection.

Figure 4.10 shows how a garbled string is decoded into legitimate ASM by the correct envelope dongle.

www.syngress.com

Figure 4.10 Enveloped Dongles

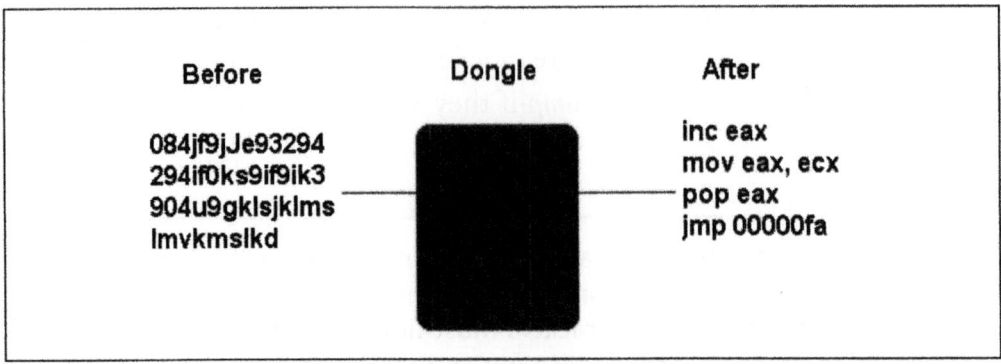

Without in-depth dongle analysis or internal information being disclosed, enveloped dongles are good opponents for crackers, since they are often complex, requiring painstaking effort to analyze. If a cracker does not defeat the dongle technology, he or she must either rebuild the application after it has been decoded, or include his or her own dongle emulator to decode it.

Cracking is an entire world within the scene; a niche division kept quiet in the darkest corners of cyberspace.

I never would have guessed how much work was involved in cracking. I thought it would be easy; a quick 5-minute job and its finished, or maybe a few hours if the target is hard. But days? Weeks? I would never have imagined that it could take so long. End users never think about the hours, often weeks of work that is invested into every crack released. Cracking requires intelligence, dedication, and creativity. Cracking is not a hobby, it is a an art form, a way of life. And to many in the warez group scene, it is a religion.

Chapter 5

The Release

A release is the result of a lot of work. It takes a supplier, a cracker, and a packager many hours to produce a final product.

A release is to a cracker what a canvas is to an artist (i.e., an expression of self and a transformation of time into a tangible product). To the end user, a release is a pirated application that is compressed and includes notes on how to install and use the product. It is the final link in the piracy chain.

Pirates take each release very seriously; it is more than just a release to them, it is an art form. It is human nature to take pride in the things that you invest time and effort into. For crackers, each release becomes a creation, something unique that the group submits to the *warez* group scene. For example:

- NuSphere_phpED_v3.2.3217_WORKING-FCN

- 321Studios.DVDXCopy.Platinum.v3.2.1.WinAll.Cracked-EAT

- Roxio.Easy.Media.Creator.v7.0-AGAiN

These are all "official" releases listed from a scene site. They are all uniform in style; the directory names are specific, stating the product, the developing company, and the product version. The directory names use underscores instead of spaces and each directory is suffixed with the group that released it. Inside each directory, the file names are eight characters long with a three-letter extension. Each release is split into disks ranging from 2.8MB to 5MB in size, and each is individually zipped. The first disk in a set contains an Info File (NFO), which provides information about the release. Further disks in each set contain a unique *file_id.diz* file that indicates the current disk number in the set of disks. (See Figure 5.1.)

Figure 5.1 *file_id.diz*

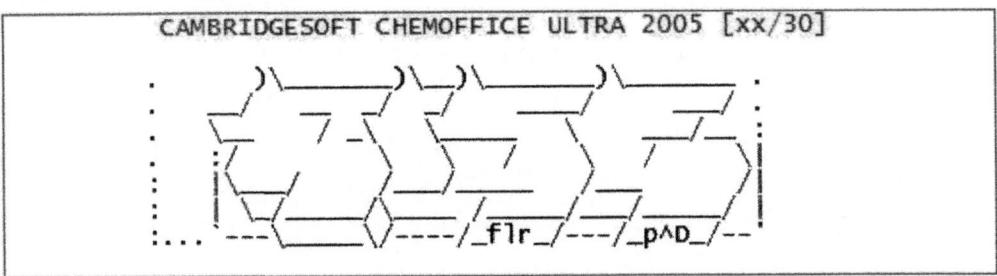

Each release must adhere to a specific set of scene rules. If a release strays from the rules (i.e., trying to be different or ignoring warez policies) scene sites will refuse the release and instantly *nuke* it.

PIRACY FACT…

When a site refuses a release, the site administrator marks it as a *nuke*, as shown below:

!NUKED-CAMBRIDGESOFT.CHEMOFFICE.ULTRA.2005.RiSE

When a release is nuked, the person who uploaded it will lose between 1.5 and 5 times the size of the release in credits. Each site has its own nuke rules; some sway a little from scene rules, but the majority share the same ideas.

If a top scene site nukes a release, many other sites will also nuke it, often without investigating whether or not it is legitimate. Because of this, it is essential that at least 80 percent of the top scene sites accept the release.

Figure 5.2 shows a nuke list from a top site that indicates the reasons used for rejecting certain pirated releases. These reasons range from being a Minor Upgrade (MU) from a past release to functional problems within an application. Ironically, pirates who steal from other pirates will have their own releases *nuked*. Honor among thieves; pirates do not steal from other pirates.

Figure 5.2 A Nuke List

```
,-------------------------------------------------------------------
.
| Nuker       | Nukee       | Amount    | Reason
|
|-------------|-------------|-----------|-----------------------------
|
| xxxxxxx     | xxxxxx      | 1x   4.4M | not.working.5.burn.limited
|
| Age:  3h 56m| Dir: Lavavo.CD.Ripper.3.1.9.WinALL.Regged-XMA0D
|
|-------------------------------------------------------------------
|
| xxxxxxx     | xxxxxx      | 1x   4.4M | not.working.5.burn.limited
|
| Age:  3h 59m| Dir: Lavavo.CD.Ripper.3.2.0.WinALL.Regged-XMA0D
|
```

```
|----------------------------------------------------------------------
|
| xxxxxxxx   | xxxx           | 1x  6.0M | grp.req
|
| Age: 12h 40m| Dir: Alcohol.120.v1.9.5.2722.Multilingual.WinALL.Cracked-
D|
|----------------------------------------------------------------------
|
| xxxxxxx    | xxxxxx         | 1x 24.4M | empty.dir
|
| Age: 15h 51m| Dir:
INTEL.CPP.COMPILER.v8.1.025.NiTROUSINTEL.CPP.COMPILER|
|----------------------------------------------------------------------
|
| xxxxxxx    | xxxxxxx        | 2x 14.3M | incomplete
|
| Age: 15h 52m| Dir:
Charles.River.Media.Mobile.Device.Game.Development.Oc|
|----------------------------------------------------------------------
|
| xxxxxxx    | xxxxxxx        | 1x127.0M | stolen
|
| Age: 16h  0m| Dir: Kao.the.Kangaroo.2.Multi-TECHNiC
|
|----------------------------------------------------------------------
|
| xxxxxxx   | xxxx            | 1x  1.7M | bad.dir.its.v1.1.1.1          |
| Age: 16h 25m| Dir: Fax.Server.Remote.Submit.v1.2.1.1.WinAll.Cracked-HS
|
|----------------------------------------------------------------------
|
| xxxxxxx    | xxxxxxx        | 1x  4.6M | mu.031705
|
| Age: 17h 43m| Dir: ACTUALTESTS.Cisco.642-
661.Exam.Q.and.A.03.24.2005.LiB|
|----------------------------------------------------------------------
|
| xxxxxxx    | xxxxxxx        | 1x  3.4M | mu.031705
|
| Age: 17h 43m| Dir: ACTUALTESTS.Cisco.642-
811.Exam.Q.and.A.03.24.2005.LiB|
|----------------------------------------------------------------------
|
```

```
| xxxxxxx       | xxxxxx      | 1x  2.0M | mu.031705
|
| Age: 17h 43m| Dir: ACTUALTESTS.Cisco.350-
018.Exam.Q.and.A.03.16.2005.LiB|
|--------------------------------------------------------------------
|
| Read site rules to avoid being nuked :)
```

The scene committee's job is to create and maintain scene rules regarding nuke and release regulations—the so-called warez police of the Internet.

There is a lot of conformity in each different release. A lot of time and effort is invested in packaging the pirated goods in the perfect manner. Why bother? Piracy is about rebellion, freedom, and choice.

It is ironic that there are more rules and regulations in the scene than there are for creating and selling software itself. Scene rules focus on quality control and usability; a spelling mistake in a directory name can result in a nuke.

PIRACY SCENARIO

Company X releases Print Master 2000, a commercial printing software package. However, the software application has a few bugs during installation and will only install correctly on a small number of computers. Company X is not concerned about the problem; management demanded that v2000 be released on time, so they will correct the problem with a patch or a fix later.

The ELITEPIRATES group obtained a copy of Print Master 2000, which has no copy protection, and quickly packaged and released it. However, scene sites nuked the application because it refused to install on many computers.

The promise of an upcoming patch is useless here, because a product must be working to begin with. Pirates are not interested in buggy or faulty software; within a few hours every scene site will have nuked the application.

Many warez groups have members called *release coordinators* that are dedicated to making sure a release goes smoothly. These group members focus on working within the guidelines of the scene to ensure that the different sites accept the releases. If a release is nuked, release coordinators quickly find out why. There is usually a legitimate reason why a release is nuked, such as the site administrator incorrectly nuking the title.

Site Rules

Figure 5.3 shows a copy of the rules from a popular ISO site. These rules dictate what releases can be uploaded and what the *nuke ratio* is (how many credits the person who uploaded it will lose after being nuked).

Figure 5.3 Scene Rules

```
-GENERAL RULES-

    1.  Do not upload releases more than 2 day old.    -> Nuke 2x
          (NO BACKFILL!)
    2.  Absolutely NO Foreign ISO, VCD, ,0Day and MP3s
                        -> Nuke 1x - ??x, Nuker Discretion
    3.  You have 12 hours to finish your upload    -> Nuke 3x
    4.  Upload into the appropriate dir          -> Nuke 2x
    5.  No inapropriate subdirectories inside releases      -> Nuke 1x
    6.  Site affils are exempt from the rules
    7.  (NO DATED FOLDERS)                        -> Nuke 2x
    8.  Staff has the right to nuke anything they deem worthy, DO NOT
        argue with them.


  -ISO RULES-
    1.  Platforms:                            -> Nuke 2x - 5x
          - ALLOWED   : Windows 9x/NT/2000/Linux/ISO game patches/dox
          - DISALLOWED: Everything else
    2.  Absolutely NO:
          - Shareware/FreeWare/Demo/Kiddie Images/Clipart/Textures
          - Releases over 3 CDs (Unless Approved by Site Staff)
    3.  All releases must be in .rar format and contain a .sfv and .nfo
          - Minimum file size : 10 megabytes
          - Maximum file size : 20 megabytes
```

```
   4.   Only true CD images in .bin/.cue or or .iso

-MP3 RULES-

   1.   Release: .mp3 format ONLY! Plus SFV and NFO compulsary.
              * Upload 192kbps Only unless by request *
         The Official RIAA MP3-Release-Rules must be STRICTLY followed.
              2003 + mp3 releases ONLY          -> Nuke 2x
   2.   No Foreign mp3, however foriegn releases of US are allowed
              ie  Danish Retail etc...
```

A majority of these rules are common sense; nothing can be free, foreign, or overly large. Releases must be fully uploaded within 12 hours of creating the directory, and only software for Windows or Linux is allowed.

PIRACY FACT...

Linux is a recent addition to the acceptance list. For many years, the only operating system allowed in a warez release was Windows.

As Linux grew more popular, scene rules adjusted to allow groups to pirate commercial Linux applications. Although MAC is not allowed on this particular site, many scene sites are starting to allow for piracy of OS X applications and games.

Any group affiliated with the site is exempt from these rules and will never be nuked.

PIRACY FACT...

When a warez group affiliates with a site, they promise to send their releases to that site first. Receiving a large title before any other site is a privilege and greatly increases the popularity and status of the warez site.

In return, sites' create accounts for group members and promise never to nuke the group's release. Strategically, this is very beneficial to the group; if 90 percent of top sites in the scene are affiliated with a

particular group and promise to never nuke their releases, the group
can release whatever they want without fear.

Dupe Checking

Dupe checking is the most fundamental and necessary step that a release
coordinator will undertake for each release. The scene is only interested
in one working copy of each title, whether it is a game, an application, an
upgrade, or a *keygen*, the first one released is the only one allowed. Any
subsequent releases of the same program are nuked as being a *dupe*.

Dupe checking is relatively simple and the majority of scene sites are
equipped with the ability to search their own online database. File
Transfer Protocol (FTP) daemons such as *gltpd* automatically add any
directory names into a dupe database, thereby allowing site members to
search the database for any dupes. (See Figure 5.4).

Figure 5.4 Dupe Checking

```
site dupe spam
120404  SpamGunner_v2.0_Keygen_Only-UCF
120904  Syngress.Inside.the.SPAM.Cartel.Nov.2004.eBook-DDU
121304  Spam.Manager.v1.18.nfo.fix-SoS
121304  Spam.Manager.Personal.v1.18.Keymaker.Only-EMBRACE
121304  Spam.Manager.v1.18-SoS
121304  Spam.Manager.v1.18.nfo.fix-SoS
123104  No.More.Spam.v2.1.4.1108.WinALL.Cracked.NFOFiX-BM
123104  No.More.Spam.v2.1.4.1108.WinALL.Cracked-BM
010305  Spam.Manager.Personal.v1.19.Incl.Keymaker-EMBRACE
```

It is essential for groups to dupe check any release. If a release is not
dupe checked, it may result in a nuke. The days of work that crackers,
suppliers, and other group members put in can quickly turn into thin air
when another group releases the product first.

Packing

When a release's dupe status is cleared and a title is ready to be released, the product must be *packed* into scene-compliant volumes.

Many groups have dedicated *packers* who pack releases night and day. Because they often have access to high-speed connections, packers are essential to a group's success.

Releases must be supplied, cracked, tested, and packed within a very short time frame; the release depends on it.

First, the files from the release are compressed using either RAR or ACE, and then split into commonly sized disk volumes (usually 1.44MB, 2.88MB, or 5MB in size). Maximum compression must be used during this stage, because the release must be under a certain size limit. Applications cannot be larger than 200MB, although some sites accept larger releases under special conditions. Games are limited to 250MB, although a majority of sites will accept a larger release if the title is worthy.

After the initial compression takes place, the group NFO and *file_id.diz* are written, that show the number of disks and other information such as serial number or a product description. These files are essential to the release; if any archives are missing the *file_id.diz* or NFO file, consider it *nuked*.

Next, each volume is zipped; the first disk with both the NFO and the *file_id.diz* files, and all subsequent disks containing only the *file_id.diz*. Zip file names must be eight-characters long with a three-point extension and a clear description of numbering (e.g., f-eraa01.zip, f-eraa02.zip, f-eraa03.zip, and so on). File names cannot change during mid-set and the numbering must be consistent. Failure to do so will result in the release being nuked.

Directory names must contain the product name and the version, correctly spelled and clearly visible. Groups can also include the name of the company that developed the product, so as to not confuse directories (e.g., "Realtek_Spam_Stopper_v1.3" with "Antisoft_Spam_Stopper_v1.3."). Directory names use underscores in place of periods and spaces.

If there is any particular reason that a product should not be nuked (e.g., the other released version did not work, or this version contains additional features), groups will try to get a nuker's attention by adding "READ_NFO" or "WORKING" to the directory name.

If a group's release is nuked, the group can choose to re-release a REPACK or a fixed version. Many groups opt to release REPACK'S.

Packers act as living tools for release coordinators, informing them when a new release needs to be packed and uploaded. It takes only minutes for an experienced packer to pack a large release and then upload it to a private group site, ready for the next stage.

Pre'ing

Pre'ing (pre-releasing) is the stage in which the release is uploaded to a group's affiliated sites and released. Group-affiliated sites want a group's release to uploaded first; therefore, many sites insist on groups using internal prescripts.

To use these scripts, a group member first uploads the release to a private directory on each group site. No one else can see these directories or the files within them. These private, hidden sections of a site are essentially not part of the warez site. Once the release is completely uploaded and ready on all sites, a simple "site pre-release Release_Name_v1-XXX" is issued. This command copies the directory and its contents from the group's hidden folder to the site's new-releases directory, therefore ensuring that the release is completed on group sites first. Pre'ing is an essential method of giving group-affiliated sites privilege, something to make the site more attractive to other pirates.

The site that receives releases from CORE (a cracking group) first, will become popular with other pirates. Couriers, who trade releases between sites, want an account of any site affiliated with a popular group so that they can get the group's releases first and upload them to their own sites for more credits.

Once a group has pre'd their release, the rush is over. Couriers pick up the group's release from their affiliated sites and trade them other sites. Within a minute, a single zip file can be copied multiple times around the world.

Art in Piracy

When a soccer team enters a packed stadium to play a game, you automatically notice a few things: players all wear the same uniforms, there is usually a mascot present, and banners carrying the team's emblem fly high in the stadium. Teams have pride in their appearance; they know that the fans come to see them and they live it up.

Piracy is much the same; groups take extreme pride in their releases and hard work. Releases are never slapped together; groups try to add sex appeal and desire into their releases, something to make the end user recognize the group and remember their name.

When I was in my early teens I was given a pile of pirated Amiga games from a friend. Keen to play the games, I rushed home and shoved the first disk into my Amiga and booted the computer. Before the game even loaded, I saw the most interesting thing, my first *introduction*, or *cracktro* as they were commonly called. "DefJam is proud to present to you, StarGlider2!," it read in bouncing, bright neon text. A cute, addictive *chiptune* played in the background, similar to that of modern day dance music. Between the music and the vibrant text, I got a mixture of uplifting, positive feelings.

Starglider 2 was horrible. The graphics were lame at best and there was no music. I was greatly disappointed. DefJam's introduction was far more amazing than the game could ever be. I went through every disk in that pile, watching each introduction and learning the names of the various cracking groups.

Fairlight, TduJam, and Razor1911 were teasers into a new digital world. Fairlight made the best introductions; they used smart 3D graphics and catchy background music, and the introduction graphics were often better than the game itself. Scrolling text thanked various group members for working hard on the current release, also greeting other competing release groups for bringing quality to the Amiga scene. I felt proud to be using a Fairlight release.

Very little has changed since the days of Amiga, except that modern releases carry more flair than ever before. From a group's NFO and

file_id.diz files (found in each zip file) to customized installers and introductions, groups' are proud of their releases and not afraid to show it.

PIRACY FACT...

One of the most outstanding examples of group pride I ever saw was
from the group PARADIGM, when they released the South Park game in
1999. Originally, when the game first loaded, it featured an animation
of the South Park characters, much like the television introduction.

PARADIGM, however, had replaced it with a customized version.
Completely re-rendered, the new animation showed Kenny being killed
by a large "Paradigm" block of text that fell from the sky.

"You killed Kenny, you bastards!," Stan would shout. Surprisingly,
the quality of the animation was top notch. Someone had spent a
great deal of time animating each character frame-by-frame, all for this
one release.

It would be easy for a group to take a game, crack it, write a small
plain text file telling users how to use the crack, and then release it.
However, piracy is not about being easy and it is not about throwing
something together quickly. Piracy is hard work; not a single stage in the
release process is easy. Because of this, groups are very loyal toward their
group name. With mottos such as "The Best Of The Best," "Sharp As a
Blade," and "We Redefine Quality," it is not just about the release, it is
also about being proud of the 20 hours you have invested in it.

NFO files usually contain large American Standard Code for
Information Interchange (ASCII)-drawn pictures, an old trait from a time
when ASCII art was popular on Bulletin Board Systems (BBS').

Figure 5.5 Hand-drawn ASCII Art

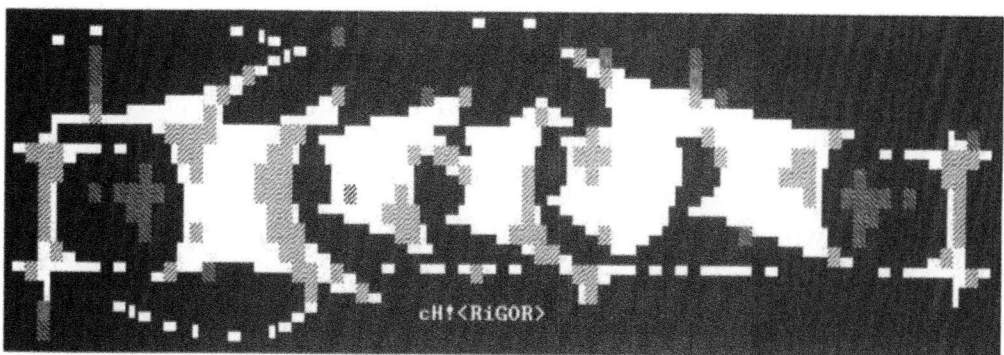

Each block of ASCII is hand drawn, painstakingly designed by an ASCII artist. Groups are recognized for their NFO files; end users read them and most have a personal favorite warez group.

Introductions have also grown from the textual days of old. Although the bright neon tunes are still used, new introductions have crisp OpenGL-rendered graphics and take advantage of the faster hardware the new generation of pirates has.

Figure 5.6 Recent Group Introductions

Like any major company, warez groups care about public relations and the image others have of them. Desired by all, warez groups want end users to dream about joining the ranks of their legendary crackers and suppliers. Groups want the best introduction, the sexiest NFO, and the coolest slogans.

Groups do not just release pirated material; they re-create software into their own works of art, showing off their talent and fearless attitudes. The quality of the product is not as important. A group may be very proud of releasing a boring game simply because it featured an incredibly complicated and convoluted protection system, which required the group to spend a week of non-stop cracking. This is what makes groups proud. The actual game is almost irrelevant.

"Sure I'm proud of my group," said a cracker from DEViANCE. "Our cracks work the first time, every time. The group name carries with it a certain level of respect. People know that we pull out the good stuff. This sounds really bad, but I've told people that I crack for deviance, and they go 'wow, dude, seriously, I love that group.' It's crazy; most of the world knows us and loves our work. So, yeah, I'm proud of that."

> "The man who does not take pride in his own performance performs nothing in which to take pride."
> — Thomas Watson, American businessman, founder of IBM

Chapter 6

Sites

Sites used for *warez* (exaggerated plural derivative of software) have long been synonymous with the underground world of *piracy*. These are the dark, shady corners of cyberspace where it all begins.

At the start of the piracy scene, Bulletin Board Systems (*BBS*) were used to distribute information; however, analog phone lines soon became obsolete. Ever-growing Internet technology offered pirates additional bandwidth and resources.

BBS' comprised of ten 19.6 Kbps lines were considered special, because they held ten users simultaneously. These days, warez sites can hold 50 users, all sharing a100 megabit connection (at a bare minimum). Much has changed in the world of technology, and piracy has evolved with it.

Logging into a true warez site is like walking into a toy store and becoming a kid again. Everything you could ever imagine is right in front of your eyes, and free for the taking.

Movies, games, applications, books, playstation2 games, you could queue up a few hundred gigabytes to download in a matter of minutes. Sites may have five or ten terabytes of storage available, all full with new releases. You could download solidly all year and never get everything.

Comparable to finding the cheat codes to life, piracy makes everything possible, it makes everything available. You could never justify buying all these games to yourself, or your wife. But here it all is, free. Neatly packaged with text files describing what each release is, you could spend hours wondering the digital warehouse of software like a kid in a toy store.

Sites are the focal point of the release process and the backbone of the scene itself. Each release group must be affiliated with several decent sites if they intend to release anything. The warez groups need the sites and the sites need the warez groups.

Sites want a group's release first; they need the group to *prerelease* their release to the site in order to increase the site's status and popularity. Groups need sites for two reasons: first, release groups need the ability to release a title into the scene and, second, they need sites to spread quickly throughout the community. With every step of the release process moving like greased lightening, it is unthinkable for a group to wait hours for a release to spread from one site to another. The crackers and suppliers in the groups also expect unlimited, ratio-free accounts to each of the group's sites. To reward members who invest long hours, groups commonly give them unlimited access to download at will, as long as they remain active within the group.

Scene sites are impressive, secure, fault-tolerant data warehouses that are used for piracy. The infrastructure and hardware involved in many sites rivals that of a mid-sized company. Some sites boast their own dedicated firewalls, multiple gigabit (GB) connections, and many terabytes (TB) of ultra-fast Small Computer System Interface (SCSI) storage space. Talking to Rodan for the first time was enough to impress me. Although Rodan did not run a *top site*, his setup was still considerable. "I use *bouncers* on multiple gig lines, HP server gear, SCSI-connected disk array with a few terabytes, all housed at one of Europe's fastest connected universities; it' really fly's."

Piracy Fact...

Bouncers are essentially data proxies that act as a method for maintaining a site's anonymity.

The following three host names are site bouncers:

- *Fisted-power1.ath.cx*
- *Fisted-power2.ath.cx*
- *Fisted-power3.ath.cx*

Each bouncer accepts a File Transfer Protocol (FTP) connection, and then forwards the user to the "real" site.

"Just how many terabytes is 'a few?'" I casually asked Rodan one day.

"We started out with 1 a few years ago and have added a few more disks since then. The current size is 6.4 TB, 4.4 TB for general warez, another TB for Mp3s, and the last TB is for movies. Most of the space goes into archives, though." "It adds up," Rodan added.

6.4 TB? Legal authorities go crazy when someone shares a few gigabytes on a peer-to-peer (P2P) network. Casual piracy is nothing compared to this; this is a professional operation. Rodan was no different than a systems administrator for a small company.

How could someone plant such a large warez site on a university network? Surely, someone must notice the massive amount of bandwidth to and from the server. I questioned Rodan's honesty; perhaps I was being fed one lie at a time. I needed more evidence. "How do you get away with all the bandwidth? Doesn't anyone notice it?" I asked.

"Well, the link owner is the network administrator at the university. He fiddles all the data usage graphs so they ignore anything that comes or goes to the site. It's been at the university for years and has never been found."

PIRACY FACT...

Sites are usually run by mini subgroups within the scene, each with different members and contributors.

Box owners, link owners, site administrators, nukers, and *artists* all make up the final product, each pulling their weight in a different way.

Box owners are the financier's of the site. They buy the original hardware and any upgrades required, and replace any broken components.

Link owners control the housing of the site, usually at large universities or Internet Service Provider (ISP) locations that are used for massive amounts of bandwidth. Student dorms are very common; however, many sites are now run by university staff.

Site administrators take care of user accounts. If someone forgets a password, needs their account changed, or has a question about the site, a site administrator is usually there to help.

Nukers troll the site looking for any releases that should be nuked: old, fake, uncracked, or minor upgrades. Nukers are the quality control on the site.

You would not think an artist has much place in a warez site; however, pride has a large influence on the scene. Warez sites are commonly highly decorated, using both color-based American National Standards Institute (ANSI) and American Standard Code for Information Interchange (ASCII) art for welcome screens and menus.

Customized FTP clients and servers exist to support colors, brining back the bright vibrant feel of the BBS' of old.

"So, you're telling me that you and a university network administrator (who probably makes a pittance of an academic wage) had the money to spend on 6.4 TBs worth of SCSI disks and expensive server hardware?

You're kidding me," my tone grew very doubtful as I waited for Rodan's response.

"Ha-ha, yeah, well, try this out for size. It was free, donated by two different groups. They just wanted someone to house a site for them, basically."

"How secure is the site?" I asked. "Anyone ever find it?"

"Well, we run *glftpd* with Target LAN Server/Secure Sockets Layer (TLS/SSL). A firewall in front of the server stops most people from finding it, and only allows connections from trusted IPs. We also only add /32's to the firewall, so it's not very open. We will also add another firewall on the box if someone plugs into the network. Oh, and an Integrated Decision Support (IDS) hung off the network firewall, well, its actually very secure. No one has ever hacked it, or even discovered the site on the network."

PIRACY FACT...

TLS/SSL is an encrypted authentication method, not originally available in the FTP protocol. This is the preferred method for keeping a site secure, because the login and any directory listings sent are encrypted. TLS/SSL is comparable to the implementation of OpenSSL within Hyper Text Transfer Protocol Secure sockets (HTTPS).

The firewalls are in place with /32 rules, which means they only accept connections from a single, specified host; no netmasks of *blocks* of IPs are allowed. This reduces the amount of hosts that can access the server, and aids in keeping its presence undetected.

IDS' are often installed to detect possible attackers. They are passive devices and cannot be detected remotely.

Types of Sites

Scene sites come in many different varieties, with each one catering to different aspects of the scene (e.g., sites that only carry Mp3s of newly released music, or large archive sites that contain every cracked application since the dawn of the electronic age). Each site is different and unique in its own way.

Speed is often the biggest governing factor of a site's success; the more bandwidth a site has, the faster a courier can upload a release to it. Popularity depends on speed; like every other aspect of piracy, it is all just one big race.

The features and types of warez that a site holds will determine whether or not the site is successful. Everyone in the scene wants something different, and a site that caters to everyone will be more popular than one that does not.

Figure 6.1 shows a diagram of different sites and explains how they rank.

Figure 6.1 Types of Sites and Their Ranking

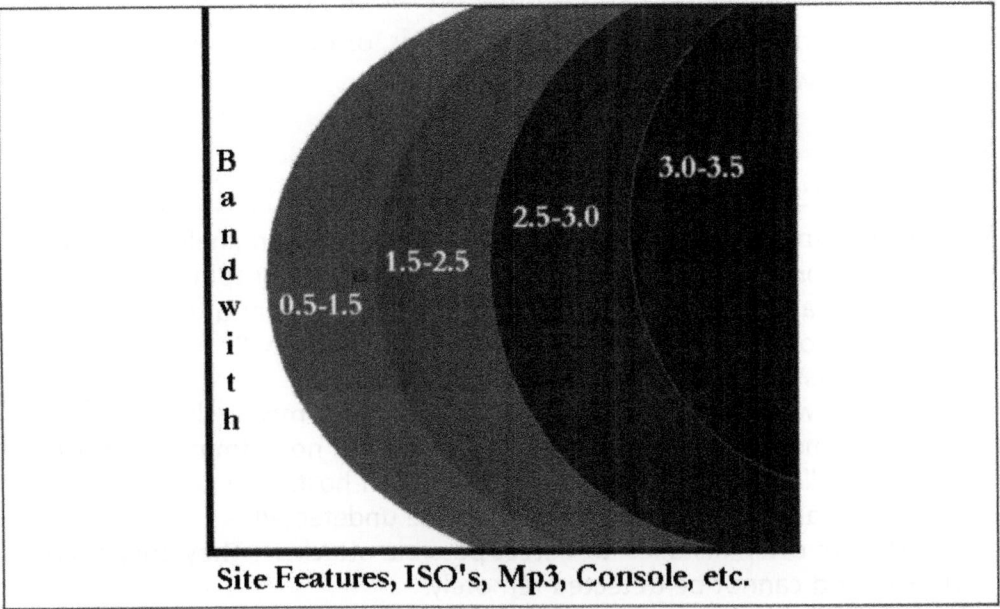

Each type of site has a distinct rank, which determines how exclusive or elite the site is. Site ranking is important; groups constantly seek the highest ranked sites. Very few sites are ranked a prestigious 3.0 to 3.5 rank. (Site ranking is covered in detail in Chapter 7.)

PIRACY FACT...

There are approximately 15 3.0+ ranked sites on the internet, only the most respected and secure of sites remain with this prestigious rank. More 2.0-2.9 rank sites exist, officially the figure is just below 30. Over a hundred 1.0 ranked sites and below exist although many are not ranked officially.

Piracy originates from these few locations, because they are considered the fastest sites in the world. Top ranked sites are the core points of the scene (equivalent to the National Association of Securities Dealers Automated Quotation (NASDAQ) and the New York Stock Exchange (NYSE). They are the backbone of the entire scene process. Large groups *pre* to these sites, because they offer the fastest method of distribution.

Top sites are often located on core Internet backbones or at major ISPs with impressive amounts of hardware. Possibly the highest risk sites in the scene, the Federal Bureau of Investigation (FBI) tends to focus on these sites, although only a handful have ever been found by the authorities.

Exclusivity is prevalent here. You must be someone important on the scene to get an account on these sites, and you must also be in a well-known group with a good reputation. User bases are small, often containing less than 100 accounts (very small in comparison to other sites).

Obtaining an account on these sites makes you one of the true elite; these are the sites pirates dream about.

Sites ranked 3.0 to 3.5 often carry large archives of releases. Boasting impressive storage space and impeccable down time, these sites tend to cater to a pirate's every need. A site ranked 3.0 to 3.5 will have everything from music and movies, to e-books, consoles, and Macintosh software.

Sites that are ranked 2.5 to 3.0 are the most prestigious of the common sites; many groups *pre* to these sites if they are not allowed to have accounts on a site ranked 3.0 to 3.5. Releases from the 3.0+ ranked top sites are quickly traded to these sites. When a group cracks a release and *pre's* it to a top site ranked 2.5 to 3.0, it takes less than a minute to be traded to every other site that is ranked 2.0 to 3.5.

Lower-ranked sites are easier to get accounts on, and often have 200 to 300 accounts in their user base. However, you still must have a decent reputation in the scene or be affiliated with a large, well-known group to get on the sites ranked 2.5 to 3.0.

These sites tend to carry the same amount of data as the exclusive 3.0 to 3.5-ranked sites do, the only difference being the quality of the bandwidth and the groups that support the site.

A minimum of a 100 Mb connection on a clean, unsaturated link is required to be a 2.5 to 3.0-ranked site. Bandwidth is usually located in Europe or in new high-speed American locations.

Sites ranked 1.5 to 2.5 are the most common; the majority of scene members have accounts on these sites. They receive every application, International Organization for Standardization (ISO), and movie, several hours after they are originally released. These sites usually go down first, often being detected shortly after going live. If a group cannot get an account on a higher-ranked site, they are forced to *pre* on a site ranked 1.5 to 2.5. Consequently, it may take one to two hours for the release to be distributed globally, thereby ensuring that the group is not taken seriously.

Piracy Fact...

One to two hours may not seem long, but it can make a huge difference in the scene.

Image this scenario:

Two groups have just finished cracking Doom 4, the highly anticipated and popular fictional title.

The popular group GAMERS releases the game first, but their sites are ranked low, mostly in the 1.5 to 2.0 range. Unknowingly, another group RENEDADESY releases the game on their high-ranking sites 10 minutes after GAMERS.

While the first release from GAMERS is slowly spreading around minor sites, RENEDAGES release has already been distributed to every top site and is quickly working its way down to the other sites.

Any top-ranked site would see that RENEGADES won the race. Because only the first release uploaded is accepted, GAMERS release is considered a duplicate and nuked. Technically though, GAMERS won the race.

Depending on their popularity, sites that are ranked 1.5 to 2.5 may receive a release 10 to 20 minutes after it is released. However, if the site has poor support, it can take several hours to backfill old releases.

The majority of sites start off ranked 1.5, but as their reputation and affiliations grow, their status grows. Because these sites often have up to 1000 user accounts, they need something special to stand out from the crowd.

The lowest rank is 0.5 to 1.5 and includes home cable connections, saturated 10 Mb lines, and limited storage space. These sites are prevalent in the scene and tend to grow quickly. Ten to 20 new sites may spring up in a week and then within another week, 10 to 15 sites may vanish. Quality is not a high priority on these sites, which usually run from desktops or slow hardware.

Many different types of sites exist. While rank is important, users often appreciate sites that offer something different. Speed is useless if a site does not carry what a user craves.

Archive Sites

Slower sites usually have the most archive space (40 TB to 50 TB). Every game, application, movie, Mp3, DVD-R, XBOX, Playstation, and Game Cube ever released can be stored on a lower-ranked site. However, it takes more time to download from these sites.

ISO Sites

The ISO is a standard used for CD image creation. It is a complete 1:1 replication of the contents of a CD or DVD. ISO's are heavily traded in the scene.

Any CD or DVD can be released in the scene as an ISO. The only condition for an ISO release is that the image must be an accurate 1:1 replica of legitimate retail media. A beta version, a homemade CD, or unfinished product will not suffice. The only difference between ISO sites is the amount of different types of ISO's they will accept.

Figure 6.2 lists the currently accepted media within the scene. Each site is different, and the acceptance list is usually decided by the amount of storage space a site has. The more media a site accepts, the more popular it will be.

Figure 6.2 ISO Accepted Media Types

```
ISO\
ISO\games
ISO\games\mac
ISO\games\foreign
ISO\apps
ISO\apps\foreign
ISO\apps\mac
ISO\movies\
ISO\movies\DVDR
ISO\movies\svcd
ISO\movies\vcd
ISO\movies\xxx
ISO\console\
ISO\console\psx
ISO\console\psx2
ISO\console\xbox
ISO\console\gamecube
ISO\console\dreamcast
ISO\console\gameboy
ISO\console\gameboyadvanced
```

Given adequate storage space, an ISO site can easily hold all of the above media in ample quantity. The only catch to ISOs is the speed at which they transfer. Even when using a GB connection, uploading a 4.3 GB DVD can take several hours. Given this, ISO releases take longer to move from site to site. ISO sites must have an enormous amount of bandwidth to deal with the amount of traffic passing through them.

Oday Sites

Although a CD can easily be turned into an ISO release, what about small applications or games that do not ship on CDs but are downloaded instead? Applications such as WinZip, Winrar, and SecureCRT fall under the category *0day*. Because of their small size, they are traded more readily and usually within an hour or two of the release, within the 0day.

0day sites were the original sites in the scene. BBS' were effectively 0day sites, and when the Internet became popular, these sites migrated to the Internet.

Because of the immense amount of 0day sites, they tend to be added onto existing ISO sites. A 0day site may only require several hundred gigabytes of storage at any given time; therefore, it can be easily accommodated within a larger ISO site.

0day sites only offer small releases, which are usually edited in size (e.g., previous ISO releases with in-game music and movies removed).

Piracy Fact...

The process is called ripping, taking a large ISO application or game and removing none essential information such as in game movies, sound tracks or unneeded files.

Ripping also involves using highly optimized compression routines. Rippers often convert in game sounds from wave files to mp3's. Once the user has downloaded the game they will run a decompression program to reconvert the mp3's to wave.

Third party applications such as Adobe Acrobat Reader and DirectX and also removed to reduce size.

As user bandwidth increases, fewer people want to download an edited copy of a game, instead preferring to download the full ISO image. 0day sites are a dying-breed. A site that only offers 0day releases will not be highly attractive within the scene.

Music Exclusive

Music piracy is very much alive in the underground music scene. Although many scene sites carry released Mp3's, only a few sites exclusively carry music releases. Using FTP servers with specialized functions for dealing with Mp3's, these sites are often the hubs of music piracy.

Music-exclusive sites often categorize music by genre and sampling rate (quality), and enforce strict policies about music encoding rates, rapidly nuking poor-quality releases.

Size is not as important with music-exclusive sites. A site with only two or three TBs is large enough to hold a massive amount of music.

Many music sites also carry the expensive sampling tracks used by DJ's. The applications used to author music and sound filters and utilities are also traded to music sites.

Private Group Sites, Dump Sites

Every scene group needs private sites (often referred to as *dumpsites*), because group members tend to dump various packages on the server for other members to receive.

Dumpsites are very common in the scene and every group has at least one. These sites are used for two reasons. First, the majority of scene sites enforce very strict rules (e.g., anyone caught downloading via anything slower than 128 Kbps will have their account deleted instantly). Dumpsites only allow ten to fifteen users to login at any given time, therefore, keeping bandwidth rates high.

What does a group do, however, if their star cracker, who has been investing hundreds of hours a week cracking the group's applications, is on a 56K modem located in Russia? This is where a dumpsite comes in handy. Group members can download anything they want from the site, even at 1K per sec.

Dumpsites tend to be supported by *mirror scripts*, applications that replicate another site automatically (similar to synchronization).

A dumpsite can contain the exact contents of a topsite ranked 3.0, receiving each day's directories at a set period (usually hourly or daily). Mirroring allows group members to download quality-assured, pre-sorted releases at their own pace.

Secondly and most commonly, group sites are used for suppliers and crackers to trade their handiwork. Crackers need a way to get an application or game from the supplier, crack it, and then upload it for the packer or tester.

Dumpsites contain directories such as "TO_BE_CRACKED," "TO_BE_PACKED," and so forth. In-boxes for each member of a group and for each release move from directory to directory until its release.

Group sites also allow crackers archive previous cracks, private tools, and documents they may have created. In many ways, the information held on a private group site is more valuable than the information on a large warez site.

Ironically, private group sites last the longest out of all scene sites. They draw the least amount of attention; several internal group sites are infamous in the scene for their ability to "always" be up.

Site Bots and Clever Pirates

Pirates are ingenious, creative, and intelligent in their quest to make piracy as easy as possible. One example of this is the creation of *sitebots*, automated scripts that announce when a new release is uploaded to a site. Acting as member in an Internet Relay Chat (IRC) channel, sitebots are a popular way to alert couriers that there is a new release. This alert allows a courier to quickly transfer the release to another site.

Through the help of some newfound friends in the scene, I was invited into a prestigious site ranked 3.5 on a private IRC network. The channel had 45 members, most of which were couriers waiting for the sitebot to announce new releases in the channel. Watching the sitebot was amazing. You could see that the main goal was to try to get a release up before any other group.

It is one big race; scene couriers and site supporters actively trade releases to and from the site. Occasionally, a group affiliated with a site pre's their release directly.

Figure 6.3 Sitebots and IRC

```
<COGB0T>   (COG-COMPLETE)
ArGoSoft.Mail.Server.Pro.with.IMAP.v1.8.7.8.WinALL.Incl.Keymaker-CORE
(total: 5MB / avg. 2401kB/s) 1. xxxx/AMN       [4.8M/1F/100.0%/2401KB/s]

<COGB0T>   (COG-NUKE) -1x-
Syngress.Publishing.Hacking.a.Terror.Network.The.Silent.Threat.of.Covert.C
hannels.eBook-TLFeBOOK (Nuker: xxxxxx Nukee(s): xxxxxxx (7.7MB) Reason:
dupe.022205.ddu)

<COGB0T>   (COG-NEW) -0519-
Flamingpear.Flexify.v1.98.for.Adobe.Photoshop.Incl.Keygen-SCOTCH by
xxxxxx(RTS)

<COGB0T>   (COG-UPD)
Flamingpear.Flexify.v1.98.for.Adobe.Photoshop.Incl.Keygen-SCOTCH (1 files
expected)

<COGB0T>   (COG-COMPLETE)
Flamingpear.Flexify.v1.98.for.Adobe.Photoshop.Incl.Keygen-SCOTCH (total:
1MB / avg. 2909kB/s) 1. xxxxxx/RTS       [1.0M/1F/100.0%/2909KB/s]

<COGB0T>   (COG-NEW) -0519-  Deadhunt_PLUS_4_TRAINER-TRDogs by xxxxxx(AOD)

<COGB0T>   (COG-UPD) Deadhunt_PLUS_4_TRAINER-TRDogs (1 files expected)

<COGB0T>   (COG-COMPLETE) Deadhunt_PLUS_4_TRAINER-TRDogs (total: 0MB / avg.
590kB/s) 1. xxxxxxxx/AOD       [0.3M/1F/100.0%/590KB/s]

<COGB0T>   (COG-PRE) NEW RELEASE ARRIVED! -->> ZWT PRE <<--
BCGSoft.Professional.Editor.v7.30.Full.Source-ZWT (1.6 MB)

<COGB0T>   (COG-NEW) -0519-  VRML_Export_2006_For_AutoCAD_v3.4.0.50317-
DIGERATI by xxxxxx(RTS)

<COGB0T>   (COG-UPD) VRML_Export_2006_For_AutoCAD_v3.4.0.50317-DIGERATI (1
files expected)

<COGB0T>   (COG-COMPLETE) VRML_Export_2006_For_AutoCAD_v3.4.0.50317-
DIGERATI (total: 1MB / avg. 1489kB/s) 1. xxxxxxxx/RTS
[0.6M/1F/100.0%/1489KB/s]

<COGB0T>   (COG-NEW) -0519-  ArGoSoft.FTP.Server.1.4.3.0.Incl.Keymaker-
EMBRACE by xxxxxxxx(AOD)

<COGB0T>   (COG-NEW) -0519-  Lavavo.CD.Ripper.v4.0.2.Incl.Keymaker-EMBRACE
by xxxxxxxx(RTS)

<COGB0T>   (COG-UPD) Lavavo.CD.Ripper.v4.0.2.Incl.Keymaker-EMBRACE (1 files
expected)

<COGB0T>   (COG-COMPLETE) Lavavo.CD.Ripper.v4.0.2.Incl.Keymaker-EMBRACE
(total: 4MB / avg. 752kB/s) 1. xxxxxxxx/RTS
[4.4M/1F/100.0%/752KB/s]

<COGB0T>   (COG-NEW) -0519-  Lavavo.DVD.Ripper.v3.01.Incl.Keymaker-EMBRACE
by xxxxxxxx(RTS)

<COGB0T>   (COG-UPD) Lavavo.DVD.Ripper.v3.01.Incl.Keymaker-EMBRACE (1 files
expected)
```

```
<COGBOT>  (COG-COMPLETE) Lavavo.DVD.Ripper.v3.01.Incl.Keymaker-EMBRACE
(total: 3MB / avg. 931kB/s) 1. xxxxxxxx/RTS
[2.7M/1F/100.0%/931KB/s]
<COGBOT>  (COG-DEL) -0519- ArGoSoft.FTP.Server.1.4.3.0.Incl.Keymaker-
EMBRACE by xxxxxxxx.
<COGBOT>  (COG-NEW) -0519-
WaveMachine.Labs.Drumagog.Pro.VST.RTAS.v4.0.incl.KeyGen.DIRFIX-BEAT by
xxxxxxxx(RTS)
<COGBOT>  (COG-NEW) -0519-  Visual.Surf.Safe.v1.0.0.61.SWEDiSH-ABSOKT by
xxxxxxxx(RTS)
<COGBOT>  (COG-UPD) Visual.Surf.Safe.v1.0.0.61.SWEDiSH-ABSOKT (1 files
expected)
```

Couriers from the groups RTS, AMN and AOD were competing for territory and the number one spot on the "Week Up" chart.

Piracy Fact...

Week Up charts (WKUs) are lists of a site's best couriers for that week, those who uploaded more than anyone else. The spot is coveted, and a popular site may have 10 to 20 couriers competing for the number 1 rank.

Figure 6.4 Week Up's on a Popular 0day Site.

##	User	Location/Tagline	Files	Megabytes	Avg k/s
[01]			130	502MB	1278K/s
[02]			124	386MB	741K/s
[03]			86	360MB	753K/s
[04]			145	347MB	1024K/s
[05]			113	291MB	826K/s
[06]			92	263MB	795K/s
[07]			58	219MB	808K/s
[08]			46	147MB	1034K/s
[09]			35	138MB	519K/s
[10]			35	123MB	1712K/s

You can see that the most prolific couriers are uploading large amounts of files at well over 1MB per second.

These couriers traded relentlessly. Each courier tended to trade an average of 4 to 5 hours a day, both to and from the site. Prolific couriers were active between 9 and 14 hours a day, uploading a new release every 2 minutes. Such dedication is comparable to stock traders buying and selling their way around the financial market.

What about P2P?

When the majority of non-*sceners* (those who are not in the scene), think about ways to obtain pirated media, P2P and other public file-sharing networks are usually the first method considered. A piracy standard, public file-sharing applications have become synonymous with piracy.

P2P is unreliable and often filled with fake or incomplete files. Downloading from a single FTP site is much easier and more convenient.

I was curious to know how real pirates felt about the controversy behind public file-sharing applications. One afternoon I placed the following question in a scene-orientated IRC channel: "So, who here likes p2p apps, good/bad?" The response I received shocked me. Real pirates think that P2Ps should be shutdown altogether, along with all other free and public file-sharing mediums.

"Pirated goods are meant for those who pirate. It's a private club, we don't want any of our stuff to be spread around by some kid on kazza or edonkey, that's just lame," said one angry pirate.

"Yeah," said another channel member. "Although if some punk kid wants to take all the heat for the piracy we do, I guess I don't mind too much."

"They steal our work! I hate p2p crap. They take our releases, mess with them, and then share them with all their friends. And everyone thinks they are so cool because they can download something I cracked last month. Either get in the scene and do it right, or buy it. P2P is evil," said another.

Such attitudes confounded me. Piracy is piracy, right? How is P2P any different from downloading from a scene site? Then it clicked. Pirates hate P2P networks because the people using them are effectively freeloaders; they do nothing to contribute back to the scene.

Crackers, suppliers, couriers, site administrators, and nukers all play their part in the scene, no matter how small that part is. The majority of scene members respect and value every member in the scene. Everyone needs everyone else; that is how the scene works. If a single role within the scene were removed, the entire scene structure would crumble.

Crackers and suppliers make releases for groups to release, who then upload them to sites for couriers to trade to other sites for additional credits, thereby spreading the release and aiding the group. It is a tight knot, a house of cards that stands perfectly, as long as everyone pulls his or her own weight. However, when members of the public get involved, things start to get messy. File-sharing networks bring a lot of media attention to piracy, attention pirates do not want and actively try to silence.

PIRACY FACT…

Some groups have become so frustrated and angry about file-sharing networks that they have started to encrypt every release they produce. Only trusted scene members are given access to the key to decrypt the archive. Attitudes like this sum up how different piracy and file sharing is; it may result in the same product, but they are a world apart.

File sharing is not piracy; it is not even close. It lacks order and class.

The scene is a classy, structured environment. Although you may picture it as an unorganized mess, it is far from that. Pirates respect this structure. They enjoy life in the scene and try to keep scene life as private as possible.

P2P and other public mediums are the result of media leaking through the cracks of the scene. Public distribution of pirated media is the last thing any pirate wants. Pirated media includes the off-cuts that the scene throws out, the runt of the litter, the digital scraps of piracy, that end up on public-sharing networks.

Chapter 7

The Distribution Chain

Distribution in Motion

Distribution is the key to piracy. A strong distribution chain is required if any structured rules or regulations are to be applied to an otherwise chaotic digital world. Pirated material needs a strict and highly efficient distribution process. Structure is the key; there must be a specific flow in place. Consider the following real–world scenario.

The *Morning Paper* is released every morning seven days a week. Newspapers come off the printing press at 2:00 A.M. and are bundled and distributed to stores and resellers from 3:00 A.M. on. .

The content of the paper is geared towards morning reading, carrying mostly business and financial news. It is crucial that subscribers have the paper before 9:00 A.M. Shops and newsstands put the paper out at 8:00 A.M. and resellers make their own deliveries. Paperboys and couriers, must deliver their newspapers to their subscribers before 9:00 A.M..

Consider how this distribution process would work if the paper arrived a day late. Would you subscribe to a newspaper that delivered yesterday's news? Imagine what would happen if all of the paperboys went on strike. Reliable distribution methods are a vital. You could say the paperboy who delivers your morning paper is just as important as the journalists who wrote it. Without a solid distribution network everything else is irreverent.

Scene distribution methods are similar to those used in the newspaper world, with equal levels of demand and complexity all under a strict timeframe. Speed is the key; ideally, a topsite receives every new release 5 minutes before it is officially released. Whoever has it first wins. It often comes down to the wire; a few seconds makes a big difference for competing topsites.

Topsites demand that all of the groups affiliated with them pre-release directly to their site. If a group is not affiliated with them, the site administrators encourage them topre-release to their site. The methods of persuasion include bribing group members with lavish accounts on other sites, or threatening them with account termination. Piracy is a cutthroat world and a topsite's status lasts only as long as it receives *every release first*.

Topsites are at the pinnacle of the distribution chain; they are the starting point of the scene and the key to piracy. Every pirated application used was originally downloaded from a topsite. Consider them to be the digital warehouses of the scene, where the first packages of media are sent to and distributed from.

PIRACY FACT...

Only a few topsites have ever been busted, because police raids tend to focus on the generic scene sites. Generic scene sites tend to have lower levels of security and a larger user base. These are the fly-by-night sites that may only be active a few months before they are discovered.

The street sellers commonly found in Asia sell counterfeit CDs; usually bootlegged video CDs or cracked games. Trying to compete in the competitive counterfeit world of Asia is tough. Street merchants only sell copies of a title that no other merchant has. It is in a street merchant's best interest to be as close as possible to the pirate's distribution chain, in order to get the CDs on the street as soon as possible.

Street merchants are often members of popular International Standards Organization (ISO) groups, whose role is to sell group' releases on the streets of Asia. For a small fee, groups often give street merchants an ISO release one day in advance of a pirated release date. The majority of scene groups have a history of selling releases to street merchants; however, recently, the attitude has changed and profiting from the scene has become taboo.

If a release group is unwilling to give a street merchant a release prior to its pirated release date, it is not uncommon for the street sellers to purchase ratio-free accounts on the group's private sites.

PIRACY FACT...

There was an interesting rumor going around the scene several years ago, just before Diablo 2 was officially released. Several counterfeiters in Asia were keen to do just about anything to illegally sell releases before their official release date.

Rumor has it that a member of a large scene group physically broke into the Blizzard offices and stole a gold CD which contained the final build of Diablo 2. The scene member was offered $10,000 for a final copy of the game. However, the offender had a flash of morality. He began to think that stealing the CD was risky enough; therefore, selling it would be suicidal.

Only Blizzard knows if this story is true, but it is not out of the ordinary.

Figure 7.1 shows a flow chart outlining the distribution process of a warez (exaggerated plural derivative of software)release; how it is transferred from point to point, and where it ultimately ends up.

The release used in this example is an application that allows user to change the look of their Windows applications by altering the colors, backgrounds, and menu styles. This release was cracked by a fictitious warez group known as "DAMMIT." DAMMIT's release contained a *keygen* application. This keygen allows users to register the software to their own username, removing any shareware protection.

Figure 7.1 Distribution Process for a Small Windows Application

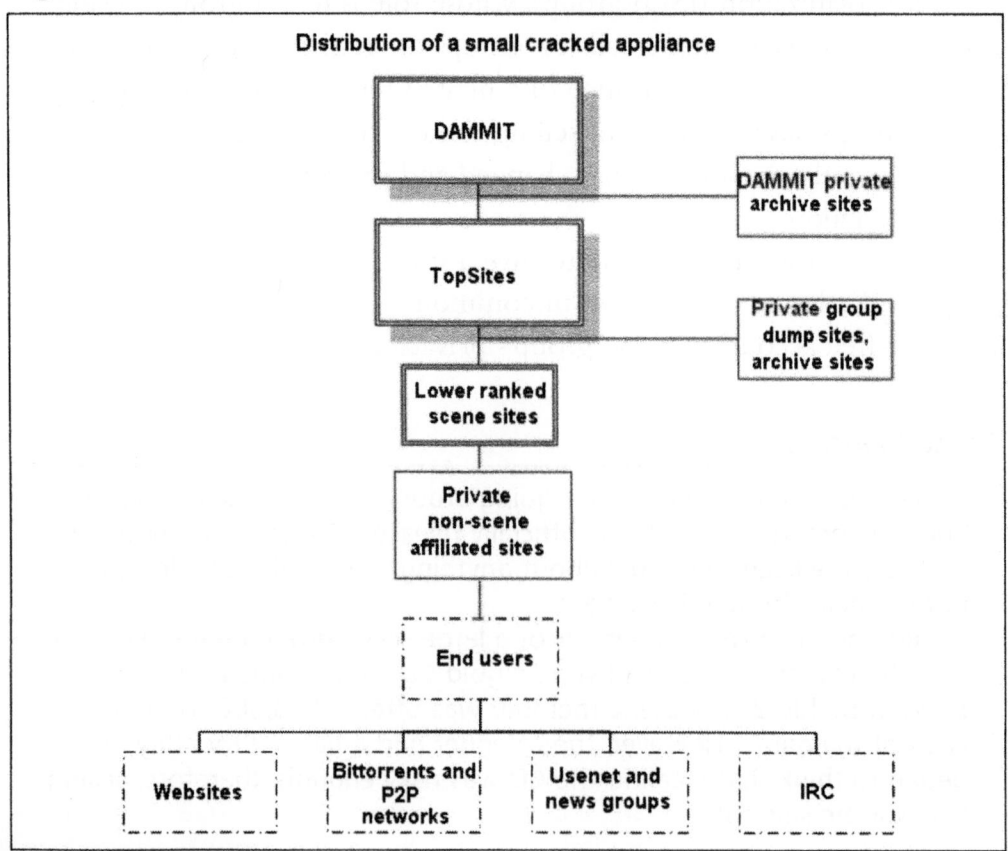

As you can see, a release flows through many hands before it reaches the majority of home users.

First, a release is created by a packager within DAMMIT. The packager makes sure that the release conforms to scene rules and has no risk of being nuked.

Next, the release is uploaded to the private, pre-release directories on all of DAMMIT's affiliated sites. Pre-release directories allow for a quick release process, because the release is only copied into the incoming directory when it is ready.

Releases are also archived on a private DAMMIT site known as "DAMMIT-HEAVEN". DAMMIT-HEAVEN has over 20 terabytes (tb) of storage online and a small active user base, which holds archives of all DAMMIT releases and private group information.

Once a release is pre-released on DAMMIT sites, the couriers see it and begin trading it to as many sites as possible, while it is still fresh. As time progresses, the release spreads to all of the sites within the scene and then makes its way into private home user sites, the most amateur of warez sites. Within days of release, the archive passes through several thousand sites and is quickly making its way towards the majority of end users.

However, at each step of the process the release is carried to fewer and fewer sites. Only a popular title will make its way from a topsite to end users. A majority of releases are never seen, because of their obscure and niche nature.

There are approximately 100 to 120 releases cracked, packaged, and released daily by various groups. However, only those scene sites with the resources to accommodate large amounts of information and the very popular or desired releases are carried throughout the distribution process to the end users.

End users receive their pirated material from easily accessible forms of distribution, such as Bit Torrent, peer-to-peer (P2P) networks, and Internet Relay Chat (IRC). Although not an exclusive scene environment, it works for many. Public transfer mediums are completely contrary to the scenes, which are designed by those who were rejected access to the scene.

The idea of everyone having an equal level of easily gained access has left public warez transfer methods flawed, clunky, uncivilized, and highly visible by the media.

Scene sites commonly run virus scanners, have high standards of quality, and remove any suspicious releases. Site administrators try to keep their sites quiet; nothing is advertised or announced and individual site profiles are unknown to the media. All information is on a need-to-know-basis.

PIRACY FACT...

Public transfer mediums are not always clean. Releases commonly contain viruses or backdoors and sometimes people try to trick others into downloading fraudulent files.

P2P networks are becoming favorite targets for hackers, who use their popular distribution methods to propagate worms and new viruses (e.g., an archive labeled *WindowsXP_Source.zip* might trick a user into downloading a malicious binary). Some people maintain that **all** pirated material contains viruses.

However, to the contrary, scene sites are too professional to distribute viruses. Any virus downloaded from a scene site, originated from the public medium that it was downloaded from.

From topsites, to scene sites, to private sites, the further along the distribution chain that a release goes, the less exclusive it becomes. No one wants yesterday's news; a release is not worth anything once it is a few days old.

After a release has been traded throughout the public arena and shared on various file-sharing networks, it reaches the end of its distribution chain. If demand for the release was high, it can be found on these public networks for a few weeks; otherwise, it will quickly fade.

The resting place for cracks, serial numbers, and keygens, and the final step in the distribution chain, are Russian or Chinese-based cracked Web sites. Such Web sites strip out any keygens or license information from within the distributed releases, posting just the keygen or license information on their public Web sites.

PIRACY FACT...

Chinese-run Web sites had until the end of May 2005 to register with the Ministry of Information, or face legal action. The registration drive was an effort to clamp down on fraud and other "unhealthy" activities on the Internet. Activities such as pornography and illegally distributing media have been disallowed; any domains supporting such activities will be removed.

From start to finish, the piracy process may take four to five days to complete for each release. However, if the title was highly anticipated, the required distribution period could be reduced to a matter of hours.

There are subtle but obvious differences between the distribution process of applications and of games. Video compact disks (VCDs), super video compact disks (SVCDs), Telesyncs, and DVDRIPs are highly popular with end users. The majority of readers would rather download a DVD of *Starwars Episode 3* than a seemingly useless Windows shareware application.

Due to the high demand, many movies and TV shows are being distributed directly to end users, often within minutes of their release. Placing end users on an even footing with many popular and exclusive scene sites makes downloading pirated video material incredibly easy.

PIRACY FACT...

In March 2005, secret service agents raided the address of a woman named Lisa Yamamoto, aged 45 and an ex-employee of FOX studios.
     Lisa was charged with using the FOX servers and networks to run a private File Transfer Protocol (FTP) site for a warez group that she belonged to. Lisa was also suspected of supplying the group with movies such as "Old School," "X-Men2," and "The Matrix Reloaded" for release.

Novice users can quickly find and begin retrieving hundreds of giga-bytes worth of pirated goods in a matter of minutes; an unprecedented amount, even in the context of the scene. A desktop and a high-speed connection are all you need to become a mainstream video pirate. Take the example below.

Group VideoFANs are active High Definition Television (HDTV) recorders that record and release new television shows minutes after they are screened in America. Users in other countries highly anticipate these releases, which are regularly collected by TV addicts worldwide. (See Figure 7.2.)

Figure 7.2 Distribution Process for a TV Show

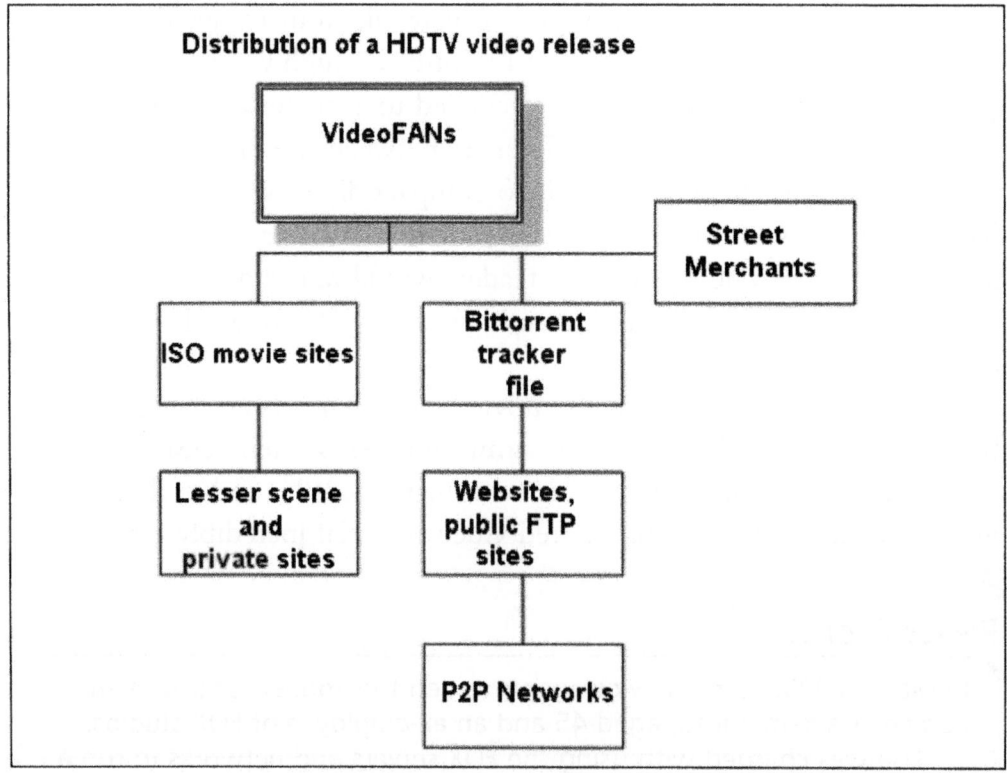

Street merchants play a huge role in pirated video media. The street demand for audiovisual (AV) content is high, and counterfeiters are often involved in the scene, using their connections in groups to obtain new movies to sell on the street.

PIRACY FACT...

Street merchants selling pirated video media are becoming such a problem in China that the country's capital, Shanghai, has dispatched piracy crime units.

In the wake of China hosting the international film festival this year, Shanghai has the near impossible task of closing down the thousands of street merchants selling pirated videos. Many of these pirated DVDs and TV shows are downloaded directly from the scene and then sold on the street.

"We want to create a good cultural environment for the international film festival and give guests from home and abroad a good impression," said Lan Yiming, the Deputy Head of Shanghai's Culture Inspection Bureau.

This distribution process is much different compared to the previous diagram. In this example, VideoFAN members create and begin sharing the release on Bit Torrent (a distributed downloading system) at the same time that they upload it to their own exclusive scene sites.

Public sharing has a huge impact on the distribution time of video content. Literally within hours of a new TV show first airing, the content will have traveled the earth several times. A TV show released and played in America on Monday night, will be downloadable by anyone in the world by Tuesday morning.

Pirated AV media is the only type of piracy that moves as fast, if not faster, than the warez scene itself. The size and popularity of public sharing methods rival those of the most exclusive topsites, and pirated video media is fast becoming an epidemic.

PIRACY FACT...

A recent study performed by Envisional, a Web tracking company, states that over 18 percent of all pirated TV shows are downloaded in the United Kingdom. Australia comes in second with 15.5 percent. Americans only account for 7 percent.

AV information, especially TV shows, is seen as fair game by pirates. Unlike software or movies, TV shows are not considered intellectual property by pirates. Such a mindset is due to the widespread use of VCR's in our society. Pirating TV content somehow seems less illegal to pirates, even though the content is still protected under intellectual copyright laws.

Because of this, TV piracy distribution has almost completely moved out of the private scene. It would take home-users weeks to find a CD of a popular game or application; however a TV show can be found and downloaded quickly.

PIRACY FACT...

One could argue that TV piracy has helped several TV shows, including "Battlestar Galactica" and "Doctor Who." "Doctor Who" was set to be British Broadcasting Corporation's (BBC's) most popular show, to be aired on March 24th.

However, two weeks before the proposed screening date, an unfinished "Work print" of "Dr Who," Episode No. 1, was leaked into the Internet through the BBC's production partner, Canadian Broadcasting Corporation (CBC). The word spread like wildfire; everyone wanted to download Episode No. 1. Even though an estimated 20 to 40 million users worldwide have downloaded and watched this episode, it still drew a viewer rating of over 10.81 million the night it screened on the BBC. This is one of the highest ratings that the BBC has ever received. Surprisingly, the BBC did not seem to care too much about the leak. There were no damming press releases and it was kept quiet in the media.

At one time, it was suspected that the BBC leaked this version into the piracy world specifically to hype the launch date, a new marketing technique known as "viral advertising." By releasing a work print version, watchers would get a taste of the final product and be more eager to tune in on March 24th.

The BBC denied such claims and then issued a media statement saying, "The leak of the first episode on the Internet was not a publicity stunt. It was a significant breach of copyright, which is currently under investigation. The source of it appears to be connected to our co-production partner. We would urge viewers not to spoil their enjoyment and to wait for the finished version."

The distribution of pirated material is complicated and structured, and requires many key players in order for it to work. Although a release is easily created and quickly sent to a handful of sites, spreading it globally takes a much larger effort.

Couriers

There are more couriers in the scene than there are crackers, suppliers, and sites combined. Couriers are the worker ants of the scene, carrying releases from site to site, ensuring that each release is spread from the top-sites down to the smallest sites.

Large, infamous courier groups exist that teem with couriers who spend countless hours trading releases from site to site. Couriers spend 8 to 10 hours every day moving releases. They live for it; it is a passion of sorts. Couriers do not care about the release. They have no preference regarding who releases it or what it does; they only care about the number of megabytes (MBs) that they can trade daily.

To couriers it is all about speed and efficiency. Couriers consider it life and death, a fusion of speed and high-paced typing, I have watched many couriers in the scene and I marvel at their dedication to a seemingly endless task.

It all begins with speed. The mark of a courier is someone who can move fast. When a release is 200 megabytes in size you do not want to try to move it on a cable modem. Considerable effort is taken by courier groups to acquire servers on high-speed connections. Ideally, such servers are housed at similar locations to the sites they trade to and from, usually universities or core backbone connections.

Common trends can be noticed in the countries that couriers use to trade from, many of them being European universities.

The following are three popular networks that couriers like to use:

- **tudelft.nl** Tu Delft is a technical university in the Nederlands
- **luth.se** Luleå Tekniska Universitet is a Swedish technical university

- ***utwente.nl*** The Technical University of Twente is in the Nederland's.

These universities offer students "high-speed Internet access" directly to their dormitory. High speed equates to a 100MB flat rate fiber connection.

Since many sites are housed at these universities, couriers can trade to and from them at 100MB. "100MB pfft," Estafari (a group courier) said to me. "I trade gig, nothing slower, when you're trading across the euro border you get raped on bw, gig can pump a few 100K faster than 100meg, only n00bs trade slow." Translated into English, this roughly means that Europe and America are connected via several large backbones, and although these backbones are capable of tremendous amounts of throughput, they can become overloaded and cause bottlenecks at peak times during the day.

A courier trading from a server in Europe to a server in America is dependent on this backbone connection; it governs the speed at which they can talk. If the backbone is clogged, the connection speed will be limited.

When using a gigabyte connection (1000MB) in Europe, the server can obtain a higher throughput to America, usually by its ability to send packets slightly faster. Although this does not drastically increase the bandwidth rate, some improvements can be found.

If a courier based in Europe with a gigabyte connection is racing a courier based in America with a 100MB connection and the European-American link is congested, the American 100MB connection will be faster. Speed equals megabytes.

With this in mind, couriers go to great efforts to obtain accounts on servers that are as geographically close as possible to the sites that they actively trade to.

Why bother investing so much time into something as pointless as copying other people's releases from site to site?

To answer this question and many others, I conducted an interview with Estafari to find out why he spends an average of 12 hours a day glued to his computer trading releases.

INTERVIEW WITH A COURIER

Me: "So, Estafari, when did you become a courier, and why?"

Estafari: "I started when I was young. It was how I got into the scene. I wanted accounts on good sites, to download games, movies, etc. The only way to get on good sites is to have a skill, and I didn't have one. So, I thought to myself, what can I do? I figured being a courier was the easiest way. It didn't require much skill and I had a lot of time on my hands (having just finished school)

I had a friend in XXX, a courier group. I asked him if I could join and try it all out. He agreed and gave me a shell on a 100MB European box. I bitched to a few site admins and sold my self as some hot shot courier, and managed to get a few accounts on some of XXX's affiliated sites.

Then the hard work began. The trick was pulling releases from one site and trading them to three others, fast. One of the sites got releases faster, so it was a good place to trade from. I was limited only by the amount of credits I had, so I really had to be creative. I would build up credits on the other sites and then trade any pre's they got back to the faster site, to get credits to trade back to the others. It's a real art form!"

Me: "Yeah, that sounds like hard work too. How long did you spend doing this?"

Estafari: "All day, every day. It's such a drug, man. I could do 30 hours at the keyboard easy without sleep. I set up a script to monitor site IRC chans and play a noise whenever the site bot announced there was a pre or new release."

Me: "So you really got into it?"

Estafari: "Yes. Soon I had accounts on sites that would make the common man cry. Trading got harder and faster; there is more competition on the exclusive sites. It's seriously mad how fast some of these sites are."

Me: "Was there any reward for doing all of this?"

Estafari: "Well, scene sites have a ranking system. Each site is given a score based on how fast it receives releases and the amount of support

Continued

www.syngress.com

it has. There are a few courier e-magazines released that have combined score cards of couriers and courier groups and how well they fare on each site.

You get points for each site you do well on, usually the top five slots. These points are then added up and the magazines show the winner of the current week. The more points a group scores, the more desirable they are to others. More sites want to affiliate with them, more members want to join.

In the end, it comes down to being 'elite,' everyone wants to be on the winning team. The group that comes in first on every site will have good offers from others. But mostly it's about being elite. When you're at the top of the courier game, you get a lot of goodies."

Me: "How far up the chain did you get?"

Estafari: "Well, as I said before, I started trading 1.0 to 1.5 ranked sites. Now I trade topsites only. I was recruited into XXX. After a while, they gave me a ton of bandwidth to use; shells, hardware. They even had cash prizes for the best weekly courier."

Me: "Cash prizes?"

Estafari: "Yeah, it's a real competition and people take it very seriously. Many of the groups work with guys who sell pirated material, and they make cash from it, and use that cash to fuel the group. Buy us new hardware to play with or just give out a few hundred bucks a week."

Me: "How do you trade? What is the process involved?"

Estafari: "It's complicated while being very simple, if you get me. To start with, you need a fast shell on a good Linux or Berkeley Software Distribution (BSD) box. Windows is no go. Although you can File Exchange Protocol (FXP) trade, it's lame, and much slower.

Couriers tend to have their own FTP clients, filled with hot keys and short cuts, but essentially it's GET/SEND. So, first you login to all your sites and get ready, you just idle and wait for a release. When site1 gets a release, you will know because you will see the announcement in the group's IRC channel from the site bot. You want to quickly download this release to your shell and get it local so that you only use one lot of credits. While the release is downloading to the shell, create directories on your target sites to upload into. When you have the first disk down, begin trading it to other sites, and do that for each additional disk as it is uploaded to your source site.

If you're quick, you can trade a release in under two seconds. You gotta be quick because others will trade a release in three seconds.

Continued

It all comes down to the speed of your shell. You need a lot of bandwidth to do this well, 10MB won't cut it trading. You need at least a gigabyte connection to trade well."

Me: "Do you also trade to America?"

Estafari: "That's a tough one. There are some good American sites I like trading to, but the majority of good sites are located in Europe"

Me: "Why?"

Estafari: "I think it's mostly due to the amount of bandwidth they have. It's mad. Every university dorm there will give the students 100MB connections for a few hundred bucks a year. Wish I had that kinda bandwidth to my room.

American sites tend to be at companies or data centers. It's just the bandwidth, really. America is only fast to other American sites. I would say 60 percent of the scene is run from Europe: Finland, Sweden, The Nederland's, Czechoslovakia, Poland, all very popular places. You wouldn't think that they have the best bandwidth, but they do, oooh boy they do!"

Me: "Do you still trade releases?"

Estafari: "Yes, although it's a little different now. Many couriers use automated scripts and applications that just trade for them. It's hard enough racing against a bunch of couriers, but racing against a bunch of scripts that do not sleep; it's pointless."

Me: "So, couriers are being replaced by applications, just like automated robots."

Estafari: "Yeah, they do a better job too. But it's sad for the people that used to trade. The scene has become so focused on speed that it's really out of human reach anymore. When you trade on some sites now you need to beat the sub-2 second mark; usually 1 second is all it takes. Every file uploaded and every directory created on one site is mirrored instantly to another site. Right now I am just a pre-er for a few small release groups."

Me: "A pre-er?"

Estafari: "Yes, I take the packed releases and pre them on the group sites. Automated scripts can't beat something they do not have. Pre's are the only guaranteed megs you can get these days."

Me: "Do you enjoy this life?"

Estafari: "Yes, it's fun working with release groups. You get to help keep releases from getting nuked and you get to work with some very smart cookies in the groups."

Me: "Any plans to stop the life of a courier?"

Continued

> **Estafari:** "I would, but I need sites to download things. I do not want to drop out of the scene. The scene gives me so many things. So, I think I'll stick around, until the machines kick me out anyway."
> **Me:** "Thanks for your time, Estafari."

The more I talk to couriers, the more I get the feeling that they are not even interested in the piracy aspect of the scene. To them it's all about who can upload the most and the fastest to the most elite sites. Like every other aspect of the scene, no one is actively trying to hurt the software industry; there is no malicious intent. Is that hard to imagine? Prior to writing this book, I thought that everyone involved in the scene was trying to use piracy for the greater evil, to rip off hard-working software developers and spread hippie-like idealisms.

A good example of this is the courier "Weekly Stats" magazines; pages of statistics of different couriers and their uploading efforts on differently ranked sites. Not once is a single release named. (See Figure 7.3.)

Couriers are happy trading any information; it's not about piracy to them, it's about distribution.

Figure 7.3 Weekly Courier Statistics

```
Site Ranking:

    3.0 >-> [B*R] [E*] [*]
    2.5 <-> [D*D] [B*] [F*] [N*] [*]
    2.0 >-> [A*L] [C*M] [T*H] [H*G] [T*S]
    1.5 <-> [A*S] [N*D] [R*N] [M*]
    1.0 >-> [P*] [A*M] [T*L] [*] [M*]


Top Ranking:
                  [THIS WEEK]                        [ALL TIME]

        < 01 >  maro      363.5 =|=  < 01 >  maro      363.5
        < 02 >  darkwolf  306.5 =|=  < 02 >  darkwolf  306.5
        < 03 >  johs      195   =|=  < 03 >  johs      195
        < 04 >  skitza    190   =|=  < 04 >  skitza    190
```

< 05 >	aj	184.5	=|=	< 05 >	aj	184.5
< 06 >	algalord	117	=|=	< 06 >	algalord	117
< 07 >	theprof	69	=|=	< 07 >	theprof	69
< 08 >	deuce	57.5	=|=	< 08 >	deuce	57.5
< 09 >	sobol	55	=|=	< 09 >	sobol	55
< 10 >	dj	53	=|=	< 10 >	dj	53
< 11 >	thedude	52.5	=|=	< 11 >	thedude	52.5
< 12 >	doakey	41.5	=|=	< 12 >	doakey	41.5
< 13 >	tohuk	41	=|=	< 13 >	tohuk	41
< 14 >	preacher	35	=|=	< 14 >	preacher	35

Group Scores:

< 1 >	AMN	349	=|=	< 1 >	AMN	349
< 2 >	AOD	317	=|=	< 2 >	AOD	317
< 3 >	MSN	296.5	=|=	< 3 >	MSN	296.5
< 4 >	LT	295.5	=|=	< 4 >	LT	295.5
< 5 >	RTS	30	=|=	< 5 >	RTS	30

Magazines such as this are not rare. There used to be several magazines that were produced and released weekly. Couriers want to know how they are faring against other groups. They want to beat the competition and be number one. Comparable to a sports match, couriers have dedication to their team.

Public Distribution

For the average Joe, the life of a professional warez courier is out of reach. Couriers have it all; unlimited access and detailed, internal knowledge of the scene and scene groups.

But it is not a typical user who sits at home and downloads the latest pirated copy of Windows. It is not typical of the massive amounts of end users. End users are forced to use many different mediums to obtain pirated material. Many are not pretty, but it is all they have. End users are resourceful and creative, often creating their own methods of distributing pirated information. This public, pseudo-scene is complete with its own groups, members, and hierarchies. However, this scene operates on a shoestring budget with little resources, bandwidth, or monetary investment.

Professional pirates have resources. It's easier to share a terabyte of information when you have your own network, servers, and infrastructure.

If you had nothing but your cable modem at home, and you wished to serve large amounts of information to thousands of public users, how would you do it? Your cable modem would reach saturation with only a few users downloading. You need massive amounts of available bandwidth to offer this service, but you do not have the resources.

With this task in hand, many methods of distributing pirated information have been developed, all based on the idea of having little or no resources at your disposal while sharing as much information as possible.

The following sections look at how the average Joe distributes and shares pirated information. Although the public scene is rarely responsible for releasing or supplying a pirated application or game, they are prolific in sharing it and public sharing methods are constantly in the media eye.

Unprotected FTP Sites

The hardest problem with disturbing a large amount of illegal information, such as warez or pirated movies, is the simple fact that the media is illegal. You cannot advertise yourself as supporting piracy. Any Web site or FTP site hosting the media must remain secret.

However, when your goal is to advertise a "cool" warez site that you want the public to log into and enjoy, what do you do? You make someone else host the media without their knowledge, thereby removing the element of risk while still allowing you to advertise and promote the site. FTP sites are commonly used for this purpose. By default, many FTP servers allow anonymous users to upload files into an incoming or public directory, usually so that a small number of users can share information easily.

However, with a massive amount of servers offering free storage place, unprotected FTP sites soon became abused. Pirates used them to house gigabytes of pirated media, which cost the FTP site owner in both resources and bandwidth.

Pirates must be sneaky and discreet in how they hide information within an FTP site. Many pirates bury the information within the deep branches of their directories. While searching the Internet, I found one public warez site hidden within a French company's e-mail server on their network. (See Figure 7.4.)

Figure 7.4 Hiding the Information

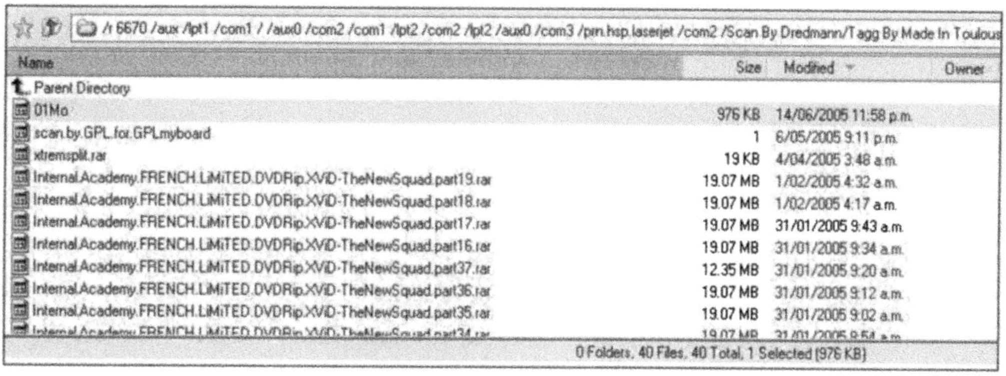

The full directory path used to hide a pirated copy of "Internal Academy", a French DVD film, is */r 6670 /aux /lpt1 /com1 / /aux0 /com2 /com1 /lpt2 /com2 /lpt2 /aux0 /com3 /prn.hsp.laserjet /com2 /Scan By Dredmann/Tagg By Made In Toulouse/Up By Membre/For Unl!m!T/Here/Internal.Academy/*. This maze of directories is designed to confuse anyone who is administering the server.

Device names such as */com2* and */aux0* and names beginning with a dot (.) are commonly used when hiding directories. Foreign language characters are also popular, because English clients and servers cannot understand unprintable characters such as those found in the American Standard Code for Information Interchange (ASCII) range.

Some IRC channels exist where pirates are free to trade the concealed locations of their varying warez. Large lists of commonly used hiding places are compiled and other pirates are encouraged to upload anything they have to share. One such channel is #freewarez, a public channel on a smaller IRC network. Just like many others, #freewarez freely gives a large list of sites to anyone who joins and types the special trigger. (See Figure 7.5.)

PIRACY FACT...

In IRC terms, a "trigger" is a special keyword such as "!list" or "!freestuff" that is typed in a channel. Automated channel robots (bots) will act on this trigger and send the user a list of sites.

Figure 7.5 Release Hotspots

```
-=oOo=-      Oo,.,,oo''Oo,.,,oo''Oo,.,,oo -=oOo=--=oOo=- Oo,.,,oo''Oo,.,,oo''Oo,.,,oo      -=oOo=-
-=oOo=-                                                                                    -=oOo=-
-=oOo=-                                                                                    -=oOo=-
-=oOo=-      Hi!                                                                           -=oOo=-
-=oOo=-      You are now looking at the biggest, the best and most                        -=oOo=-
-=oOo=-      wanted FTP list on the net: The #freewarez List!                             -=oOo=-
-=oOo=-                                                                                    -=oOo=-
-=oOo=-      This list provides you with thousands of FTP sites that                      -=oOo=-
-=oOo=-      are all working, non ratio, often on fast connections,                       -=oOo=-
-=oOo=-      contain the latest warez and are ready to be leeched from.                   -=oOo=-
-=oOo=-      That means you will not see FTP's saying "Ratio 1:3,                          -=oOo=-
-=oOo=-      current credit 0 kb" here!                                                    -=oOo=-
-=oOo=-                                                                                    -=oOo=-
-=oOo=-      Warez are free. That means we don't earn money with what                     -=oOo=-
-=oOo=-      we do. We will never ask money from you, to get our list!                    -=oOo=-
-=oOo=-      Please report cheaters, that sell our list, put it on                        -=oOo=-
-=oOo=-      their website next to a big banner or post it somewhere else.                -=oOo=-
-=oOo=-      FTP's are very unstable, so about 20% of all sites                           -=oOo=-
-=oOo=-      in the list go offline every day! Keep on posting to keep                    -=oOo=-
-=oOo=-      our list big and good!                                                       -=oOo=-
```

Each site listed above contains no more than three or four releases. Although hardly a 20tb warez storage warehouse, these public FTP sites fulfill a need for many.

A solid distribution method is required for every type of internet pirate. From the small FTP sites to the professionals, everyone takes piracy very seriously. It is more than a hobby to a dedicated pirate.

XDCC IRC Bots

Multiple Direct Client-to-Client (XDCC) is an extension of the IRC protocol's Direct Client Connection (DCC), a method commonly used to communicate directly between two clients without using an interim chat or IRC server.

DCC has been used since the dawn of IRC, mostly for sending files to other users or holding private conversations with them.

XDCC works on the same principle of communicating directly between two users, only it operates from an automated, autonomous robot. This automated bot sends users the file or package that they request.

When applied to piracy distribution, bots offer an effective method for distributing files discreetly to users.

A bot will sit in a public IRC channel and replay advertisements of packages it currently has to offer. Packages are composed of each release broken down into smaller archives, usually between 50 and 75MB.

When a client finds a package they desire, they issue a request to the bot to receive that packages number. The bots will then try to send the user the desired package by DCC'ing them the archive. Alternatively, if the bot is currently sending too many files, the client is placed in a queue until a slot becomes available. (See Figure 7.6.)

Figure 7.6 XDCC Bot Example

```
<superbot> Slots 6/10 open: Files offered: #10: "/msg superbox GET
#packagenumber" to receive a package
<superbot> Package: #1: Friends, Season 5 - Archive 1 of 10
<superbot> Package: #2: Friends, Season 5 - Archive 2 of 10
<superbot> Package: #3: Friends, Season 5 - Archive 3 of 10
```

Although IRC bots offer a powerful and simple method for pirates to distribute their wares, they receive practically no media attention. File sharing networks such as kazaar and edonkey are widely known by law enforcement agencies that pursue those who use these illegal networks.

XDCC bots have been present on the Internet since 1994; however, there has not been a single arrest from either using or operating these file-serving bots.

During my travels in the scene I managed to find one such bot owner, a man who goes by the handle Lazarus. Lazarus runs several bots that offer ISO images of Xbox and Playstation2 games. He agreed to a short interview with me to discuss why he runs these XDCC bots and what it means to him.

INTERVIEW WITH A BOT OWNER

Me: "Lazarus, firstly, do you mind telling me how long you have been running XDCC bots and just how many you run?"

Lazarus: "Sure, I started running filebots in 2000 for an IRC channel called *freeconsolewarez*. The idea was to offer games to people for download. XDCC seemed logical, since we all sat in the channel and just chatted anyway.

I run three filebots now, two from a connection at my work and one from home."

Me: "You run two from work? You're not worried about someone finding out?"

Lazarus: "Not really. They don't use that much bandwidth. I send out maybe 150 to 200 gigabytes (GB) a week at the most. No one has noticed yet and its been five years."

Me: "Why do you run these bots?"

Lazarus: "Why not? I download a lot of console ISO's from other places, and I have many friends online who like to play games. I like to share; why not be honest."

Me: "Ever worry about being caught?"

Lazarus: "Not really; no one seems to really care. I had to sign an agreement at work recently saying that I would never use a file-sharing network, or risk getting fired. It didn't say anything about IRC."

Me: "Are the XDCC bots hard to maintain?"

Lazarus: "Nope, not at all. They run as egg drop processes on any UNIX server, I set them up and just leave them going. I update the content files each week and give them new packages to distribute. I am currently serving up to 45 people."

Me: "What do you think of all the recent legal action against software pirates? Do you think it's justified? How do you feel about piracy?"

Lazarus: "Yes, I mean, it is stealing someone's work, but it's more complicated than that. I am a console gamer from way back. I have bought every console and the majority of games I play, but I am just sick of paying now. Everyone wants money from you. I figure they get enough of my money; I deserve some things for free. Most console gamers feel the same way. It's all one big scam to get your money.

We pirate the games to escape. To be honest, it feels really good to just get a game and play it. I know it's stealing, I know it's against the law, but it just feels so good."

Continued

Me: "So, you don't have any plans to stop? You know, you could land in jail for longer with a piracy charge (especially distributing) than you would for a rape charge?"
[In some countries? –mb]
Lazarus: "Really? Well, I'll be honest, that scares me. It's not worth that, but I don't have any plans to stop. Actually, I am thinking of setting up another fileserver bot some time soon."
Me: "If you had any thoughts or suggestions for the game console industry on how to combat piracy, what would it be?"
Lazarus: "Easy; make games better and cheaper. I would buy every game that came out, if they only cost $10 each. I am so sick of spending $40 on a game and finding out it's a horrid, buggy crap. Most stores don't give you a full refund, so you're stuck with the nasty game. If you want to stop piracy, don't make it harder, make it easier. Make it so easy to get a game legally that no one would bother pirating it. Reverse psychology 101."
Me: "Thanks a lot for the interview. Good luck with the file-serving bots."
Lazarus: "Thanks."

File-sharing Networks

File sharing networks have become the most popular form of sharing digital media between large numbers of users. Originating from humble roots, Napster was the first and original file-sharing network. It was designed solely with music in mind, and only allowed users to share mp3 files. Each user joining the network offered the music they had stored locally, and in return they were given access to the music everyone else offered. It is a simple, noncommercial idea that seemed too good to be true. There was no cost associated with Napster; you did not need to know the right people or belong to some exclusive group. You simply downloaded the client and selected your music.

It did not take long for both recording artists and publishing labels to realize two fundamental facts about Napster. Firstly, it was breaking the law and almost all music shared was copyrighted. Secondly no one had comprehended just how successful Napster was becoming. If Napster's community was only a few hundred in number, the recording industry would not care too much. However, when companies began to realize the growth and popularity of Napster, they began to worry about the future of music and CD's.

Next a giant wave of lawsuits came that soon engulfed the Napster project. Artists such as Dr. Dre and the 1980s metal band Mettalica personally funded these lawsuits, aggressively attacking the software vendor. The music industry was waking up to the fact that downloading music freely was becoming hip. Napster did not seem illegal or immoral to those using it, to them it was simply a great idea and it was going to change the music industry.

However, Napster did not last. Between the lawsuits and the negative media attention, the beloved service was soon out of action. Napster enlightened many, since no one had ever tried using a distributed network to deliver media. It was the beginning of a new revolution of Internet piracy distribution; a revolution that would have a prolific effect on the Internet.

File-sharing networks offered a reliable, functional, and free method for millions of average Internet users to share media among themselves. Soon after Napster's demise, Gnutella (an open source network based on the design and success of Napster) emerged. Gnutella allowed users to search for any file type (not just music) and became a hit with those looking to share videos. Napster's demise taught the file-sharing community a very valuable lesson; centralization implies legal liability, meaning that any central server used to house content or links to content is legally liable for that content. Napster used their own servers and infrastructure to allow users to share content with one another. When Napster was hit with lawsuits, it only took one server being unplugged for the entire Napster network to fade.

Gnutella's design was that of a decentralized network, meaning there was no centralized server or service. It was distributed and anyone could run his or her own server. This made it practically impossible for someone to catch or shut down the entire network. When a single network owner is forced to shut down, many other networks still existed.

Decentralization became a key point in the design of file-sharing networks, and as more networks emerged, each offered a higher level of decentralization.

PIRACY FACT...

File-sharing networks are not just threatened by legal authorities; hackers and script kiddies often use Denial of Service (DOS) on key elements of the network, in order to take it off line.

By using a decentralized architecture, there are no single points of failure and no server or service that can be attacked.

Recent-sharing applications use multiple networks and services, with a single client able to search many different networks simultaneously. With such a vast diversity of networks, law enforcement agencies are powerless to do anything.

PIRACY FACT...

Law enforcement agencies may be powerless to shut down the networks that run the file-sharing servers, but private companies are not so powerless. In true American style, if you can't defeat them, sue them.

Recently, the Recording Industry Association of America (RIAA) has become infamous for searching file sharing networks, looking for any user who shares a substantial amount of pirated media, and then blindly suing them for millions of dollars in supposed lost revenue. Sarah Seabury was falsely accused of sharing a wealth of rap music (see RIAA vs. 66-year-old Sarah Seabury). Sarah, a computer neophyte, did not even know what file sharing was, and was said to be so shaken after the accusations that she began to have heart palpitations.

RIAA lawyers dropped the accusations after Sarah was proven innocent. Oddly enough, the 66-year-old admitted to having no interest in rap music.

Another lawsuit involved Brianna LaHara, a 12-year-old who was accused of sharing pirated music, thereby costing the recording industry millions. Brianna, who paid $29.95 to access file-sharing network Kazaa was convinced the service was legal. "I thought it was OK to download music because my mom paid a service fee for it. Out of all people, why did they pick me?" said Brianna.

File-sharing networks are simply too hard to shut down. There are too many of them and they are too popular with the youth today. Suing users is the only method for attacking the service.

Many of my friends spend countless hours searching various file-sharing networks for new things to download. To them it is the equivalent of Google. It is not malice, these people are not cut throat criminals and they are not cracking and distributing pirated media, it is just downloading.

I recently caught up with a friend of mine named Peter. I took him out for a drink and to chat about piracy and file-sharing networks. Personally, I have never used any type of file-sharing application, so I figured it would be best to interview Peter.

INTERVIEW WITH A FILE-SHARING USER

Me: "Peter, what type of media do you download on P2P networks and why?"

Peter: "Music videos mostly, but I get some TV episodes and music too."

Me: "Why?"

Peter: "Why? Because I can; I like music videos"

Me: "Do you know that this is illegal? Previously the RIAA has tracked down users by their IP address and forced ISP's to give out customer information. This is a real threat"

Peter: "Yeah, but everyone does it"

Me: "So you accept the risks? It is till worth it?"

Peter: "Yeah, I don't see what's wrong with it. I get to listen to a lot of new stuff."

Me: "That's a good point. So, you see file-sharing networks as a 'trial' of the music. How many albums have you bought this year?"

Continued

> **Peter:** "Probably 15 or 20, I only buy the ones that I really like. I buy more albums now that I use file sharing though. I dunno what the big deal is; it helps their sales if you ask me."
>
> **Me:** "What do you hate about file sharing networks?"
>
> **Peter:** "There's always a lot of fake stuff on it; porn, viruses, adware. I only get music videos because they tend to be what you expect. I wouldn't download a zip file from a P2P net, though. It would contain a virus for sure."
>
> **Me:** "Would you pay for access to a file-sharing network?"
>
> **Peter:** "What? No; of course not. The only reason I use it is that it's free. I already pay for the damn albums. I don't want to pay more money. The Internet is meant to make things easier and cheaper, not cost me more."
>
> **Me:** "A perfect file-sharing network would have what?"
>
> **Peter:** "Virus scanners, no fake stuff, quality control, good search engine."

After a few more beers, Peter told me that he was very worried about the future of file-sharing networks. "I need them to find new bands to listen to; otherwise, I only listen to what the radio tells me to. The Internet rocks for giving you more choices".

File-sharing networks may be immensely popular with those looking to share media, but as Peter pointed out, they are key distribution points for those looking to propagate a virus or worm.

Piracy Fact…

Bruce Hughes, director of malicious code research at security firm TrueSecure, found that out of 4,778 files downloaded from file-sharing network Kazaa, nearly half contained a virus.

On average, 45 percent of executable files contained viruses, worms, or Trojan horses. Malicious code was intended to steal sensitive information from host PCs, such as bank account details or America Online (AOL) account passwords. These Trojan files were aggressively advertised on file-sharing networks, with many misleading filenames. A single user may be sharing thousands of executable files with sneaky, unsuspecting file

names such as *winzip_keygen.exe* or *windows_xp_keygen.exe*, all containing the same virus or worm. Any user who is tricked into downloading the files is instantly infected with the virus.

File-sharing networks are still growing in popularity and remain a
favorite with many. Recently designed networks are so well integrated
with each other that they offer an unparalleled file search engine for
users. However, virus and worm authors perceive this usability as an ideal
method to propagate malicious code, pumping many malicious binaries
into the file-sharing community and decreasing the general enjoyment of
the service.

Bit Torrent

Bit Torrent is a novel and unique approach to file distribution; and its
popularity is growing far beyond that of file-sharing networks. Bit
Torrent is not just for computer pirates; it's being used by many legitimate organizations as a reliable method of distributing large files. For
example, Linux distributions are now commonly available via a Bit
Torrent file.

Bit Torrent works on a unique philosophy, which is the reason its
growth has been so rapid in the technology sector. Unlike standard file
distribution methods that share single streams of bandwidth until completion, Bit Torrent is completely the opposite; every user downloading a file
is simultaneously sharing that file with other users. Therefore, the more
users downloading a file, the faster it will transfer for everyone.

A user may begin downloading the first 2 percent of the file from
one particular user and the last 10 percent from another user. Each user
offers a different segment of the file and each segment is joined together
at the end.

The ability to share a file while it is still downloading is one of the
reasons Bit Torrents are so successful. A user with 1 percent of a file
downloaded can help another user with 99 percent of that file finish
downloading by offering the missing bytes they require. Many Bit Torrent

Web sites exist that give users a way to search what is offered from different Bit Torrents. Remember, the more people who download the file the better.

Bit Torrents range from 50MB to 5GB. After some searching online, I managed to find Bit Torrents that offered complete seasons of TV episodes, some up to 7GB in size.

Figure 7.7 Bit Torrent Searching

Games	9.4d	[DL] Golden Palace Casino and Poker Games [simp...	317.44 KB
Misc.	27d	[DL] A Fapalot presents Ten Sexy Girls [sin ci... A Fapalot presents Ten Sexy Girls [sin ci...	5.16 MB
Unclassified	57.1d	[DL] **joey**.121.hedtv-lol.[BT].avi	174.95 MB
TV	34.8d	[DL] TV-**Joey** > **Joey** - The Full 1st Season!! (bn... **Joey** full 1st season (bnl)	4.37 GB
TV	133.9d	[DL] **joey**.01x16.hdtv-lol.avi	171.04 MB
Unclassified	85.1d	[DL] **joey**.120.pdtv-lol.[BT].avi	176.39 MB
Unclassified	133.9d	[DL] 198 **joey**.116.hdtv-lol.[BT].avi	171.04 MB
TV	1.8d	[DL] TV-**Joey** > **Joey** Episodes 17 a 20 en Francai... **Joey** 1X17 a 1X20 UP By BiGFooT	929.56 MB
TV	35.6d	[DL] **Joey**.S01E24.HDTV.XviD-TCM	184.41 MB

The only Bit Torrent requirement is for a tracker file, a unique Uniform Resource Locator (URL) to which each client communicates. Trackers act as intermediaries, passing on requests for additional bytes of a package or offering to share a section of a file to others.

Bit Torrent technology is best described as a hybrid-centralized distribution server. Even though each client receives the data directly from another client, a centralized tracker server is still required. Having this central tracker server is a weak point for Bit Torrents, because the same Napster methodology applies and the tracker host is liable for the content it provides.

PIRACY FACT...

Recently, RIAA efforts have been focused on suing any Web site found to be offering Bit Torrent services that include pirated content. Sites such as the one shown in Figure 7.7 are becoming a rarity, and many Web sites are quickly taken offline because of a legal threat. Bit Torrents have the music and film industry worried, because its popularity is endless compared to file-sharing networks.

Even Microsoft has admitted how impressed they are with the Bit Torrent design. They recently announced their own Bit Torrent clone protocol called Avalanche.

Meanwhile, a further development in the Bit Torrent application by *supernova.org* (a Web site shut down by the RIAA) will see Bit Torrent become completely decentralized, thereby removing the need for any central tracking server.

Newsgroups

Possibly the oldest and well known Internet service used, newsgroups are making a come back into the public piracy scene.

Similar to modern day bulletin boards or e-mail lists, newsgroups are a way for a server to relay information to many users at once. Usenet.com, possibly the oldest and most established newsgroup provider still running, is one example of how well newsgroup networks work.

The newsgroup *alt.binaries.multimedia*, a popular channel on the Usenet.com newsgroup network, has quadrupled in traffic since 2001. In an average day a staggering 100gigabytes of pirated movies will be posted to the thread. Usenet.com threads and newsgroups in general are seen as a less-policed area of the Internet and piracy has flourished because of this.

Many new pirated movies are becoming available on newsgroups before they are available on any file-sharing networks. Newsgroups are growing in popularity and many close to the professional piracy scene are happy to upload new releases to it.

Anonymity is a major factor in the lasting success of newsgroups. Being one of the first internet services developed, newsgroups have little accountability and leave behind a very thin audit trail. Source IP addresses of those who upload and download are not recorded. Additionally, information is stored remotely on a server so clients are not legally responsible or liable for distributing pirated information, as is the case with peer 2 peer.

How long will it last? Who knows? Do the RIAA even know what a newsgroup is?

Even Usenet.com is aware of its success in the piracy market; new accounts created now cost a fee. Users are billed extra for excessive downloading and Usenet.com is treated as a giant piracy market by many.

Legally Usenet.com is liable for the content it publishes; therefore, given the additional media attention, there may soon be pending lawsuits.

Usenet.com is just one example of a newsgroup service, but many more exist. Newsgroups function like a giant digital message board, users can post files or messages and other readers can download them.

Since the files are stored on a central newsgroup server the service is designed very similarly to an FTP site.

Judging from past RIAA-filed lawsuits, it is easier to prosecute someone for sharing a piece of media than it is for downloading it. Sharing means you have the intent to distribute, that you are fueling the problem of piracy. Downloading, however, only shows end-user piracy; you are not distributing this to anyone else, you are keeping it quiet. Legally, newsgroups are much better for the end user. Although still illegal, it is a lesser crime and harder to successfully prosecute.

Newsgroups have recently seen a huge boom in usage; some newsgroup providers now claim several terabytes of data traffic each day.

Playground Trading

High school friends and primary school buddies are the final step in the public chain of piracy. When I was young, I traded copies of games with all of my friends. One person in our group would receive a copy of a new game, quickly duplicate it, and pass it on to the rest of us. We would race each other to see who could complete the game first.

I was no more than 11, and to me it was all for fun, it was not illegal. We could not afford even a single copy of a game, so we had no choice. Our floppy disk swapping club ended when one member's mother was worried about all the games her son had acquired and the legality of it. Soon after, all of our parents were called and each of us was banned from using the computer.

Playground disk trading was the starting ground for several of my friends, and piracy is still a part of their life. They download everything from the Internet and run their own private warez sites for friends.

Similar casual piracy is seen in the office and throughout families.

How many times has an uncle, friend or colleague offered you a bootlegged copy of a new film or offered a gold CD version of a new game.

Piracy is social, and for many who are simply casual pirates they see no harm in offering a CD to a friend.

Chapter 8

The Piracy Scene

The Many Faces of the Piracy Scene

When individuals change the environment they live in, they eventually adapt to their new environment. For example, city people are used to a fast pace, and people in small towns are used to a slow pace. If a city person moves to a small town, they will eventually adapt to their new lifestyle, just as a small town person will adapt to the city. If someone is not happy in their present environment, they can move to one they like better.

The piracy scene is very similar to society. Within one scene there are countless smaller scenes, each complete and functional in their own way, but very different. There are different pirates for each different type of media, who have specialized skill sets and a varied level of commitment to their trade. Each corner of the scene is completely different than the other.

Game pirates (those who specialize in cracking and releasing PC games in either International Organization for Standardization [ISO] or ripped form) are under a large amount of stress and pressure. Games are fast and hard hitting, and require a tremendous level of dedication. With few games released each year, the competition is huge. Crackers go days without sleep because they love the rush of piracy; however, all of the high stress and work they invest can easily turn into a waste of time if another group releases the game first.

Application groups may have a release for weeks or even months, before they release it. With so many applications on the market, there is less rush and less competition.

The video piracy scene is also different than the other scenes. These pirates are video buffs that commonly work in projection booths and video distribution companies. To them it is all about risk, about pulling out their beta-CAM recorder during the first screening of a highly anticipated movie. It is a thrill beyond compare.

These greatly varied and contrasting environments create very different types of pirates and many different piracy scenes. Each scene essentially shares the same goal—pirating media as fast as possible—but that is where the similarities end.

This chapter examines the sub-scenes within the piracy scene (e.g., consoles, e-books, videos, movies, and recording television [TV] channels).

Console

Consoles are the new groups of the scene. From XBOX to PlayStation, Nintendo Gameboy Advance, and GameCube, anything being sold for consoles has been pirated. Initial versions of most console machines had little piracy protection; therefore, all you had to have to pirate most original games was a small modchip installed in your console, or a low level Compact Disc Recordable (CDR) capable of copying the original CDs.

As counterfeiting grew, technology evolved and piracy became more complicated because of the additional layers of copy protection that were implemented. Modchips for new consoles can take years to develop; security has become tighter as consoles have become popular.

PIRACY FACT…

A reliable source told me that the original XBOX copy protection was first defeated by a member of a popular ISO group, who was also a developer for the console. It took three weeks for the cracker to develop a method of ripping the CDs into image files.

The first few games for the XBOX and PlayStation 2 took months to be released. Technology was new and crackers were unable to find a reliable method of creating an image of an original game disk. As time progressed, the methods became more refined and the modchips were made available to the public. Console piracy soared.

Games are now ripped and released quickly, often before the official publishing date. Inside suppliers (many at publishing and distribution companies) leak games to piracy groups. Console piracy is becoming an established scene and will soon rival the PC game scene. Although the majority of home users have PCs, many more have consoles and demands for games are much greater.

Recent technology from Nintendo and Sony has produced a handheld console with adequate graphics and rendering abilities. PlayStation Portables (PSPs) and Nintendo DS' have grown greatly in both popularity and piracy.

More recently, the Nintendo DS was cracked by pirates, who found a way to copy read-only memory (ROM) images to flash cards and then transfer them to other DS' to play.

PSP piracy will undoubtedly be huge when it reaches its pinnacle. Per current status, there have been several successful exploits on the PSP, which allowed pirates to run homemade applications.

There is a lot friction between the console and PC ISO scenes, although some groups work well together. PC ISO groups are exclusive and elite, with massive amounts of resources, while console groups are smaller, with public channels and an open attitude toward new members.

The new generation of consoles will decide which piracy scene wins—console or PC. If piracy copy protection methods are implemented into new consoles, console piracy will cease. However, if the protection methods are defeated, the piracy paradigm will shift. Console piracy will see thousands of new members, as PC ISO groups dissolve and reform into new console release groups. Suppliers and crackers would retrain, honing their skills on a particular brand of console and specializing in console piracy.

Movies

"He keeps downloading these movies from the Internet," a woman said loudly to her friend. "The quality is horrible; you can hardly hear any sound." After hearing this one morning, I started thinking: Why do people enjoy watching movies of such poor quality? Obviously, this lady is being forced to watch a movie that was shot with a hand camera in a cinema, a release known as a "CAM" in the movie piracy scene.

Special effects and surround sound are key elements of a movie, and we demand them from modern day films. So, why bother with a low grade copy? As I thought about this further, the woman added, "What's more, I have to wait another three weeks until it comes out in cinemas. I don't know why he bothers."

Then it dawned on me. Movies are considered the modern day theater, the pastime of many who enjoy relaxing and being entertained for a few hours. However, this media is governed by demand and time limits. A movie is released on DVD weeks after it has been screened in the cinema, thereby maximizing possible revenue and allowing film makers to double up on release dates. However, many die-hard fans want the media now. They want to watch the movie first, and then brag to their friends that they know the secret ending.

Media hype and frenzy is fueling piracy. Many hardcore movie buffs do not want to wait for the release date, so they download recorded copies (often of poor quality) or unfinished workprints.

Collectors also become fueled by music piracy. Having the ability to collect thousands of DVD images is highly irresistible, and many of the video piracy scene members are collectors.

Pirated digital movies come in many forms of size and quality. Maximum compression rates can read an average-quality movie into 500MB, which easily fits on a CD, while many released DVD images of movies come complete with movie extras and untouched Moving Picture Experts Group (MPEG-2) quality.

Releases are usually categorized by their source and the quality it provides. A movie shot with a CAM without a tripod is very different than the same movie being captured from the retail DVD. Movies sites often only accept certain levels of quality. Most movies are released from several different sources, and some are re-released five or six times from higher quality media. The following sections discuss the quality standard levels.

CAM

The lowest of the low, CAM movies are shot using portable cameras that people sneak into cinemas. Often, the camera falls down mid-session or its view is blocked by someone standing up in front. The sound is usually lacking and the picture quality is often grainy.

PIRACY FACT...

Very few scene sites allow CAMs, because they are considered too low in quality to be useful. However, it was not always like this. Before DVDs became mainstream, all movies released in the scene were shot with portable cameras.

Workprints

Workprints are unfinished, pre-production materials that often lack scenes and additional sounds. They are of higher quality than CAM movies, and usually contain a *ticker* somewhere in the picture.

PIRACY FACT...

A ticker is a small clock that shows the current frame that is running. It is usually used for reference purposes by directors and animators.

Workprints are usually leaked from production houses. Most recently, a StarWars Eposide 3 workprint was released hours before the first official screening. The workprint was of relatively high quality because it originated from a DVD; however, it had two tickers at the top of every frame. (See Figure 8.1.)

Figure 8.1 Star Wars Episode 3 Workprint Release

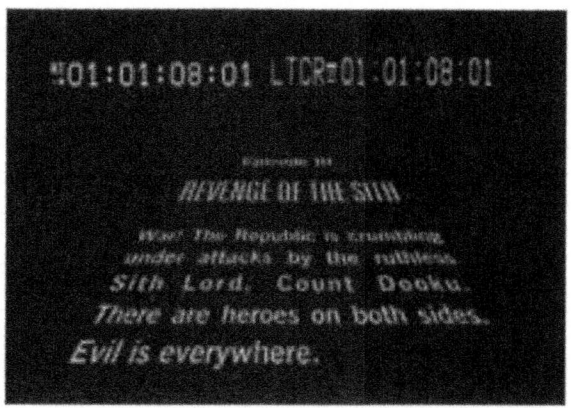

Workprints are rare, and only a highly anticipated film's workprints are released by pirates. The majority of watchers are only interested in watching the final product.

Telesync

A telesync is a film recorded on a professional camera (often a digital beta-cam). The cameras are placed on steady tripods and the films are recorded in an empty cinema from the main projection booth. The sound is often recorded straight from the mixing board, giving the telesync a high quality of sound. Some releases even include surround sound in Audio Compression 3 (AC3) format.

Telesyncs are the most common of early releases, often being the first release a movie site accepts. Telesync movies are easier to watch than their CAM counterparts, although the picture quality is usually slightly washed out and the contrast is often out of balance.

Telesyncs are commonly traded on movie sites. They are the lowest quality allowed, but are still popular with many file traders.

Telecine

A telecine is the result of capturing each frame of footage directly from the film reel. This is achieved by projecting each frame of the film onto a charge coupled device (CCD). CCDs capture and record the projected video, giving Telecines a substantial increase in picture quality over both telesync and CAM.

Although telecines are essentially an analog film capture, the film quality is close to that of a DVD. If a pirate has the technology and the time to produce a telecine, chances are it will pass as a DVD copy on the black market. Telecine audio comes directly from the mixing desk, which makes the telecine version of a film hard to distinguish from the real DVD.

However, creating a telecine can take days of work. CCDs operate slowly, and a standard movie will take six to seven hours to capture. After capturing the video, the sound must be included and synced with each frame of video.

Because they must be re-mastered, cleaned up, and packed, the full process of creating a telecine can take three to four days.

Screener

Prior to Academy Awards and other Hollywood award shows, judges are sent high-quality versions of the films they will be judging. Called *screeners*, these DVD or VHS copies are sent to reviewers, press agents, and select business partners under strict Non-disclosure Agreements (NDAs) from publishing companies. Although screeners have a good level of sound and video quality, they are usually watermarked.

Watermarking involves placing moving distribution notices at both the head and the foot of each film frame. Often, unique serial numbers or identification tags are shown on the screen, which are designed to track each copy of the screener. In such circumstances, video pirates crack the screener by placing blurred patches over visible serial numbers and identification tags. Although the movie is still watchable, the tags and blurred patches are still noticeable. Other common screener traits are brief durations of black and white video and temporary loss of sound.

PIRACY FACT...

A recent study found that during the 2004 Oscars, "Lord of the Rings, Return of the King" was the only film out of the 23 films reviewed that was **not** leaked to the Internet, because NewLine Cinemas did not distribute the movie in screener format to its reviewers.

DVD Retail

DVD Retail is the final, commercial product. Often released in several versions, the majority of movies are released from the DVD source.

Groups will commonly release a Digital Video Compression Format based on DivX (XVID) and Super Video Compact Disc (SVCD) of the movie. Some groups will even release the complete Digital Versatile Disk Recordable (DVDR) image of the movie, fully intact and with DVD extras.

PIRACY FACT...

XVID and SVCD are different encoding methods. XVID is high compression and can reduce the size of a movie to fit on a single CD. Size comes at a cost though, and the quality of the video and sound is often noticeably reduced.

SVCD is a straight MPEG-2 copy of lower quality than the original DVD. SVCD files are twice the size of an XVID and often come with surround sound in AC3 format. Using an uncompressed format such as SVCDs has an added performance benefit and does not require a powerful central processing unit (CPU) to decompress and play the video.

Next to ISO and console piracy, the video piracy scene is becoming a large and competitive environment. New groups are formed daily that rip, compress, and release a variety of media.

PIRACY FACT...

The video piracy scene is becoming so popular, that a short download-able Internet TV series was produced. Dubbed "The Scene," each episode follows a fictitious video piracy group called CPX. The group has structure, with various members acting as release coordinators, suppliers, and rippers. Watching the TV series is hardly action viewing, since essentially everyone is just sitting on Internet Relay Chat (IRC) talking to each other about a new release, but it does give you an insight into the video piracy world.

The scene can be downloaded at http://www.welcometothescene.com

Although this book focuses on software piracy, it is clear that a very similar group structure is also used in video piracy scene.

ISO piracy groups and video piracy groups often share sites, with both groups uploading new releases and their members given access to a more varied amount of data.

KQS...

"You can get just about anything from KQS, I can't believe they have the complete James Bond collection of DVDs," Jamax said to me. An idler in a group cracking channel, I was sitting in on IRC.

"You like James Bond?" I replied.

"Yeah man, it's the best."

"What site is KQS? Who do I talk to about getting an account?" I curiously asked.

"Oh, XXXXX would be your best bet. Man, they got so many movies there, like 3,500 DVD images online. It's bigger than my video store!" he added.

KQS was a group site that I was not privileged enough to access. An internal or group archive site of 3,500 DVD's is impressive, and would require almost 13 terabytes (tb) of storage space.

Although the crackers around me have no involvement in video piracy and have never copied a DVD in their life, their skills in the ISO scene give them access to the video piracy scene.

KQS is probably on a very large, underused bandwidth connection, likely at a university or large corporation. The site owner has the resources to cater to the two groups by inviting both the video and

Continued

software piracy groups to affiliate with the site . The two groups share an equal level of respect for each other and both benefit from each others presence on KQS.

TV

Although TV piracy is not as epic as Hollywood movie piracy, it is growing in popularity and becoming a full-fledged piracy scene. Originally, TV shows were banned from many sites that carried movies, because they were considered junk. "Why bother, it's on TV anyway." No one saw the need for pirated TV.

As the TV piracy scene became more sophisticated, the quality of TV shows increased and they began to surface on the Internet before they aired on TV. The rest of the piracy scene began to take notice.

With the recent price drop in large volume hard drives and the growth in Personal Video Recorder (PVR) software, pirates could run their own personal TV stations, showing only the content they wanted to see. TV piracy is now common on most movie and ISO sites, and is an accepted part of the video and ISO scene.

Groups are becoming very efficient at releasing high quality, digital TV versions of sitcoms, cartoons, and other popular late night shows. Suppliers of pirated TV range from professionals to home users.

Professional satellite junkies with large satellites capable of picking up many broadcasted video streams, are responsible for much of the TV piracy. These video hackers eavesdrop on private video broadcasting frequencies used by TV stations. With many TV stations now running from a completely digital environment, technology requirements often demand that the TV station be sent the content prior to broadcast. Usually one or two days before an episode is screened on TV, video distribution companies will broadcast the content. Although this broadcast is on a private, unknown frequency, it is often unencrypted. Anyone that can tune into the satellite frequency can watch the TV episodes in advance.

PIRACY FACT

Many professional TV pirates live close to Las Vegas and Utah, so that they can broadcast video streams from the desert where there are no buildings or mountains to obstruct the signal.

By recording content sent to a TV station, professional pirates are able to release full quality TV programs without any commercials or faults, days before it is screened on air. Although the number of professional TV pirates is relatively low (no more than ten), they account for the majority of releases in the TV scene. All other releases come from home users who record the content they watch on Pay per View (PPV), standard cable, or other digital TV sources.

Releases are compressed in either XVID or DIVX format and released on the Internet to scene sites, bit torrents, and file-sharing networks. An average 30-minute episode of Fox's "The Simpsons" would take only 10 minutes to download on a cable modem because it is less than 180MB in size.

With download times so short, many pirates choose to run their own TIVO-like services, downloading the day's TV viewing each morning.

Although ripping TV can require a specified skill set, TV piracy groups are often very small. Many of these TV groups spread their releases directly to file-sharing networks first, and then upload them to scene sites.

E-books and Bookware

E-books have grown in popularity. The latest piracy fad is releasing digital copies of printed material (known as *bookware*) such as fiction, non-fiction, technical manuals, and comics. Anything with a price tag is copied, turned into a digital format such as Portable Document Format (PDF) or CHM, and released on the Internet. (See Figure 8.2.)

Figure 8.2 A Short List of Bookware Releases

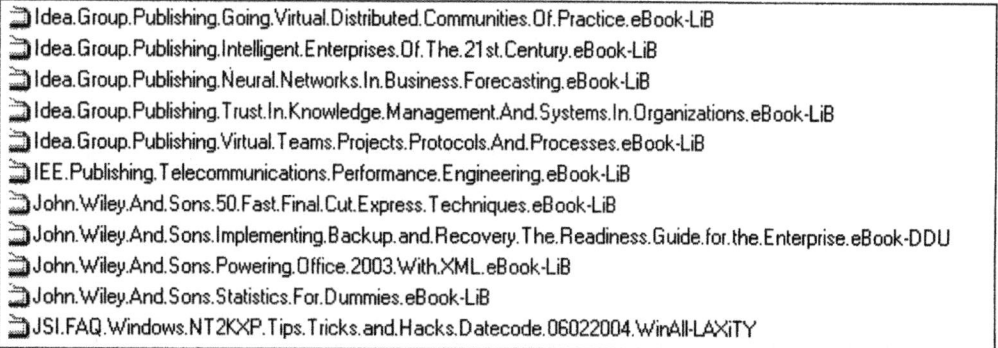

```
Idea.Group.Publishing.Going.Virtual.Distributed.Communities.Of.Practice.eBook-LiB
Idea.Group.Publishing.Intelligent.Enterprises.Of.The.21st.Century.eBook-LiB
Idea.Group.Publishing.Neural.Networks.In.Business.Forecasting.eBook-LiB
Idea.Group.Publishing.Trust.In.Knowledge.Management.And.Systems.In.Organizations.eBook-LiB
Idea.Group.Publishing.Virtual.Teams.Projects.Protocols.And.Processes.eBook-LiB
IEE.Publishing.Telecommunications.Performance.Engineering.eBook-LiB
John.Wiley.And.Sons.50.Fast.Final.Cut.Express.Techniques.eBook-LiB
John.Wiley.And.Sons.Implementing.Backup.and.Recovery.The.Readiness.Guide.for.the.Enterprise.eBook-DDU
John.Wiley.And.Sons.Powering.Office.2003.With.XML.eBook-LiB
John.Wiley.And.Sons.Statistics.For.Dummies.eBook-LiB
JSI.FAQ.Windows.NT2KXP.Tips.Tricks.and.Hacks.Datecode.06022004.WinAll-LAXiTY
```

With the growth of portable e-book readers and the growing popularity of digital media, e-books are fast becoming the preferred method of reading media. Also, many e-library Web sites now exist (e.g., *safari.oreilly.com*), where subscribers can quickly pay for access to any printed book or just a chapter of a book.

Ultimately, e-books are the way of the future. They offer readers a streamlined method for getting information quickly. However, e-books currently lack any solid form of Digital Rights Management (DRM), which makes them easy targets for pirates. The growth in the piracy of e-books has become epic. In 2002, there were just over 150 e-books released into the piracy scene, a relatively low number considering the amount of books printed. A majority of scene sites refused to accept the bookware, and e-books were greatly frowned upon by most in the scene.

E-book release statistics have grown significantly since 2002; in 2004 there were over 2,000 digital copies of books, magazines, and printed media released. In the first six months of 2005, there were 1400 e-book releases, thus showing the general acceptance and market demand for the material within the scene.

E-book groups are now common and accepted within the mainstream piracy scene. Many consider the releases to be "Smart Aids," which help pirates learn new skills and advance their own Information Technology (IT) careers.

The book you are reading now will probably be pirated and released in a digital form within a few weeks of its official publishing date. As an author, it is something you grow to accept. Piracy is everywhere, and books are possibly the hardest media to protect from piracy.

So, how do e-book pirates obtain copies of books within days of their official published date? Scanning each page of a book is highly time-consuming, and purchasing each book is expensive. The piracy methods used are simple and, more often than not, printed books are never involved in the process.

Pirates focus on e-library sites such as *safari.orielly.com* and *books24x7.com*, which offer digital portfolios of reading material. Accounts to these sites are either fraudulently purchased or unlimited education accounts are compromised and used by the groups. Next, pirates develop their own applications that digitally read the books online by scanning each page from the e-library, collecting the words and pictures displayed. This content is then rewritten into another document, along with any pictures or formatting, thus creating a digital replica. Although still time consuming, this method does not require any physical media; pirates simply use a computer to replicate the already digitally created pages.

This brings up an interesting question. If ripping software is as simple as reading, remembering, and replicating content that is already published online, what can publishers do to stop it? Sadly, little can be done. Even though pirates operate actively and publicly, to date there have been no arrests or prosecutions for the stealing printed media; therefore, there is little incentive to stop releasing the e-books.

Online e-book converting applications are common, and e-books are now released within days of their official publishing date. Fringe printed media is also growing in popularity, as seen in the following Info File (NFO) for the group Enigma of Esoteric Nothingness (EEN), an e-book group that specializes in esoteric literature. (See Figure 8.3.)

Figure 8.3 Group Recruitment for Suppliers of Fringe Printed Media

```
EEn is looking for any and all suppliers of
occult, conspiracy, weaponry, and any other
esoteric literature (books, magazines, pamphlets,
initation ritual manuals, and sacred texts).

Books from action library publishers such as Loompanics
and Paladin are always welcome!

Experienced IT book suppliers (must have own accounts
and be experienced at ripping & compiling technical
books)

If you have a scanner and are willing to help
preserve and spread lost knowledge, then
contact us. beefjerkey[-=at=-]hushmail.com
```

In many instances of e-book piracy, a home scanner and a few hours of patience is still required. Many groups have taken to releasing scanned copies of comic books such as "Xmen" and "Spiderman." Although the magazines only cost a few dollars, the digital versions are easier to collect and will not fade or crumple.

Scanners are also used in pirating game guide books, which are popular with enthusiastic gamers who like to read up on secret tricks and complicated plot walkthroughs.

E-book piracy is becoming the new craze for online collectors. Because the books are small (most are under 100MB), collectors can easily store large amounts of e-books with a minimal amount of bandwidth and storage space.

In the beginning, most mainstream scene sites rejected bookware because they considered them books with no "fun factor." However, the majority of sites now accept all new book releases.

What will this do to the print industry? When mass media catches onto the idea and books are actively traded online, the print industry will suffer and books will become more expensive. Given the capabilities of future technology and the ease of reading an e-book, printed media may soon become a thing of the past. Piracy has a powerful effect on technology.

Music

Music is the most widely pirated media in the world today. From singles to albums to recording demos, music of all genres is ripped and released into the music piracy scene. Music piracy is unlike any other type of piracy and receives a lot of media attention. It is smaller and easier to transfer than other digital media, unlike ISO piracy where each release must be supplied, cracked, and packaged. Music piracy is practically autonomous, and single individuals can pirate hundreds of new tracks daily. Many applications have already been developed to aid in ripping CDs, thereby leaving little work for the pirates. Additionally, massive amounts of music are released daily, so there is always a new CD to be ripped. Unlike the ISO game scene that may have only ten releases a month, more than 500 albums are released each week

Originally, the music piracy scene had their own MP3 sites that were exclusive to music groups only. MP3 ripping groups would upload their releases to the site, identical to the way other piracy scenes operate. However, everything changed when Napster was released. Napster was the beginning of something much larger. As more people joined the "Napster piracy scene," many began to see the MP3 piracy scene as obsolete. Napster obtained albums before MP3 release groups did, had more users contributing, was easier to use, and you could find any type of music you needed.

More recently, public file-sharing networks and the music piracy scene have become increasingly interwoven. Release groups still release albums to sites that carry MP3s, but pirates now supply the music from file-sharing networks.

Many music piracy release groups are known for pirating music themselves. As strange as that seems, pirates effectively take tracks from public-sharing networks, rename them so they look authentic, and then claim that they ripped the latest album themselves.

Although many legitimate release groups exist in the music scene, file-sharing networks have had a huge impact. In many ways, the public arena is better equipped for music piracy; everyone enjoys music and most people like sharing it. However, exclusive music piracy sites are more reliable, with sorted and dated directories and no waiting times or slow connections. The difference is arguable, but the public music-sharing area is as large as the private one.

Piracy Fact...

Several MP3 groups have been known to team up with other ISO groups. One such group was Fairlight, an infamous ISO piracy group. Fairlight worked with large MP3 release groups, giving them private access to internal Fairlight resources. In return, the MP3 groups added Fairlight members to their sites, giving them access to hundreds of gigabytes (GBs) of pirated music.

Suppliers to the music piracy scene work in every corner of the music industry. The majority of CDs are given to press agents, distributors, and promoters. Unlike the video industry, music is sent to radio stations, promoters, and the press weeks before its official release. Because more people are gaining access to the media, a higher percentage of it is pirated.

Piracy Fact...

At first, major record labels attempted to stop music piracy by filing lawsuits against file-trading networks such as Napster. Now, they have turned their attention to who they believe is leaking albums to the Internet prior to their official release. Universal Music Group, Universal Records, and Warner Music Group's Reprise Records have begun stamping press CDs with a digital watermark. Similar to how DVD screeners are marked for distribution, music will now carry a digital watermark containing the recipient's name embedded within the music.

Journalists and press agents are suspected to be the largest source of the leaked media. However, the MP3 scene is not particularly worried about the new watermarking technology. I talked to one music pirate who had this to say on the matter:

> *Watermark's... hahahahahahahahaha... morons... I don't need to crack anything - I can hear it - I can re-record it - and I can release it without watermark.. You cant hide that much information in sound, and if you try to use high frequencies that people cant hear, ill just filter them out.*
> *This is not going to stop anything.*

Many record labels now use some form of DRM on all of their CDs. Although any form of protection will protect music from casual copiers, the majority of pirates have little problem circumventing them.

Music is not protected as strongly as games or applications, and music groups do not require dedicated crackers to focus on the protection routines. Oftentimes, bypassing a CD protection scheme is as simple as forcing a player to write the song back to disk in an unprotected form. It can be even easier when the music pirate has an extensive audio component system that allows him to play and record the CD simultaneously.

Music piracy requires less time commitment than other types of piracy, and although pirating music can be risky, there have been only a few pirates arrested for releasing music into the piracy scene.

Adult Entertainment

Pornography is the largest and most successful type of media sold on the Internet. Several pornographic movies are created daily, and adult production companies flood the market with as many pornographic films as possible.

Needless to say, pirates are also interested in pornography. The entire adult movie scene exists in one piracy scene and is dedicated to releasing pornography and celebrity sex tapes. There are no more than 10 release groups in the pornography scene, and they keep very busy. On average, six new DVD releases of adult films are released daily. Think about it. On every day of every year, six new adult films are released, and it is still growing. That means that 2,190 pornographic films are produced every year, and then ripped and released by pirates.

In 2004, there were 554 movies released to Hollywood and over 1000 pirated movies released to the movie piracy scene. The movie piracy scene also releases any movies that were not released to Hollywood (e.g., film festival films and small budget films), which accounts for the difference in release numbers.

PIRACY FACT...

"Every time we put a finger in the dam, we spring another leak," says Jay Gradina, president of adult superstar Jenna Jameson's production company "Club Jenna."

Piracy consumes as much as 20 to 30 percent of a large pornographic company's revenue. These figures are based on the amount of pirated CDs that have been confiscated from the street. If you walk into a store and see 100 movies on the shelf, you can be sure that at least 20 of them were pirated.

Adult filmmakers are the hardest hit by piracy, because twice as many movies are pirated and released on the Internet than in Hollywood.

While searching the Internet, I managed to catch up with Dirty Old Man (known as DOM) who is a video ripper from the large adult movie piracy group "PR0NSTARS."

INTERVIEW WITH A DIRTY OLD MAN...

Me: "Who are you, and what are your affiliations in the scene."
DOM: "I am Dirty Old Man and I am only affiliated with PR0NSTARS, although I use to be in a TV ripping group called LOL."
Me: "Why do you pirate adult videos?"
DOM: "It's simpler than you think. Believe it or not, I am not a pornography freak, I don't really like pornography."
Me: "Explain?"
DOM: "Well, I work as an editor at a film company; I piece together the films and cut out any parts that we don't want to show. A few years ago, we noticed that the majority of our clients were pornography directors and we decided to go exclusive. We only deal in

Continued

pornography now. It's a niche industry and there is much more business in it than any other video industry.
I package and release the films that I edit through PR0NSTARS. I know
some of the guys in the group; there's only seven or so of them in it. I
give them movies, they give me accounts on sites."
Me: "How many movies per week do you work on?"
DOM: "On average, one every two days. It takes approximately one day
to edit 50 minutes worth of sex, because there's a fair bit of tidying
and overlaying you have to do."
Me: "How many of those are released?"
DOM: "Every one; ripped, packed and uploaded."
Me: "Don't you worry about getting caught? You're leaking three
movies a week to a piracy syndication, which will end up on the black
market eventually."
DOM: "I don't see any police trying to catch us. No one really cares
because it's the pornography world. These days, if a director called the
police demanding an investigation, there would be a demonstration
regarding police man-hours being wasted on pornography."
Me: "So, you feel confident that you won't ever get caught?
DOM: "Yes. To date, no one has been sentenced for ripping adult
media. This isn't the ISO scene. Companies like Microsoft would sue
and invest the money. Pornography directors would hire more girls and
make more films."
Me: "Thanks for your time."

Adult video piracy is not considered criminal; therefore, those who
pirate pornography do not have to fear being caught. No one will even
look for the supplier of "Teen Scream Lesbians #36." By virtue of its
content, the black market has turned adult videos into something far sin-
ister. Although pirated Hollywood movie releases eventually end up on
the black market, street merchants are usually low-key and low-scale.
Pirating a Hollywood blockbuster costs large film production companies
a lot of money; if you get too big selling pirated movies, you will be
arrested.

However, no one seems to care about the theft of pornography. This
has lead to many organized crime syndicates selling pirated adult films on
the street. Copy protection methods are non-existent and the film pro-

ducers can do nothing to stop them. A Hollywood blockbuster can cost as little as $1.00 on the black market for a DVD version. An adult film on the black market will cost $5.00. A DVD at an adult sex store costs as much as $30.00, and you will not be able to tell if it is a legitimate copy or a fake.

 **PIRACY FACT...**

"One Night in Paris," the infamous Paris Hilton sex tape, was recognized at the Adult Video News (AVN) Awards in Las Vegas earlier this year, as the year's bestselling DVD, with 500,000 units sold.

"Red Light District" owner, David Joseph, who published the DVD, estimates that there are more than half a million pirated copies of this product in circulation.

Others at the conference said it was not uncommon to open a box of returns from a retailer only to discover that half of the copies are pirated knock offs.

Although the adult scene is huge, it mostly goes unnoticed in the general piracy scene. Some movie sites allow pornographic movies, giving pirates in the ISO/MP3/TV or MOVIE scene access to adult video content. Others ban the content, because each movie can take several GBs worth of space.

Everything Else

If it has a price tag, someone will pirate it, and if it has a copyright, someone will distribute it. This is the nature of piracy. All you have to do is look at the piles of specialized software being released daily; applications that only a handful of people know how to use.

Often, the goal is not to release an amazing product, but to release something with a large price tag. Pirates want to be the first to release large scientific applications, programs that only a small percentage of people know how to use. Other releases are more bizarre and have a smaller following and their own private scene.

The Personal Digital Assistant (PDA) scene is dedicated to cracking and releasing any application or game that runs on a portable device such as an iPAQ or Java-capable phone.

In 2001, when the growth of e-books was just beginning, another form of printed piracy emerged—schematics. Although the information was usually hand drawn, releases showed detail descriptions of how to make cell phone connector cables interface directly to the phone. Such information was considered valuable in the hacker arena, and many sites allowed it.

Warez sites that accepted e-books also allowed cell phone schematic releases. Downloader's could get their favorite games, applications, e-books, and cell phone schematics from one handy location. Although the releases were accepted on some sites, cell phone schematics did not attract a lot of attention and the piracy fad soon died out.

Stock media is still released, with some ISO groups releasing countless DVD packages containing royalty-free images of various objects and scenes.

Other strange releases include "learningware," which contain various procedures such as how to use medical analysis software to analyze human stool, how to use utilities to map menstrual cycles, and even an application for designing power plants and managing high-voltage electricity distribution.

The pirate attitude can be applied to anything.

Blurring Scenes

Although each corner of the scene is unique and distinct, the different scenes blur in many places. Members from one group are also members of another group from a different scene. Group sites are affiliated with MP3s, consoles, games, and e-books.

This shared group gives each scene a brief view into the world of another scene, where console pirates can watch feuds between MP3 groups, and e-book groups can download the latest XBOX modchip Basic Input Output System (BIOS), direct from the programmers who wrote it.

Meeting places are often on IRC, where members from different scenes can share ideas on the things they have in common. On some private channels, you will find game console crackers and PC crackers chatting about life, the universe, and cracking. Although each genre of pirate is unique, all pirates share the same desire, the same bloodlust for free media. No matter how obscure or how large the target is, it will eventually be pirated, copied, and distributed.

Each year, a new type of piracy emerges; a new form of copy write-protected information. Anything that attracts the attention of other pirates stays in the scene, and eventually forms its own scene and subculture.

With change and evolution being the only consistent factor in piracy, it is little wonder that piracy has lasted so long. With the pirate dream still very much alive and no sign of diminishing, piracy will continue to exist and any new technology developed will eventually be broken down, compressed, and distributed.

Chapter 9

Piracy and the Law

Piracy is Illegal?

"I am a personal friend of Tyson from Newfoundland, Canada I just called his house about 20 minutes ago and his mom told me that he was taken away by the police. They took five or six of his PCs. That's all I know."

"Halfmoon2 has been busted. Thirty-two boxes were confiscated with 200+ DVDs, CDs. HM2 was affiliated with Centropy!"

"FBI agents came to Avec's house at 9:30 A.M. CMT with a federal search warrant. They took 271 CDs and watched her computer for several hours, monitoring site IRC channels she was in!"

These are words of terror to a pirate. This is when the law finally catches up with you. Until now, for many it was just a game, a race, a competition. People who pirate software do not see it as malicious or harmful, it is just a hobby.

When companies get tired of trying to protect their software, and when new copy protection methods are effortlessly defeated, many turn to the Federal Bureau of Investigation (FBI) for help.

"Organized crime" is the term used to link crackers, suppliers, and couriers to the illicit trade of black market media in Asia and abroad. A small minority of the scene is linked with known organized crime syndicates. For many in the scene, piracy is just a hobby that they do not profit from. For these pirates, when the FBI breaks down their door, reality very quickly comes crashing down. Yes, piracy is illegal, and your hobby will see you in jail for the next five years.

Piracy Fact...

Software piracy is considered organized crime and is classified as a federal offense. Federal law offenders, as defined by the Sentencing Reform Act of 1984, have no chance of parole. Additionally, good behavior has little impact on their sentence.

The Sentencing Reform Act of 1984 abolished parole eligibility for federal offenders—except military offenders—who committed offenses on or after November 1, 1987.

The FBI and police crime units are getting better at penetrating the scene, even getting into the most exclusive scene groups. Law officials are not stupid; they know warez (exaggerated plural derivative of software) groups exist and how they function, they know about structure within the group, and they know how to get into a group.

The most common tactic used by law enforcement agencies to bring down warez groups, is joining a group as a member. Groups are not easy to join. You need connections, resources, and the ability to offer something useful, something that is in demand.

Sites are the FBI's favorite method of infiltrating a group. Because of the impressive amount of hardware and bandwidth being offered to scene groups, other groups will affiliate with the site and its popularity will grow within the scene.

Over time, FBI agents watch hosts that login to the site such as different courier groups, users, and release groups. Sites can also affiliate with multiple warez groups, giving FBI agents connections to other groups of pirates.

Because the hardware of the site is owned and operated by the FBI, all evidence from it is credible in court. Server logs upload statistics and releases that can all be used in court. Because of this undeniable evidence, every pirate arrested so far has been successfully prosecuted, with a minimum sentence of five years and a maximum sentence of ten years.

Piracy Fact...

The average sentence in America for a convicted rapist is nine years, while the average time served is only five years. In many circumstances, a pirate receives a longer jail sentence than a convicted rapist. Law agencies are trying to make a point to the Internet community: **do not be a pirate**.

When a raid happens in the scene, everyone runs, everyone swears that this is it, they are going to retire. Everyone backs into their corner and is thankful they are not in jail. Raids scare the scene senseless and new levels of paranoia are reached with every consecutive arrest.

Figure 9.1 Closing Doors after Operation Site Down (PHXiSO)

```
This is by far the hardest nfo to write to date 1999-2005.
PHXiSO has been here like our best friend, and addiction for
far to many of these FBI bullshit shakedowns..For fucks sake as
 if George Lucas, or Autodesk needs more money? Get fucked you
know yer doing this so they pad your pockets you fucken cunts!
ANYWAY we have seen to many good groups come and go. And for us
its time to pull the plug. To the haters Fuck you. To the people
who have helped us We have much love and respect for you.

A simple goodbye, and be safe from your friends at PHXiSO..
```

As the entire piracy scene scuttles away into the dark corners of the Internet, many pirates fear things will never be the same, that it is over, that the scene is finished. Like a bear in hibernation, the scene will sleep after a large raid. Groups fade away, members retreat to other pastimes, and those who were arrested are slowly prosecuted and locked away.

Once the media hype dies down, and members begin to forget their fallen comrades, the scene comes back to life. Retired crackers and suppliers cannot stay away. Many rejoin groups and begin a new season of piracy. A year after a large raid, the scene is completely healed. Everyone has forgotten what happened, the levels of paranoia decrease, and pirates feel confident that they will not be caught, that they are somehow bulletproof. That is, until the cycle starts again.

The following sections look at the different key operations the FBI has undertaken against the warez scene and its members.

Pirates with Attitudes

Pirates with Attitudes (PWAs) were one of the most infamous warez groups of the 1990s. PWA dominated the scene. The group released every major application and had countless suppliers and crackers at their disposal. Respect and admiration for the group was huge, and they had a large cult following of wannabe pirates. The resources that PWA had at its disposal were beyond impressive; the group owned its own site hardware and infrastructure worth many tens of thousands of dollars.

Until now, FBI agents had stayed clear of the Internet and piracy. Little attention was paid to pirates, and law enforcement usually only moved in when money was changing hands. Even though the PWA was not selling anything and the group never made any profit, the PWA was a turning point for the FBI, and the first time the No Electronic Theft (NET) Act was used in court.

PIRACY FACT...

The NET Act amends the definition of "commercial advantage or private financial gain" to include the exchange of copies of copyrighted works even if no money changes hands, and specifies penalties of up to five years in prison and $250,000 in fines. It also creates a threshold for criminal liability, even if the infringer neither obtained nor expected to obtain anything of value for the infringement. Additionally, the Act allows individuals to be held liable for statutory damages of up to $150,000 per work infringed or actual damages or lost profits (whichever is greater).

Officially, the PWA arrests were groundbreaking. However, the operation was never given a title such as "Operation Buccaneer" or "Operation Site Down."

PWA was a different breed of warez group. They had strong social ties; its members were more than friends, they were family and would do anything for each other.

The group had grown impressively over time and many top crackers and suppliers in the scene wanted to join PWA. Why? Because it was a known fact that PWA "looked after" their members.

Within PWA were five Intel employees who currently work in the hardware division of Intel. These members were hardware suppliers for PWA. Between the five of them they could sneak a lot of components and chips out of Intel and send them to PWA leaders for distribution.

Each month, PWA gave the group's top cracker and top supplier a brand new desktop computer or laptop, or a bag filled with Random Access Memory (RAM) chips. This reward scheme encouraged group members to compete among themselves, and made the group infamous.

PWA was unstoppable; wave after wave of releases flowed into the scene, all carrying the "Tude" trademark of Pirates with Attitudes.

Eventually, this was the group's downfall.

> "CHICAGO – Seventeen defendants from across the United States and Europe were indicted by a federal grand jury today for allegedly conspiring to infringe the copyright of more than 5,000 computer software programs that were available through a hidden Internet site that was located at a university in Quebec, Canada, the Justice Department announced. Twelve of the defendants, including an Aurora, Ill., man, allegedly were members or leaders of an international organization of software pirates known as "Pirates with Attitudes," an underground group that disseminates stolen copies of software, including programs that are not yet commercially available."

The Canadian site mentioned above was called "Sentinel," which was a private PWA member site that was considered to be the largest and oldest site in the scene. Sentinel first came online in 1995, when many scene groups were still using bulletin boards to trade files. PWA supplied the site with hardware, disks, RAM, and CPU upgrades. The infrastructure was impressive and completely owned and controlled by the PWA.

PIRACY FACT...

It may have been supplied by PWA, but it was paid for by Intel. The five Intel employees shipped the hardware to Canada through Intel's own internal shipping system. Intel funds also paid the customs' fees and for the hardware to be shipped directly to Sentinel.

Sentinel was discovered by the FBI in late 1999, who then called the FBI. The FBI agents were lucky; they had stumbled into the largest and most infamous piracy group of the era, and they did not want to let it slip.

The two individuals who previously ran Sentential were given an ultimatum: work with the FBI and help catch other PWA members, or be held responsible for Sentinel and all of its files.

Within a year of the two site administrators working with the FBI, agents had enough information to issue 17 search warrants within America and Europe. PWA members were tracked down by the packages of hardware they received. This also provided evidence for obtaining search warrants for each member.

In January 2000, PWA crumbled. Other scene groups were horrified: for the first time in history, an entire group was brought down. Key PWA members were now facing up to five years in jail.

All 15 members pled guilty to copyright conspiracy or copyright infringement, and all were sentenced to jail time, fines, or both. The highest ranking member of PWA, Marlenus, aka Robin Rothberg, received the harshest sentence of 18 months, while other members were sentenced to one year or less. Although 17 warrants were issued, only 15 were sentenced. The remaining two members of PWA are still fugitives and listed on the United States Department of Justice (USDOJ) Web site.

The alleged members of PWA who are fugitives are:

Mark Veerboken, aka "Shiffie," of Belgium

Kaj Bjorlin, aka "Darklord," of Sweden

☠ PIRACY FACT…

If you were a wanted fugitive, would you go back to a life of piracy or play it clean?

Shiffie, aka Mark Veerboken could not stay away from the high life. In 2003, Shiffie formed a new warez group that focused on releasing plug-ins for graphical applications such as Lightwave and 3DSMAX.

The group was called S.C.O.T.C.H, and as you can see from the NFO snippet below, Shiffie still holds some "tude" from his PAW days.

> ³ S.C.O.T.C.H wishes to greet following groups: FCN, DWP, FALLEN, DOD, RBS ³
>
> ³ SSG, FSN, BHF, UCF, and THCISO, and wishes to honour the warriors of the ³
>
> ³ T.U.D.E who have lost the fight against piracy. You will live forever in ³
>
> ³ our memories!!!!   ³

My sources in the scene say Shiffie was not caught by the FBI, because his name is not Mark Veerboken. FBI agents were looking for the wrong man.

Operation Buccaneer

Operation Buccaneer was the FBI's second major scene raid, which focused almost entirely on two groups: Drink or Die (DOD [an application release group]), and Razor1911 (a PC game release group).

Operation Buccaneer was also the FBI's most successful raid to date. Every active member of DOD was caught and arrested, with a total of 15 pirates sentenced to between 5 and 15 years in federal prison. Several key members from Razor1911 were also caught, with the former leader of the group receiving a 50-month jail term.

Operation Buccaneer was such a success primarily due to two former DOD members who were willing to give information about other members' to lessen their own jail sentence. Kent Kartadinata and James Cudney both gave information via video link at the various court trials, stating who the group members were and what their role within DOD was.

The success of Operation Buccaneer gave FBI agents their first real glimpse into the infrastructure of an established and sophisticated warez group. This information helped them greatly, and bringing down the DOD was a key turning point for legal authorities.

DOD had impressive resources and many dedicated members and was considered one of the oldest groups in the PC scene. Many members of DOD worked at large software development companies such as Symantec or Checkpoint. Because of these internal suppliers, DOD was infamous for releasing Symantec applications, often only hours after the product was announced final, as was the case of PC Anywhere v10.5.

 PIRACY FACT…

The DOD was also infamous for their release of Windows 95, which the group managed to release days before the official release date.

They went on to develop and release their own utility called DVD Speed Ripper, the first DVD ripping application to decrypt the Decryption of Contents Scrambling System (DeCSS).

Although "DVD Jon," aka Jon Johansen from the group Masters of Reverse Engineering (MoRE) took the media credit for the crack, it was actually first developed by DOD and an unaffiliated German programmer.

Bandido

Bandido, aka Hew Raymond Griffiths was the leader of DOD, a disabled Australian citizen who was unable to work and lived on a disability benefit with his father in New South Wales. Neighbors described Hew as a quiet man who kept to himself and who was not a troublemaker.

Bandido ran DOD for many years. He was also a senior in Razor 1911 and RiSC; by all means a very established and respected member of the scene community. Bandido played a large part in the majority of all software piracy that occurred in the early 1990s. He ran sites, supplied releases, and ensured that his groups stayed on top.

When Australian authorities raided Hew's New South Wales home, FBI agents in the U.S. were worried because Australian law is relaxed when compared to U.S. law. Hew would face a significantly lesser jail term if he was tried on his home soil. He may even escape any jail time.

FBI agents immediately began an extradition case, forcing Hew to be tried as an American citizen on American soil. Hew argued the extradition, stating that he was an Australian citizen and had never been to America, why should I be tried as an American? Under U.S. law, Hew would face a maximum sentence of ten years in federal prison and $500,000 (USD) fine as compensation for the damage he caused. A grand jury eventually agreed that the extradition was required, and Hew is due to be sentenced as an U.S. citizen later this year.

Bandido is an interesting case, because Hew is very adamant he did nothing wrong by being in DOD. In an interview that Bandido gave to an electronic scene magazine in 1999, he commented, "I cannot be busted, I have no warez here. And it is not a crime to be in a group."

When Bandido was arrested, this interview was picked up by many media organizations. In many ways, this published interview will help prosecute Bandido when has his day in court.

The full body of the interview can be found below, where Bandido talks about his life in the scene and what he does in DOD/Razor. He even gives away such information as his country of citizenship and his age.

AN INTERVIEW WITH BANDIDO

[biXen]: Hello BanDiDo. Let's start with your age, full nickname, nationality, and which groups you have been in.

[BanDiDo]: Ok, to start with I was born in 1962....I am English (I live in Australia). I started my *Career* back in the BBS days way back. Then I founded ViCE couriers in 1995 I think it was, then I joined DRiNK OR DiE and Razor 1911. I was also in RCN at one point before it died. I am currently RiSC council and DOD council.

[biXen]: Can you tell us a bit about your work in the groups, for example in RiSC and DOD as council. What is it that you do for them?

[BanDiDo]: Well, in terms of RiSC, I help with site add since I am a site op on about 20 sites. And I do some PR and logistical work. In terms of DOD, I basically am part of the few people who actually run DOD in terms of operations. I concentrate on site duties mostly, although I recruit and do release work as needed. Basically, I do it all as needed.

[biXen]: When did you first notice that there was something called the scene, and how did you notice it?

[BanDiDo]: Wow, that is a question that makes me think. Well, I started off during the BBS era, I found my way onto the local pirate boards, and eventually onto mainstream systems. I suppose all those mysterious NFOs made us all wonder what more there was (some of us stuck around to find out:). I miss analogue days, the scene is a sad place to be now in some ways. It is changing and not for the better.

[biXen]: Do you have any skills, like cracking or coding?

Continued

[BanDiDo]: No, personally I don't code, I can barely write a batch file that doesn't hate me:) I do however have a rather nice team capable of coding and cracking anything.

[biXen]: So, how did you actually get into the scene without having any special skills?

[BanDiDo]: Ah skills... well I have always led groups, so I suppose I have a measure of organizational ability. I was always a trader, too. I suppose I have proved over time to many in the scene that I have some ethics and tend to work rather hard. DOD doesn't tend to have incapable people running areas of responsibility. If you mean skills in terms of coding and such, no, as I mentioned, I have others that are capable of all those things. I myself sadly never had the patience to learn to code. I wish I did though. Coding is the real "essence" of the PC world, and I admire anyone who has the patience to develop skills.

[biXen]: Why did you start the group ViCE and how did it go?

[BanDiDo]: ViCE was the first group I was ever in. I suppose it arose out of a desire of one or two people to enter the larger scene. ViCE was great for years, until the scene started to change. That is a long story. The current bunch of morons using the name "ViCE" have no sanction to do so, and most of the scene knows it. It was a great group for the years it existed. It's death almost had to happen because the courier scene is in danger of becoming extinct. With the recent busts and more on the cards, more sites will abandon couriers. The new group doesn't verify their people; any fool can join a group and get on some site. Very dangerous.

[biXen]: What policy does DOD have about couriers? Do you use your own group or external courier groups?

[BanDiDo]: DOD uses internal couriers only. We have several good ones from RiSC and DEV, etc. DOD has a strict policy: we release only to DOD HQs. We never send DOD releases to other sites, no matter how "good" the release is. And we send to **all** DOD sites. Even the slowest and smallest and most obscure gets DOD pre. We have a great relationship with our site ops, and most DOD sites have been with us a long time.

[biXen]: How about member application. What do you demand from people who want to join DOD?

[BanDiDo]: DOD has one major criteria, we look first to "friendship," and from that all else springs. Of course, applicants need to provide whatever is needed as per their reason to apply. But the main thing is long-term friendship. Most DODs have been with us for years, and I cannot remember when anyone left DOD. I have personally rejected a

Continued

great number of applicants who did not fit our personality type. We have no need of egomaniacs. We seek those who wish to be part of the family, and unlike some other groups, DOD actually is a close-knit family.

[biXen]: Since you didn't have any "real" skills, how did you end up in DOD, by friendship?

[BanDiDo]: I have been in DOD for many years now. I started out as a trader, then a site coordinator when I was promoted to Senior, and finally Council. As I stated previously, I do all things.

[biXen]: What in your opinion is the biggest difference between the scene when you joined it and how it is today?

[BanDiDo]: Oh easy... once upon a time the scene was elite for real. You had to know a guy who knew a guy who knew a guy, etc. And trading was legit. Nowadays there are a million newbies, which infect us, most of which are never checked out. And, after PFTP, the whole courier scene is a complete joke, and thus is fast becoming redundant. We have lost a lot of the allure and what little secrecy we had. I fear the scene is far too open and few pay enough heed to the real dangers of what we do.

[biXen]: Have you ever been close to getting busted or anything like that? Any incidents with members or something?

[BanDiDo]: I cannot be busted; I have no warez here. And it is not a crime to be in a group. I have however, known many people who have been busted over the years. Some due to their own stupidity, but the majority due to "narcs" (another unwelcome part of the newbie attacks we suffer from).

[biXen]: What is a "narc?"

[BanDiDo]: A narc is a wholly loathsome creature who, for personal reasons, gains much pleasure out of informing authorities of the activities and/or personal information of those he or she calls "friends." Many sites and a number of individuals have fallen to such low-life creatures. Sadly, the Internet attracts such bottom dwellers, people who in real life have no one to talk to. The anonymity of IRC is a place they revel in. Some of us, though, still maintain ethics and standards.

[biXen]: Did or do you have any idols?

[BanDiDo]: Ahh scene idols! Well, let me tell you a story. I remember in my local BBS days, reading things like DOD NFOs; all those site names and those mystical nicks. Then, years later I found myself invited to the channel #DOD (I had a supply or two), and finally saw some of the nicks. Well it was meeting pop stars, and to this day, old legends like EViLTEA, Thepep, bob226, and many others are my real idols. But my

Continued

true idols are old friends, like bcre8tiv, PsedO, fo_twenny, and so many others. In short I idolize true friends on IRC.

[biXen]: Do you ever regret your time spent in the scene?

[BanDiDo]: Nope, and for years I was online 12 hours a day, 7 days a week. Loved every minute.

[biXen]: Do you ever keep your eyes on other groups, and if so, how?

[BanDiDo]: Oh, I have spies all over. I get intelligence on almost everything that occurs. Everyone knows I tell no tales, and I have a lot of friends in all groups. So I am fairly well informed. At a high level, some of it is important intelligence that affects all groups. When I say spies I mean tongue-in-cheek. I care little for what other groups do, although I am told most of the things that go on.

[biXen]: Name the things you would do to have the best day of your life.

[BanDiDo]: Hrmm. Win a few million dollars in the lottery, then I could go to Europe or something and buy some 100MB pipies. Money baby. With money the rest is just shopping for what you want)

[biXen]: Any things you want to tell the people that read this? Some hints to help them not to not act like lamers when trying to join the scene or something?)

[BanDiDo]: Getting into the scene is not so hard nowadays. Remember, the scene is a wide. Groups like ZERAW who concentrate on public-type site work do amazing things. As far as major league, well it takes time and contacts. You don't build trust in one day. But anyone stupid enough can easily wastehundreds of hours a year in the warez scene, it just takes some time and effort to get in.

[biXen]: Okay, any final words or greets?

[BanDiDo]: Oh, I am happy to greet anyone who still holds true to the core values of the scene. I hope more people start to realize that we play a dangerous game. We are not protected by obscurity, we are not invisible, and when you play with fire, you can indeed get burned. I hope folk remember, make damn sure who you are talking to on IRC, verify anyone close to you. Be careful , this is not a game we play, and prison is not a nice thing.

Although Bandido is still facing sentencing, many other members of DOD/Razor1911 have already been sentenced and are currently serving time. Some members have already served four of their five year sentences, and will be released shortly. Table 9.1 is a conviction list of U.S. citizens. It is interesting to note that even DOD members who did not partake in piracy, only running group resources such as e-ail or Web servers, still received significant sentences for their role in the group.

Table 9.1 The Conviction List

Defendant	Nickname	Affiliations	Role In Group	Sentence
John Sankus Philadelphia, PA.	eriFlleH	DrinkOrDie, Harm	Co-leader DrinkOrDie	46 months
Barry Erickson Eugene, OR	Radsl	RiscISO, DrinkOrDie, POPZ	Supplier of Symantec releases	33 months
David A Grimes Arlington, TX	Chevelle	DrinkOrDie, RISC, RTS	Supplier of Checkpoint releases and site admin-istrator	37 months
Stacey Nawara Rosenberg, TX	Avec	RTS, Razor1911, DrinkOrDie	Release Courier	Unknown
Nathan Hunt Waterford, PA	Azide	CORPS, DrinkOrDie	Senior and top DrinkOrDie supplier	Unknown
David Russo Warwick, RI	Ange	DrinkOrDie	Tested group cracks to ensure they worked correctly.	Unknown
Sabuj Pattanayek Durham, NC	Buj	DrinkOrDie, CORPS, RTS	Software Cracker	41 months
Michael Kelly Miami, FL	Erupt	RiSC, AMNESiA, CORE, DrinkOrDie	Ran IRC bots for DOD from his place of work.	Unknown
Andrew Clardy Galesburg, IL	Doodad	POPZ, DrinkOrDie	Unknown	Unknown

Continued

Table 9.1 continued The Conviction List

Defendant	Nickname	Affiliations	Role In Group	Sentence
Christopher Tresco Boston, MA	BigRar	RiSC, DrinkorDie	Site Administrator and maintainer.	33 months
Derek Eiser Philadelphia, PA	Psychod	DrinkOrDie	Unknown	Unknown
Mike Nguyen Los Angeles, CA	Hackrat	Razor1911, RISC	Site Admin of *The Ratz Hole*	Unknown
Kent Kartadinata Los Angeles, CA	Tenkuken	DrinkOrDie	Ran DrinkOrDie mail server	Unknown
Richard Berry Rockville, MD	Flood	POPZ, DrinkOrDie	Hardware Supplier, CTO of Streampipe.com	Unknown
Kirk Patrick	thesaint	DrinkOrDie	Site Admin of *GodComplex*	Unknown
Robert Gross Horsham, PA	targetpractice	DrinkOrDie	Unknown	Unknown
Myron Cole Warminster, PA	t3rminal	DrinkOrDie	Unknown	Unknown
Armvid Karstad	ievil	DrinkOrDie, Razor1911	IRC Admin	Unknown

With many more arrested in Sweden, Norway, and Germany, Operation Buccaneer had an impressive hit list and the amount of information the FBI acquired was impressive. DOD had approximately 60 members, although only currently active members were prosecuted. Authorities now had lists of scene handlers, groups, and other site names.

The level of paranoia reached new heights after Operation Buccaneer. Pirates were scared, petrified that the FBI were coming for them. During the initial stages of the raid, a Web site was set up to supply information about who had been caught. This page can still be viewed at its archived location at **www.defacto2.net/web.pages/scenebusts–1.htm**. It shows how the scene ran in terror, with a majority of pirates abandoning the groups they were in. Sites closed in such a rapid fashion that there was a brownout in the entire scene, nothing was released and no sites were active.

Many thought the FBI were still watching and speculation began to circulate that two IRC servers were now operating in debug mode and logging all conversations. Although this was just speculation, it was enough to strike fear it into the hearts of many.

It took months for the scene to forget DOD and Operation Buccaneer, but, eventually everyone came out of hiding. Groups and sites re-opened and it was business as usual.

Operation Fast Link

WASHINGTON, D.C. - Attorney General John Ashcroft announced today the most far-reaching and aggressive enforcement action ever undertaken against organizations involved in illegal intellectual property piracy over the Internet. Beginning yesterday morning, law enforcement from 10 countries and the United States conducted over 120 searches worldwide to dismantle some of the most well-known and prolific online piracy organizations.

"Intellectual property theft is a global problem that hurts economies around the world. To be effective, we must respond globally," Attorney General Ashcroft said. "In the past 24 hours, working closely with our foreign law enforcement counterparts, we have moved aggressively to strike at the very core of the international online piracy world."

So began Operation Fast Link, the FBI's piracy raid of 2004.

Operation Fast Link was a continuation of Operation Buccaneer. FBI agents learned a lot from the previous raid. They knew how the scene worked and what its weak points were. For the first time, undercover agents operated their own topsites and used them to infiltrate large groups within the scene. (See Figure 9.2.)

Figure 9.2 Leading FBI Agent on Operation Fast Link

PIRACY FACT...

Operation Fast Link was originally named Operation Higher Education, which was an attack plan focused exclusively on FairLight. However, when FBI agents discovered the amount of pirates involved in the operation, it was renamed Operation Fast Link.

Operation FastLink focused on the game and movie piracy scene, with the majority of members from the popular scene group, FairLight, arrested.

PIRACY FACT...

FairLight was originally a Commodore 64 and Amiga release group, who released their first game in 1987. The group re-emerged on the PC scene in 2003, and released many hit titles including "The Simpsons," "Hit and Run," "Lord of the Rings: Return of the King," and "XIII."

In cooperation with U.S. customs agents, the Dutch anti-piracy group Fiscal and Economic Crime Service (FIOD-ECD) raided 20 universities within the Netherlands. The groups FairLight and Kalisto had significant European resources and many key sites hosted at technical universities within the Netherlands. The Netherlands is infamous for its fast and abundant bandwidth. Two topsites were detained from local universities along with one major archive site belonging to the Kalisto group.

PIRACY FACT...

FBI activity focuses on game and movie piracy, not because the FBI considers this to be the largest threat to the online industry, but because this is where the money is.

Operation FastLink was "assisted" by various intellectual property trade associations, including the Business Software Alliance, the Entertainment Software Association, the Motion Picture Association of America, and the Recording Industry Association of America. Some of the biggest names in anti-piracy. The Business Software Alliance alone has millions of dollars at their disposal to spend on anti-piracy. The investigation was probably bankrolled by these companies and the FBI hired to catch FairLight.

Further evidence of this can be seen in the official FBI statement that thanks the organizations for their assistance and contribution to the FBI. The offical statement can be seen at http://www.fbi.gov/pressrel/speeches/reigel063005.htm

---

Although FairLight was one of the primary groups targeted by the FBI, the group was unaware that they were on the FBI's wanted list. FairLight knew there was an increasing level of law officials watching their every move, when a key German FairLight site was raided by European police a year prior to Operation Fast Link. Many suppliers and crackers left FairLight shortly after, and the group went into temporary retirement for several months.

When FairLight came out of retirement in August 2003, members thought they were safe and that the whole situation had blown over. Little did they know that it had taken the FBI eight months to coordinate an attack on the group, and using the information gained from the initial raided German site, Fairlight was hit very hard. (See Figure 9.3.)

Shortly after the raid, FairLight had this to say about the current situation in a release entitled "Fairlight_Council_Statement-FAiRLIGHT"

Figure 9.3 FairLight, Wounded but Alive

```
Legends never die!

You all read the news - Operation Fastlink struck hard to the heart of the
scene and hit the FairLight ISO section, but mind that the demo activities
on the PC and C64 are still naturally untouched, as there is nothing to
complain about from a legal point of view on what they are doing.

So, let me underline it for you again: FairLight's ISO section is lethally
wounded, but the group as such is still alive and kicking!
FairLight is built stronger to last longer.

FairLight is bigger than one and even all of the sections.
FairLight is and you can rely on the fact that FairLight will continue to be!

Respects to the Fastlink people for finding the core of the scene, which is
not an easy thing to do.
They are doing their job and we're not whining! In war, people take bullets
- we are aware of this!
If you can't stand the sight of body bags, then stand back and let the
real men do the work for you.

We attack, adapt, improvise and survive!

We are FairLight and will continue to be FairLight.

FairLight IS the delight of ETERNAL might!
```

Although the FairLight group was adamant they would make a come back and that the group was not dead, they managed to release only one other title ("Conflict: Vietnam") before the group was abandoned several months later.

Considering the number of members who left Fairlight before operation Fast Link was executed, FBI agents were still able to arrest several key group members including:

Jathan Desire

> In entering his plea today, Desire admitted to conspiring with other individuals to construct and operate two separate computer sites that provided a library of copyrighted software, including movies, games, music, and business utility programs.

Jathan Desire was a University of Iowa student and a site administrator for FairLight. Jathan was the site administrator of two different warez sites, both affiliated with FairLight. Jathan pleaded guilty to two counts of copyright infringement and conspiracy to commit copyright infringement.

When convicted, Jathan faces a maximum 15- year jail term, and an additional $200,000 (USD) fine due to the damage he caused to the software industry.

Seth Kleinberg

Seth Kleinberg, executive Editor of *www.game-over.net*, a PC and console game-reviewing Web site, pleaded guilty to one count of conspiracy to commit criminal copyright infringement. Seth faces a maximum sentence of ten years with additional costs for the damage he caused the software industry. Seth, or Basilisk as he was known in the scene, was a supplier and cracker for the group FairLight and a supplier of console games to another group called Kalisto .

Seth was supplying titles that were given to *www.game-over.net* as review copies. Being able to supply such a large stream of releases helped Seth become a senior member in FairLight and a leading supplier in Kalisto.

PIRACY FACT...

Stephen Riach, President of *Game Over Online, Inc.*, published this press release shortly after Seth's arrest:

As President and Editor in Chief of Game Over Online, Inc., I can't emphasize enough that what Seth did, he did on his own. We do not condone Seth's actions nor do we participate in them. With that said, Seth has been relieved of his duties and the site will continue without him. I'll say it again, what Seth did has absolutely nothing to do with Game Over Online, it's an isolated incident.

Joshua Abell

A resident of San Antonio, Texas, Joshua Abell pleaded guilty to two felony charges: copyright infringement and conspiracy to commit copyright infringement. Abell faces a maximum sentence of 10 years in jail, and admitted to playing a key part in the distribution of FairLight releases.

Operation Site Down

June 30, 2005, 9:00 A.M. A courier frantically begins making directories on every topsite currently online in a desperate attempt to warn others.

"FBI_BUSTS_MANY_ARRESTED_TIME_TO_GO_HIDE-IND"

Welcome to Operation Site Down, the latest raid on the piracy scene conducted by the FBI.

That eventful morning, over 90 search warrants were issued in ten different countries, designed to disrupt and dismantle many of the leading criminal organizations that illegally distributed and traded in copyrighted software, movies, music, and games on the Internet. Operation Site Down targeted release groups and the sites they use, with specific focus on the larger scene groups.

Conservative estimates of the value of pirated works seized in yesterday's action exceed $50 million, which is only a fraction of the losses attributable to the online distribution hubs also seized in this operation. Top-level release groups like those targeted in Operation Site Down are primary suppliers to the for-profit criminal distribution networks that cost the copyright industry billions of dollars each year.

FBI agents were operating two undercover sites located in Canada. These sites were affiliated with many scene groups, and gave each members' access site an impressive 15 tb worth of storage. Sites *Chud* and *Lad* were popular with the groups that affiliated with them, and pirates did not suspect anything. Griffen, the site administrator and FBI undercover agent, asked to be added to other sites that the groups were affiliated with. Since his own site was so impressive, no one had a problem creating an account for him on other group resources.

This is how the FBI infiltrated so many groups. Although Griffen was added to only a few sites, those sites were also affiliated with many different groups.

In total, 22 groups were affiliated on the sites that Griffen had accounts with. These groups included RISCiSO, Myth, TDA, LND, Goodfellaz, Hoodlum, Vengeance, Centropy, Wasted Time, Paranoid, Corrupt, Gamerz, AdmitONE, hellbound, KGS, BBX, KHG, NOX, NFR, CDZ, TUN, and BHP.

Although many of these release groups were not internally brought down by the FBI, their affiliated sites were. As the name suggests, Operation Site Down was targeting only site administrators. The majority of arrests were for site administrators, although some couriers and suppliers were also caught. Log files from both *Chud* and *Lad* will be used in court to prosecute many of the pirates.

Although the official FBI statement made it seem that many groups were completely destroyed by Operation Site Down, my own contacts in the scene say otherwise.

"No, we are fine. Only two of our sites were done, no other group members were caught," said the leader of one piracy group. Operation Site Down was said to have dismantled.

However, many arrests did occur in other groups, especially game and video release groups. Video release group CENTROPY was hit particularly hard by the bust. CENTROPY was best known for releasing Telesync versions of blockbuster movies only hours after they first screened.

Shortly after Operation Site Down, CENTROPY released a Telesync version of "Herbie: Fully loaded," a remake of the original hit film. Within the *centropy.nfo* file was a taunting message to FBI agents. (See Figure 9.4.)

Figure 9.4 CENTROPY Taunts FBI Agents

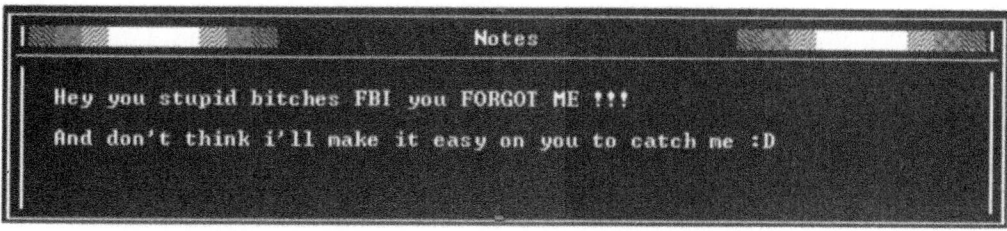

It is believed that several who were arrested on June 30th have given FBI agents the names of other members in groups and more arrests may be around the corner.

The following is an interview with someone we will call "Jacob" for the sake of his privacy. Jacob was a member of a large scene games group that was hit particularly hard by Operation Site Down.

AN INTERVIEW WITH "JACOB"

Me: Jacob, can you tell me what you do in the scene and why?

Jacob: I am a senior in a XXXXX. I mostly make sure everything goes smoothly, releases get from suppliers to crackers and sites stay happy. I am a middle man but I also supply the odd title or two.

Me: Why do you do this?

Jacob: Hard to say, even harder to say now after all of this. I guess it's fun, social, I get to make a lot of new friends.

Me: How long have you been with this group?

Jacob: Two years with these people, in one form or another in various groups.

Me: What happened the morning of July 30th?

Jacob: I got up early, checked my mail, I went to go check sites to see what had been released overnight, but my sites were down. I thought that was a little odd, so I looked at my IRC session and found the topic of the group channel something like, "BUSTS, XXX, XXX, XXX CONFIRMED DEAD, GET OFFLINE."

Me: Were you scared?

Jacob: I can't think of anything worse to read. I mean, I have always known the FBI was a possibility, a risk, but you don't really think it will happen. I went white, I grabbed some clothes and left my house. Spent the day in town. I figured I didn't want to be at my place if the FBI was going to raid.

Continued

www.syngress.com

Me: Did they?

Jacob: Well, when I got back at around 6:00 P.M. I didn't see any cars, the lock on my door was still intact. Some how I escaped this. I don't really know how, everyone knows me.

Me: What happened in the group after that?

Jacob: Well, I went back online that night and caught up with some other people who didn't get busted. It really bites; a lot of my friends got knocks on their doors. Now they are looking at a maximum of 11 years, I think.

I talked to one friend of mine who's out on bail at the moment. He said the FBI quizzed him for hours about his site. Every user account, who the user was, what group they were in. It's like they are building a database of the scene.

The FBI knew all about XXXX, our members, suppliers, crackers, sites. Impressive amounts of knowledge by the sound of it.

Me: Who within XXXX did Operation Site Down target?

Jacob: Oh, mostly site owners, suppliers, and good couriers. They went though the site logs and just grabbed the top few people who uploaded the most. It seems as though on our private sites they went for suppliers, people who uploaded many supplies to release. I think they only care about people uploading, because the majority of our sites have 100 to 150 users each. Hopefully they don't care about people like me too much.

Me: So, you're really worried about this? Do you have any nightmares of the FBI knocking on your door, or coming home to find the lock smashed in?

Jacob: Sleeping is harder now, yes. Now I really don't think piracy was worth it, I have a life, a girlfriend, a job. I really don't want to give it all up for this. I guess I have to accept my fate. I don't think I will go back to piracy again, though. I am too young for this shit!

Me: Why do you think the FBI targeted XXXX?

Jacob: Well, we have released a lot over time, about 350 games I think. I guess we were a good target for them.

Me: If there was one thing you could say to all of the active pirates in the scene and those trying to get into piracy, what would it be?

Jacob: The scene is fun, its great, it's a passionate life, but it's also dangerous. I won't say don't be a pirate, because for many that's just impossible. But I will say, understand that it may cost you your life, that 11 years in jail is a long time. Just make sure its worth it. The worst thing about the scene is how fast you are forgotten; nobody really cares too much after a few months. Is that worth the jail time?

Continued

Me: You don't think so?

Jacob: No, I don't think so. Pirates become very self absorbed. It's a private world, you think it's everything, you need it, you can't picture life without it. But there really is a very large world out there, many people in the scene could use their skills legally, and probably have more fun.

Me: What line of work are you in?

Jacob: Oddly enough, software publishing.

Me: Thanks a lot for your time, Jacob. It has been good talking to someone who has lived through such a close brush with the law. I hope it remains only a brush for your sake.

Jacob: hahah, yeah, thanks. My closing words are: "Just pirate it."

Operation What's Next?

Although Operation Site Down did not successfully dismantle as many groups as previous FBI raids, agents have gained an immense amount of information. With 22 different scene groups compromised and speculation that some have already traded additional group information for a reduced sentence, future raids are certain.

From a legal perspective, FBI agents are not bothered with P2P users; home users who download media is not that important. Downloading pirated media is a lesser offense and it is harder to prove in court.

Legally, you have a better chance of a successful prosecution if the defendant was distributing media. Either supplying titles to release groups or operating large sites that distribute releases to others, thereby increasing the spread of piracy, is far worse than partaking in piracy.

Proving intent to distribute is also easier. Log files and NFOs are all that is required, and the sentence is significantly larger than simply downloading.

To any in the scene who may be reading this, think carefully. The FBI knows as much about the scene as you do. They know groups, releases, nukes ,and pre's. They know how it works, can talk the lingo, and would find little problem with blending in. You could be sitting in a channel right now talking to an FBI agent, and you would not know the difference.

Judging from previous raids, it is clear that legal authorities will continue to use sites as a method of infiltrating a group. FBI agents do not know how to crack or supply, so they will go for the easy option and simply log everyone who enters their site.

Many groups now take extra precautions. Group NFO files no longer display the names of crackers or suppliers, and many scene sites do not allow unknown members access. This is not adequate protection for scene groups; I believe that with time even the most exclusive group can be infiltrated. We have seen it with FairLight, DOD, and PWA, all well-established groups who never actively promoted their presence.

Having talked to Jacob about his current situation, I feel that piracy is not worth ten years without parole. Although many consider piracy simply a hobby, law officials do not and the consequences are real. Its not a matter of if, it's a matter of when.

Chapter 10

The Future of Piracy

Where Now?

Between the Federal Bureau of Investigation (FBI), the Business Software Alliance (BSA), and the media, you would think digital piracy has drastically degraded the quality of our lives. Reports often show lost revenue amounts in the billions and pirates are literally killing the Internet and our economy, according to the press. But is this really the case? Piracy is essentially a new form of forgery, a digital take on one of the oldest and most prominent crimes in the history of our civilization. Forgery can be found in history as early as 670 BC, where counterfeiters in Lydia first created casts of originally minted coins, later filling the casts with metal and producing a replica counterfeit coin.

Romans adored Greek design and Roman artists produced thousands of forgeries based on original Greek art. Forgery was so prolific in this era that Roman and Greek art are now almost indistinguishable; even art scholars find it hard to tell them apart. Despite this abundant piracy and forgery, our society flourished. You could even say that piracy has had a positive effect on our society.

The currency used today is practically impossible to forge. The technology has evolved to a point where counterfeiting is no longer viable. If no one had tried to copy coins in 670 BC, would we have invented the watermark? It is because of people like software pirates that we no longer use notes made from hand printed paper.

The truth is that piracy is a natural part of evolution. Although we like to make piracy out to be evil, we really could not live without it. We need piracy to help us evolve; piracy has shaped and crafted the design of our technology and how we deploy new ideas.

A good example of this evolving technology can be seen in computer operating systems. Originally, Windows 95, 98, and 2000 were very open, communicative systems. Firewalls existed, but home users would never think of running one. Most computers on the Internet were accessible even if you were not local to them. End-user security did not really exist five or six years ago, although in theory everyone was vulnerable to exploitation.

When the first prolific worms began to surface in 1999, the Internet community immediately began to feel the effect of exploitation. Everyone was vulnerable and they were being rapidly exploited.

"Worms are destroying the Internet," said one popular computer magazine. Sure, worms could have destroyed the Internet if no one did anything about it, but we did do something.

Technology evolved. Microsoft released operating systems with more security restraints. Firewall and antivirus software boomed in popularity. By mid-2003, almost every home user ran an anti-virus client. The adoption of firewall software also grew, with 40 percent of home users commanding their own firewall. The latest versions of Windows XP now come with an built-in firewall, which is turned on by default with a secure rule set.

Although worms still exist, their future looks bleak. Within five years, very few Internet clients will be exposed to attack. Only the minority will be vulnerable, and worms will need to evolve in order to survive.

Technology was exploitable, but software developers changed their mindset and found ways to create new versions of software that fixed the apparent flaws. Comparatively, modern operating systems are light years ahead of their predecessors in security, and increasingly harder to exploit. This added security is greatly due to worms. Worms have had a similar effect on software that pirates have. Pirates are forcing software developers to evolve, to write smarter applications that cannot be defeated. Eventually, piracy will become impossible. Already there are applications and technologies released that are immune to piracy. Software developers are finally beginning to win the war.

This chapter looks at the future of different forms of media and how technology is evolving to combat piracy.

Software Piracy

The original and most apparent form of media piracy, games and applications, have been copied since floppy disks and home computers became available. Traditionally, this form of media has relied on anti-piracy techniques to keep piracy at bay. CD checks, serial numbers, dongles, although this technology decreases the rate of piracy, it does not inhibit it. With time any protection routine can be understood and defeated, and although anti-piracy software helps protect digital assets, they are by no means failsafe.

PIRACY FACT...

On average, a PC game takes 3 to 4 days after its official release date to be pirated in the scene. Applications take on average 12 days before they are cracked and released.

Technology is evolving, however, and key mind shifts in the design of games and applications are making the life of software pirates increasingly hard. Software piracy has always relied on having the media in hand, being able to take one copy and replicate it flawlessly using a computer. No matter how many layers of protection you wrap your software in, you are still trusting user's not to copy or distribute it.

Recent advancements in PC game software have seen developers use a different business model to sell their software. No longer are developers keen to ship a completely standalone version of their flagship product. Instead, they are choosing a service-based, online model. The idea is simple. If the user never has the game in its entirety, it cannot be replicated or pirated.

Massively Multiplayer Online Role Playing Games (MMORPGs) are the latest breed of PC game to date and not one online game has been pirated. The success of these games comes from their service-based design. Even if you were to copy and distribute the game CD, you would still require a valid account to play the game.

Playing the game offline is not an option. Game content such as maps and characters are all kept on a controlled game server. CDs are essentially just clients; they are not games themselves and are not standalone. Short of hacking the online service and distributing accounts, pirates are unable to copy the online titles.

Games have been using online services for years and there is a steady trend of software developers choosing service-based models over the more traditional standalone CD.

Blizzard once dominated the PC game world, with hit titles such as "Diablo," "Diablo2," "Warcraft," and "Starcraft." Their games are legendary and still sell in stores years after their official release. However, the software giant has now become an online-based game provider with their latest title, "World of WarCraft." This MMORPG is an epic world where gamers compete or play alongside millions of other gamers globally. Although many have tried to Denial of Service (DOS) and attack the W.o.W servers. No one has ever been able to pirate the game or generate their own account information.

W.o.W has become possibly the most profitable Internet-based service ever created. Blizzard boasts over 3.5 million users, each paying $15.00 a month for access to the game. W.o.W turns a revenue of over 52 million dollars a month. Although Blizzard faced some expense from maintaining and developing the service, it probably did not exceed 50 million a month. Blizzard first attempted an online service with *Battle.net*, an online portal where Diablo and Warcraft users could play games together online.

In short, a service model works. Gamers do not mind paying $15.00 a month, because the service is good and the game is fun. Pirates are unable to crack the game; in fact, no one even bothers to try. It is a well-known fact in the scene that to play an online game you will end up paying real money.

Other software developers have also tried the service-based model. Valve software unsuccessfully attempted it with HalfLife 2, where developers attempted to create a hybrid online game. Users were to download and unlock sections of the game as they were required. Cracker, however, found methods of circumventing this and eventually a pre-unlocked version of the game was released.

Microsoft has also hinted at a service-based operating system some time in the distant future; one that is completely thin and very similar in design to terminal services, although this technology requires the user to have access to high-speed Internet such as fiber or broadband. It would be very attractive to a novice computer user. It is possible that you will see this service bundled with high-speed cable providers. For the majority of home users, such a service would be ideal. Microsoft would personally take care of updating and securing your desktop. New vulnerabilities within Windows could be globally patched within a matter of seconds.

It is estimated that by 2010, 80 percent of the U.S. will be connected via broadband. That is an increase of 37 percent over the 2004 statistic of 43 percent of U.S. homes. As broadband Internet connections become common, service-based models will grow in popularity.

In order for piracy to survive, pirates will need to evolve, and find new methods of copying or tricking the service-based products into operating in a standalone fashion.

As technology evolves and grows beyond the reach of pirates, it is very likely that only a small minority of software will be pirated in the future.

Multimedia Piracy

Multimedia is by far the most problematic media to secure from piracy. By definition, multimedia is an experience you partake in by either listening to an album or watching a movie. However, sound and video can be captured by other devices also, such as video and sound recorders.

It is certain that video and audio piracy are here to stay. The demand for entertainment media is huge; no one would say no to a free movie or album.

The often trivial copying process of CDs and DVDs is also making it virtually impossible for multimedia piracy to simply fade away.

PIRACY FACT...

I read an interesting article published last week when I was thinking about the future of audio piracy. A summery of the article is as follows.

According to Entertainment Media Research, legal downloading has made a huge increase and soon will pass the pirates. A survey concluded that 35 percent of music listeners now use the Internet to download music tracks legally from music download stores like iTunes and Napster. Piracy is just ahead with 40 percent of listeners admitting they use P2P services to download and share music with other users on the network/tracker. To get to this conclusion, 4000 consumers answered the 2006 Digital Music Survey in association with the media law firm Olswang.

Thirty-five percent of users now use a legal download service. These statistics are mostly fueled by a recent Apple announcement of reaching an epic 500 million downloads from *iTunes.com* since its original launch. On an average day, iTunes users download 250,000 songs!

Although these statistics sound impressive, Peer 2 Peer networks have been drastically underestimated, Apple does not distribute anywhere near 35 percent of music.

Yankee Group's Michael Goodman puts the number of legal Digital Rights Management (DRM) downloads at 330 million last year, compared to 5 billion downloads from P2P networks. For every legal purchase, there are 16 illegal downloads. Compared to the 35 percent from Entertainment Media Research, the Yankee Group estimate of only 6 percent of downloads are legal.

My own investigation has personal download estimates much lower than the Yankee 6 percent, with an estimated 2 percent of downloads being legal. I came to these statistics after sharing a selection of my own MP3s on a popular P2P music network. Six point seven (6.7) million users were currently logged into the P2P service and sharing files. During a period of 24 hours, 35 songs from my own collection were downloaded by other users around the world.

My music collection is small, only a few hundred MP3s at most 3 gigabytes (GBs) in size, so I assume that everyone sharing music has at least the same amount as me.

With 6.7 million users online, each transferring 35 songs per day, you will see 234,500,000 daily downloads. Although these statistics only come from the one P2P network, there are three networks of similar size and user base.

Apple averages 250,000 daily song downloads from iTunes, while a single P2P network can average 235 million. According to my statistics, legal music downloads amount to less than 2 percent of all music downloaded. Furthermore, if my results encompassed all means of distributing pirated music, my estimate would be lower. In theory, the figure could be as little as 0.5 to 1 percent of music is legally purchased. This figure differs slightly from the 35 percent announced, and shows that the piracy problem is not that easy to stop.

Videos and music will never be immune from recording. Many of the audiovisual (AV) releases today bypass DRM restrictions by simply playing the media and capturing the output with another device.

High-quality component stereo systems are capable of playing a CD that is protected with DRM technology and then sending the audio output via digital optical cables to a recording device. Even the smartest DRM DVD could be played on a high-quality LCD TV and recorded with a digital hand cam. There is no way to stop this type of piracy.

Looking forward, there is going to be a definite change in the distribution methods of video. Cinemas are a thing of the past; DVDs on average make twice as much money as the big screen. DVDs are immensely popular; many of us are too busy to go to a movie and instead invest in home cinema equipment such as big screen TVs and digital projectors. With high-quality digital audio and video, a home cinema experience can be just as good as the big screen.

Personally, I have been to the movies five times this year, mostly for films I wanted to see when they first came out, such as Star Wars Episode 3. I usually rent the standard films, the ones that I do not consider noteworthy, from a local video store. I do not have much free time and although I do like to get out to the cinema, it is often easier to stay at home. This paradigm shift is going to become more apparent in the coming years, and that is bad news.

Currently, pirates are limited by release dates. If a DVD is not available while the movie plays in the cinemas, then chances are it will not be pirated until it is released to DVD. The theater-to-DVD window is typically two weeks for an average movie, with the exception of highly popular films such as Lord of the Rings, where the delay can take months. New studies forecast that in the future this window will be non-existent and media will be released simultaneously to multiple distribution channels.

"One day, if "King Kong" is going to be released on Friday, December 14, it will be released theatrically around the world, DVD around the world, pay-per-view around the world," says Peter Sealey, an adjunct professor of marketing at the University of California-Berkeley's Haas School of Business. That's where the marketplace is going. Cinemas will be for those who do not have expensive AV equipment at home. DVD's and Internet video on-demand services similar to TiVO are the way of the future.

Internet video distribution methods are seen as the next high-profit industry. Actor Morgan Freeman and Intel Corporation are among investors in a venture named ClickStar, Inc. The new digital distribution company is focused on bringing top Hollywood movies directly to consumers over broadband Internet. ClickStar connects filmmakers to film fans worldwide, delivering first-run feature films and talent-branded channels. It offers branded online services where consumers can easily access, purchase, and download pre-DVD, first-run Hollywood films, and artist-created entertainment channels through numerous viewing portals. ClickStar will bring the best of the movies to its audience in a brand new home entertainment experience.

The future of multimedia will be in your remote; the latest block-buster movie will only be a few clicks away. This same technology will probably also be used for music distribution. Online music services such as iTunes will grow in popularity as more people choose to download music instead of buying a CD. Consider how easy it would be if all of your music was held on a physically small, 100GB RAM drive. No worries about scratching a CD or having to hunt around for the right CD.

Music is going to become incredibly easy to download. Expect many iTune-type services with micro-payments per track. Such ease of use is going to cause problems when trying to protect this media from piracy. If the content is available in a high-quality digital format, it is going be a very attractive target for both audio and video pirates. Pirates will be able to obtain high-quality DVD images of brand new movies; films released only minutes ago could potentially be pirated and released faster than ever before.

Music will see similar attacks. As different DRM technology is used, there will undoubtedly be flaws found that allow music to be copied.

Piracy Fact...

Bypassing DRM technology is not as complicated as you may think it is. Recent DRM technology was bypassed by simply by using WinAmp and an audio output filter.

By playing a DRM-protected CD and using a WinAmp filter to redirect the audio stream to a physical file, a CD can effectively be written to a file minus the DRM. Attacks like this are common against DRM and can result in the creation of an unprotected audio CD in a matter of minutes.

If media is available for all to purchase, protection technology has to survive a possibly brutal attack from pirates. Even if the DRM technology protection is strong enough to thwart all attempts of direct copying, copying from screen will still exist in video piracy. Capturing audio directly and recording video from a high quality digital screen will result in a good quality replica. Pirates currently do this with hand cams in cinemas, releasing Telesyncs and CAMs of popular movies. If the recording was done at home or in a semiprofessional studio, the quality would substantially higher.

"Once you start giving the customer what they want, when they want it, and how they want it, they will pay you for it," said one of the Click Star investors. We all want to be lazy and sit at home and watch the latest movie. Who has the time and effort to go out to the cinema each night?

Price will be a huge factor in the future levels of video piracy. If customers are forced to pay DVD prices to download and watch a movie, then piracy may just be a cheaper alternative. Spending an hour finding and downloading a movie may still be worth your time and be cheaper than paying $16 to watch it. However, if a movie only cost a dollar or two to watch, piracy would not exist. Would you bother spending hours finding and downloading a movie, only to save yourself two dollars?

DVD is also due to take a drastic turn, with the soon-to-be-released Blu-Ray and HD-DVD technology. DVD's will be holding between 30 and 50GBs worth of video, depending on the technology used. Pirates will have trouble transferring and storing the huge DVD images that are almost ten times the size of existing DVDs. Even with storage capacity at its current rate of growth, you could not store many 50GB images on even a terabyte, not to mention the bandwidth required to serve that much content.

New DRM technology is also nearing completion and DVD's of the future will have stronger protection against piracy. Whether or not this technology successfully thwarts pirates' attempts is anyone's guess, but protection will only last a finite time; eventually it will be broken.

Will the Piracy Scene Continue?

FBI raids are becoming more frequent in the piracy scene, almost to the point that they are common and expected by most large groups. Recent attempts from law officials to stamp out those who are involved in software piracy have seen harsh sentences dealt out to anyone involved. Pirates are beginning to think twice about being involved with piracy; is it really worth it?

I found this out firsthand when I interviewed "Jacob" in the previous chapter. Pirates are beginning to realize that the FBI considers their harmless piracy groups, acts of organized crime. Although this has a positive effect on reducing the amount of people trying to get into the piracy scene, the long-term effects may be counterproductive. When law enforcement agencies actively try to shut down something as widespread as piracy, they often only end up making the situation worse.

Prohibition days (1920 to 1933) are a good example of how an idea that sounded good on paper quickly became something much worse when implemented. When alcohol became illegal, most people stopped producing and selling liquor. The risk was high, and getting drunk was not worth being thrown in jail for, so many backed out of the liquor business. However, the true hardened criminal, those who had a financial motive in producing and selling liquor, soon flourished.

The law efforts pushed liquor production into dark alleys and into the hands of mobsters and true organized crime syndicates. Outlawing liquor made gangsters famous and incredibly wealthy. Previously, alcohol was sold by many people and it was easy to get. When mobsters began to control prohibition days, alcohol prices rose drastically. Gangsters could afford to charge any price they wanted, because no one else sold liquor and there was a huge level of demand.

If pirates are aggressively forced into hiding, would this happen again? Sure. The majority of pirates will quit the piracy game, pack their bags, and become law-abiding citizens. But not everyone will leave. Those who stay will be pushed into the black market arena, working for gangs or counterfeiters and those interested in using piracy to make a profit.

Currently, the image of piracy is very innocent, and although some pirates try to make a profit, it is definitely not the norm. Pirates love the challenge of piracy, because they find it entertaining and they like the social interaction it provides. Although in the eyes of the law piracy is a crime, warez pirates have little criminal or financial incentive. If the black market became the only element of piracy, more and more money would exchange hands. Pirates would join the scene only to make money, and digital gangsters would begin setting up operations.

By 2010, the demand on software will be huge. If estimates prove correct and 80 percent of the U.S. is using broadband, everyone will need software. For someone financially motivated and not scared of the police, this will be a very tempting market. In my opinion, organized crime is much worse. Warez groups are not organized crime, and however malicious they may seem, they are the lesser of two evils.

Stopping piracy is not as simple as arresting everyone involved. My time in the scene has taught me that pirates are smart, keen, and creative and they design, create, and implement highly complicated technical tasks. Each member of every group is highly skilled at his or her task. These are not drones selling CDs on street corners, they are students from Harvard, Stanford, and Cambridge.

Although convicting pirates is relatively easy, it is a waste of potential. Pirates know how to defeat technology in ways very few do. Why not use this skill productively? For every crack produced, a cracker can tell you what the developer should have done and how the protection was defeated.

In order for piracy to be truly eradicated, developers must evolve their own practices. Technology needs to take a page from the piracy book and present a challenge that no one can defeat. Until now, pirates have always succeeded in defeating copy restrictions. Most software packages are available from the piracy scene. If the technology cannot be beaten, then it will not be pirated. It is that simple.

Piracy boils down to theft. If people can't steal it by beating the technology, they will steal it some other way, such as carding, scamming, phishing, etc. Although locking up anyone who defeats the technology may satisfy many, the long-term effects will be much worse. Arrests will not stop the levels of piracy and you will not see a decline in warez releases. It will, however, push the piracy scene into a much darker place.

Chapter 11

Closing Notes

I have seen it from both sides. I have seen piracy in a way that only few people have. I have been among the scene and I have become friends with many crackers and suppliers. I know the scene buzz, that strange energy that motivates pirates to excel in something highly immoral and illegal. The dedication in the scene is so strong that it is hard to hate these rebellious computer geniuses.

I respect anyone who invests so much energy and resources into something as bizarre as computer piracy. But I also know the other side of the story. As a professional writer, several of my own works have been pirated. It hurts. You feel as though someone has stolen so much from you. It is hard to rationalize the loss, because it is so nameless and cold. Pirates work under pseudonyms hidden within cryptic group names.

However, after being so close to piracy, I now know that nothing is done maliciously. While previously I would have happily seen a pirate in jail, now I am not so sure. After seeing pirates at work, seeing their dedication and effort, I can only marvel at their skill.

Currently, there is a great divide between those on the side of piracy and those against. For years, software developers have been creating protection methods and designing technology that they claim is undefeatable. Pirates are simply curious; they find pleasure in tinkering with things. Software hackers were the children that took apart small toys to see how they tick.

The media often portrays pirates as dark, shady characters, people living in the underbelly of society. This stereotype is ridiculous, and is sending a bad message about pirates and piracy to the rest of the world. When a 20-year-old graduate student is arrested and sentenced to ten years in a federal prison without parole, you have to wonder if the punishment really fits the crime. Are software companies simply lashing out at someone?

After seeing pirates at work, I understand that piracy is not something you can stop. For every pirate arrested and locked up, another one will take his place in the scene. Sure, it takes time, and perhaps the scene will be lacking in members for a few months, but curiosity is a very common human trait. Piracy will not stop anytime soon, and arresting pirates will only exacerbate the situation.

As a writer, I have documented and detailed the work of the world's most elusive digital thieves. I have rubbed shoulders with crackers, suppliers, and site administrators, and have seen countless applications when they were first cracked and then released. I cannot stress the level of talent present in the scene. My final closing note is a plea to all software development companies who may be reading this: please, hire a cracker. Look into the scene and find those people who steal your software. The software industry is leagues behind the underground world. A 15-year-old from Russia can defeat the most complex of copy protection routines designed by the U.S. Instead of asking for help, software developers should join the BSA band wagon and hunt down the pirates.

Our copy protection technology desperately needs to evolve. Piracy hurts the software industry; there is no argument about that. However, our current developers are unable to stem this wave of piracy. It is time for software companies to ask for help. With time, piracy will only grow in popularity. Even if it is pushed into the darkest recesses of the Internet, it will eventually become huge.

A resource that the software industry needs in order to fix the piracy problem is sitting in a federal prison right now.

Appendix A

Pirating Software: Attitudes and Reasons

Solutions in this chapter:

- Attitudes About Piracy
- Why is Pirated Software So Readily Available?
- Specific Reasons for Using Pirated Software
- Summary

Introduction

There are many reasons why software is pirated. However, before examining specific reasons, it is important to examine how we feel about the fundamental issues of stealing. Our attitudes about stealing shape our views concerning software piracy. Specifically, why are so many otherwise responsible computer users downloading pirated software? Why is pirated software so easy to acquire? Why is the practice so widespread? Where does it come from? This chapter attempts to answer these questions.

Attitudes About Piracy

Why people use pirated software and how they justify doing so is based on their personal opinions regarding stealing. The following sections examine the different issues that may have an influence on whether or not a person uses pirated software.

Morality

What constitutes stealing? Sticking a gun in someone's side and demanding money is undeniably stealing. Are "white collar" crimes (e.g., embezzlement and security fraud) stealing? Is cheating on your income tax or padding your expense account a criminal offense? Is it stealing to "borrow" a pen from work to use for non-company business? Is making personal phone calls on company time, taking an extra hour for lunch, spending hours daydreaming, or putting in less than a full days' work stealing from your employer? A lot of people consider these minor infractions, nothing more than normal and acceptable human behavior. Even though the law distinguishes between petty theft and grand larceny, what constitutes "stealing" for most of us is a matter of personal opinion.

Justification

Just because "thousands of people are doing it" doesn't mean it is ethical or legal. However, for many people, going along with the crowd provides all of the justification they need. Fashion and fashion advertising is all about being trendy. Political parties love it when voters "jump on the bandwagon" alongside their candidate. Religions are based on a common doctrine. Some people behave differently in groups than they might otherwise.

"Group think" also affects computer users. Some otherwise honest computer users justify downloading pirated software by saying that they are "just one of the thousands" of users who download and crack software. Other ways that people justify stealing pirated software are "the company charges too much" or "they're so big, they don't need the money."

Blame and Responsibility

Software companies employ various security techniques to prevent their products from being pilfered, while software pirates are determined to find a way around the obstacles placed in their path. While it is impossible to secure a program completely, some programs are harder to "crack" than others. It is a continual cat and mouse game between the software companies and the pirates.

Say you left the keys in the ignition of your car and it was stolen. Right or wrong, a lot of people would say that it was your fault. If your shopping bag were stolen after leaving it unattended in a public place, you would probably be criticized for being irresponsible. In each case, your only mistake was being careless; however, a certain degree of diligence is expected . And like us, software companies should also exercise a reasonable measure of diligence. They must work harder to improve the technology that safeguards their products. Understand, however, that software companies that neglect to properly protect their products are not guilty of a crime and that not properly protecting software does not make pirating software any less wrong or illegal. It simply points out the fact that better security measures must be implemented.

While it is hard to justify software piracy, it is easy to explain: it is the desire to get something for nothing. However, software piracy would not be a threat to the software industry if that were the only reason. There would still be pirated programs, but they would remain closely guarded secrets. Why then is so much pirated software readily available?

As we all know, it is good to get something for free. The only thing better than getting something for free is telling others that you got it for free. And that's the reason why so many full programs, cracks, serials, and patches are on the Internet. The "real" software pirates, the skilled computer wizards who come up with the "cracked" software, do it for the same reason Sir Edmund Hillary gave in 1923 for climbing Mt. Everest—"because it is there!" People crack software because they can; it is a challenge. When they succeed, they are proud of their accomplishment and anxious to tell the world. Aside from individuals, there are organized "crack groups" racing to see who can crack the newest programs. As the expression goes, there may be "no honor among thieves," but there is a degree of camaraderie and competition. Likewise, those who obtain pirated software from others are anxious to share their "good fortune." There are hundreds of specialized Web sites that facilitate this, and much of the sharing is done openly.

There is no need to spend countless hours dissecting and analyzing a program's code to develop a workaround. For that matter, there is no reason to understand how the software works. All of the real work has already been done. However, people intent on stealing software must know where to find the information and how to use it.

NOTE

The main reason that software piracy is so widespread is because it is readily available and easy to use.

Specific Reasons For Using Pirated Software

There are several reasons why people use pirated software, although not all of the reasons apply to everyone. Saving money is one reason, however, it is not always the main reason.

We have all seen stories in the news about famous celebrities caught shoplifting. Because most famous celebrities are very rich, their motivation probably involved something other than saving money. It is the same way with pirated software. It is the thrill of getting something for nothing.

Saving Money

Saving money is also a huge motivation for using pirated software. Software costs up to $1,000 per copy, while pirated software is free. Saving money is important to most people, and it is easy to see why, given a choice, some people choose pirated software.

That's not to say that we are all thieves, but as Melanie Griffith said in the movie *A Stranger Among Us,* "Within every honest man is a thief struggling to get out." It is incredibly easy to download "cracked" software from the Web and make perfect copies of CDs and DVDs. We can steal intellectual property to our hearts content from the privacy of our own homes. People that normally would never think of taking something that is not theirs behave differently where software is concerned. Meanwhile, there is safety in numbers, and the risk of being caught and punished is almost nonexistent. Such temptation is hard to resist.

Since the beginning of financial civilization, humanity has been infatuated with buying everything for the cheapest possible price. Our culture actively promotes this attitude with large-scale sales and higher levels of inter-corporate competition that often furthers the already massive price reductions on products. Piracy takes this mindset one step further. Although a price for a product may be inexpensive and already greatly reduced from its original value, it still costs money. If you could have the same product for no cost, would you take it?

Piracy fuels this money-saving desire. Why spend $20 on a DVD when you can download an exact copy from the Internet for free? When faced with an ethical decision of either not paying for a product or sacrificing part of a long-term dream, it is often easier to not pay. It is this attitude that draws the majority of people to piracy: to play the latest games, listen to favorite artists, and watch the latest blockbusters for free. In a world where everything has a price tag, piracy is often seen as a "sigh of relief," the one thing that comes without a price tag attached and no marketing swing.

Like it or hate it, piracy has found a place in our society and has been widely adopted by both young and old. Its inherent grip on modern day technology means it is here to stay and is widely seen as the preferred choice for the younger generation. Piracy is hip, piracy is cool, piracy is being able to tell your friends that you have already seen the movie that will be released next week, or to boast frame rates in a game that no one else can even order yet. Piracy is having the upper hand in a money-oriented world, to be able to have something for free with no strings attached.

The core idea behind digital piracy (e.g., DVDs and CDs) or entertainment (e.g., software) is the attitude that information and digital entertainment should be free for all to try and then to buy it if they like the product. This attitude stems from how digital media has become the center piece in our life. Digital media has become our own private personal space. Advertising gurus have managed to turn the general public into digital junkies and now every entertainment avenue comes with a price. It has become very easy to not pay for something that you crave and depend on so much.

It is easy to classify piracy as theft and to state that all who pirate digital media are thieves, but the subject is far more complex. For example, the majority of home computer users who download pirated software will usually buy the software if it works well, and many game players choose to support developers and buy a game if they enjoy playing it. It could be said that the actions of pirates are not those of thieves, but rather of consumers who want to be "sure" of their purchase.

Evaluation

One of the semi-legitimate reasons for obtaining software without paying is to see if it meets your needs. It is not uncommon for a product to fall short of expectations. And while many products come with guarantees and many stores have decent return policies, software is usually in a class by itself.

I once returned a computer to Best Buy within one week of purchasing it. My old computer finally "bit the dust" and I needed a new one in a hurry. Even though the computer I selected fell way short of my "dream machine," I figured that a new name brand computer running at several times the speed of my old one would at least be a step up. It wasn't! It crashed ridiculously often and I couldn't "live with it." Luckily, I was able to return it and get my money back. However, if I had purchased a $20 software program and did not like it for *any* reason, I would have been stuck with it.

As posted on Best Buy's Web site (*www.bestbuy.com*) and prominently displayed in their stores, full refunds are offered within 14 or 30 days from purchase date, depending on the merchandise. However, the following items are specifically listed as exceptions:

- Computer software
- Video games
- Prerecorded videos
- DVD software
- Music

To receive credit for these items, they must be unopened. This is typical of return policies at most stores. Essentially, when it comes to software, if you bought it, you own it! You cannot blame the stores. If they permitted software to be returned, more than a few "customers" would undoubtedly view the store as a "lending library" (i.e., buy, use, copy, and return). To be fair, many software manufacturers offer "try before you buy" trial versions of their products.

The Right Version

I wish I had a dollar for every time I've heard of someone buying *upgrade* software only to find that they really needed the full-blown version or vice versa. The choice is sometimes confusing. To confuse things further, the differences between upgrades and full versions are not always indicated plainly on the packages. As shown in Figure A.1, the packaging of different programs is sometimes so close in appearance that it is difficult to tell them apart even when you know what you need.

Figure A.1 Full Version vs. Upgrade Packaging Differences

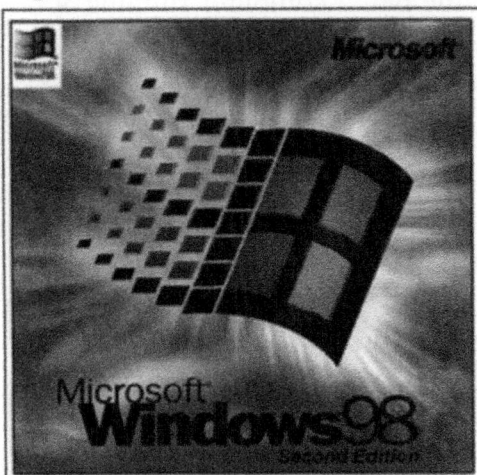

Upgrades cost less than full versions; however, buying the wrong one by mistake is usually only discovered *after* you try to install it. What seemed like a bargain turns out to be a waste of money. Subtle or misleading packaging is not an excuse for pirating; however, if you have ever tried unsuccessfully to return opened software, you might feel differently.

Compatibility

As part of evaluating software, it is equally important to make sure that it is compatible with your hardware and other software. Every software manufacturer's Web sites should list their system requirements and all software should have them printed on the box. Typically listed are the required processors and their speeds, the operating systems, the minimum and recommended amount of random-access memory (RAM), and the amount of required hard disk space. These days, most requirements also list a CD-ROM drive and sometimes a video card and monitor specifications.

Still, it is not unheard of for a newly installed program to be incompatible with another program. If that is the case, one of the programs can be closed while the other is being used. However, sometimes that is not possible or desirable. It is good to know these things *before* buying a new program.

Sport

"Borrowing" software can become a very challenging and competitive hobby. On one side is the software companies who are trying to keep their products secure, and on the other side are crackers racing to see who can crack the latest programs first. It doesn't matter if a pirate has a use for the program; the challenge and fun is in obtaining a working copy.

New programs come out every day and software pirates are always among the first in line. However, aside from the dozen or so programs that everyone wants, the vast majority of lesser-known pirated programs are never purchased. How much this hobby contributes to the overall piracy statistics is impossible to know, but I suspect it represents a huge percentage. That still doesn't excuse stealing the programs, but it is something to consider.

Nearly all cracks originate from a relatively small number of very knowledgeable computer enthusiasts who post them on the Internet for all to see and use. How they actually go about cracking the various programs is complicated and somewhat analogous to breaking an enemy's code and deciphering their communications. It requires an understanding of various programming languages, the ability to extract and disassemble source code, a solid familiarity of assembly language, and a working knowledge of the various techniques used to secure programs. Most of the same skills needed to write software are needed to crack it. It would not be surprising to learn that the vast majority of crackers are employed in the software industry. While producing cracks is complex, using them is simple, which is one of the reasons that software piracy is so widespread.

Curiosity

When it comes to pirated software, curiosity can substitute for the usual research and forethought that might precede the purchase of a product. An application that ordinarily would hold little appeal becomes very interesting when you can download, install, and "audition" it without leaving your chair. Likewise, it is just as easy to try out several programs before deciding which ones to keep.

Up-to-date Versions

Software is a work in progress. New versions and revisions to existing programs are constantly being released that introduce new features, improve performance, and fix existing bugs. Sometimes upgrades are given to registered owners for free or for a discounted price, but more often than not they charge full price. When the changes are extensive, a whole new version may be released.

Few customers who purchase software in stores realize that they are probably buying obsolete products. Often, the software being sold is one, two, or more revision levels behind the current one. If a product is identified by the year on the box (e.g., Norton Antivirus 2002) and it is already 2004, it cannot be disguised as the current version. However, for the most part, there may only be a small letter or serial number on the back of the box to distinguish between versions. Unless people do their homework, they will not know if the software is current. With pirated software, it is usually possible to stay current for free.

Not only is a lot of pirated software up-to-date, it is often possible to obtain the latest programs and upgrades before they are announced on the company's Web site or placed on store shelves. A great example is Windows XP. Due to an abundance of hype and high hopes, it is doubtful that the launch of any software product was more highly antici-pated by honest consumers and software pirates alike. Amazingly, pirates had their copies of XP over a month before anyone else.

"Devils' Own" was the code name for the pirated version of Windows XP Professional. The so-called "corporate version" was intended for volume licensing to large corporations and did not require product activa-tion. That made it ideal for being pirated, because the only item that had to be entered during installation was the "FCK…" product key.

Knowledge

As stated earlier, even if you have no use for pirated software, you may still want to learn more about it. "Why?" Many gambling books point out that the best way to avoid being cheated is to learn how the cheaters cheat (i.e., "it takes a thief to catch a thief"). As software companies have discovered, seeing how the pirates crack their programs provides key information toward defeating them. It is a known fact that many software creators "camp out" on crack sites and message boards to get a feel for the security, or lack thereof, of their products. If you want to make some-thing more secure, study how the thieves do it.

Summary

People have different ways of looking at and justifying pirated software. However, none of the reasons for pirating software excuses the fact that it is stealing. In a halfhearted attempt to mitigate things, many Web sites hosting pirated software urge their visitors to consider buying the software if they want to continue using it.

However, this is not a book about morality. This is an expose showing the extent of the problem, why it is being done, how it is being done, and what is being done to stop it. As already stressed, one of the main reasons piracy is such a huge problem is because it is so easy.

Appendix B

Why Software is Pirated

Solutions in this chapter:

- Extent of the Problem
- Cost or Availability
- Curiosity
- Corporate Policy

Introduction

Digital integrity is crucial in the electronic environment, and computer users go to great lengths to ensure that the applications they run are legitimate. Because viruses, worms, spyware, and key loggers are common on the Internet, there is good reason to be vigilant when installing software or running a new application. The opportunity to distribute a worm or virus through pirated software is a very real threat.

End users are forced to trust that the people who pirate the software do not embed any viruses or malicious code within it. This blind trust is easily exploitable and creates a large window for attack on users of pirated software.

This chapter focuses on people that put themselves at technical and legal risk to use pirated media. It also discusses why these people do not see the risk in using pirated software.

Extent of the Problem

One out of every three programs is pirated, and while it is impossible to know the exact extent of the damages, the losses from pirated software (e.g., lost sales, lost tax revenues, lost jobs, diminished software development, increased prices, and stymied innovation) are most likely in the many billions of dollars per year. The risks associated with using pirated software include:

- Incomplete or defective programs
- No written manuals or other documentation
- Virus infections
- No warranty protection
- No upgrade options
- No customer support
- Personal and company liability resulting from copyright violations

The Business Software Alliance (BSA) (www.bsa.org), an anti-piracy group established in 1988 that spans 65 countries and is comprised of some of the largest software manufacturers, estimates that nearly two million Web pages contain links to pirated software. They also estimate that over 60 percent of all software sold over the Internet is counterfeit, and that more than 90 percent is being sold in violation of the manufacturers' licensing agreements. The problem is global in scope and nowhere near being resolved.

Pirated?

Pirated software is easily passed off as legitimate, and end users are often are tricked into buying the "heavily discounted" software. This software may look real but it often lacks manuals and technical support (see Figure B.1).

Figure B.1 Piracy, Direct to Your E-mail

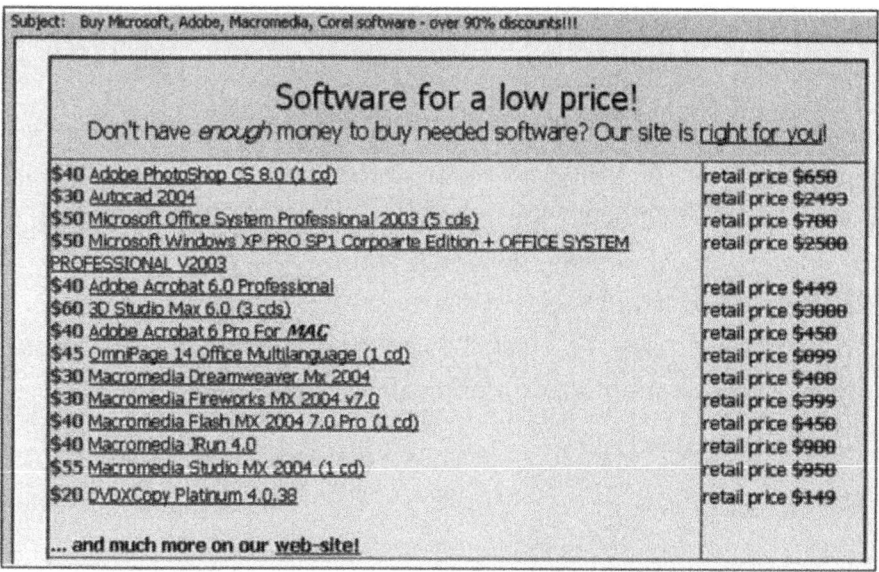

Often called Original Equipment Manufacturer (OEM) software (although OEM software legally cannot be resold), pirated software is becoming a favorite commodity on the black market because of the large profit margin involved. In 2001, a Microsoft warehouse was broken into, which held millions of copies of Microsoft software worth millions of dollars on the black market. However, the thieves did not touch any of the software. Instead, they stole millions of "CERTIFIED PRODUCT" holographic stickers and product authenticity certificates, which are used to verify the authenticity of a Microsoft software package. Thieves can easily copy a CD, but only high tech operations can preprint the holograms. These product stickers and certificates are the worth more than the boxed software on the black market.

PIRACY FACT…

Microsoft offers an online service you can use to verify the legitimacy of any Microsoft Windows products (*www.microsoft.com/resources/ howtotell/uk/windows/default.mspx*). The site uses an online ActiveX control to check the product key of any Windows installation.

The site also has key information that can be used to verify the legitimacy of the holograms and the CD covers of most Microsoft products.

Recipients of pirated software usually find out that they bought into a scam when they contact Microsoft looking for support or trying to upgrade their software. Software products are often identified through a CDKEY or serial number, each of which is unique and identifies the owner of the product and the type of license that accompanies it. Although pirated software may install and function correctly, Microsoft will eventually notice the many different users with the same serial number.

PIRACY FACT...

Because the piracy of Microsoft products has become so huge, the software giant has launched a new campaign in the UK targeted at helping the millions of users who purchased pirated copies of Windows XP. With the launch of Windows SP2, new Microsoft policy inhibits known pirated serial numbers from being used to upgrade a copy of Windows. Leaving end users without the ability to fix critical security problems causes a lot of frustration, especially when the user is unaware that the software they purchased was pirated.

Microsoft's new campaign gives anyone who bought a copy of a pirated Microsoft Windows product the ability to swap it for a free, licensed copy.

Another common piracy practice is selling new computers with copies of Windows or Office "pre-installed." Computer companies attempt to save money by selling pre-activated copies of Microsoft products, even though they don't have a valid Microsoft license. Eventually, however, everyone who uses pre-installed software will find out that they lack support and the ability to upgrade.

PIRACY FACT...

Microsoft has developed a licensing system known as Windows Product Activation (WPA), which is a private/public-based key exchange system, where clients unlock his or her copy of Windows by entering a corresponding code, thereby ensuring that each license is unique and legitimate.

When installing Windows, clients are asked to enter a unique CDKEY (often called a "Product Key") found on the CD jewel case. The product key itself varies. If the user enters a Volume License Key (VLK), Windows activation is not required after installation. VLKs (often called "Pre-Activated Keys") are commonly sold to large corporations that do not want to deal with product activation. However, these keys are often leaked on the Internet and used when counterfeiting Windows or pre-loading computers with Microsoft products.

> Retail copies of Windows products come with a different type of key, and require the user to activate the product within 30 days of installation.
>
> WPA was the first instance of a large corporation using the Internet for license authentication, and although the system works for many home users, it still has flaws.

Often, those who buy pirated software have no knowledge that they did so. Naivety is a very exploitable attribute of human nature and our lust for buying something at the lowest possible price can turn into a legal and ethical dilemma for many.

Cost or Availability

Cost is often the main reason why software is pirated. From hardware to software, the Information Technology (IT) industry is never cheap, especially when it comes to niche software.

A friend of mine was studying for a PhD in organic chemistry. In order to write his thesis he needed a specialized piece of software that the university didn't own. Without this software, his thesis would be greatly lacking. Even so, the university refused to buy a copy.

My friend told me that the software cost over $9,000 dollars for a student license. To make matters worse, the company did not provide a trial version. Because my friend only needed to use the software once or twice, a demo version would have sufficed. Luckily, he was able to contact someone who had a copy of the software and who was willing to send him a copy. He told me afterward that he would have bought it if he could have afforded it.

Piracy as an alternative to purchase was created through a simple "cause and effect" process; the price of software is often too high for the individual, so the software is pirated. If the software sold for a much lower price, would piracy still exist?

An interesting case for this argument can be seen in the recent launch of iTunes and other Digital Rights Management (DRM) online music stores. For less than a dollar, you can download a favorite track from any album or the entire album for under $10.00. Reduced prices appeal to the end users. Many would rather spend $1.00 up front than 30 minutes of their time hunting the Internet for a high-quality version. The time that my friend invested looking for a copy of the chemistry-specific software cost him three full days of work. If the software had cost only $100.00, he would have bought it, because the time involved was worth more to him.

According to a recent study by the BSA, the 13 to 18-year-old age group contains the highest percentage of pirates, with 90 percent of teenagers preferring to pirate digital media rather than purchase it. A lack of financial independence is the driving factor for why teens pirate digital media.

Similar statistics and trends are seen when comparing countries that pirate digital media. Macedonia has the highest percentage of pirated Microsoft products currently used. Only 8,000 licensed copies of Windows exist in the entire country, but there are over 100,000 computers running Microsoft products.

In the majority of cases, computers have to run Microsoft products for interoperability between applications and technology. However, when the price of Office XP costs the average Macedonian two months salary, it is much easier to pay street merchants $1.50/USD for a copy. Piracy is so huge in Macedonia that an estimated 1.5 percent of the country's Gross Domestic Product (GDP) is derived from piracy.

PIRACY FACT...

Recently, Microsoft announced the availability of a reduced price, cut-down version of Windows XP for third-world nations. However, unlike the normal version of Windows XP, the new "Windows Starter Edition" does not contain any local networking support and can only run three applications simultaneously. This software initiative only reinforces the fully functional $1.50 pirated copy.

Many Computer-Aided Design (CAD), Computer-Aided Milling (CAM), and encryption-enabled software is not legally allowed to be sold anywhere but in America. Many third-world countries are rejected when they try to buy software that contains a strong or un-exportable encryption routine or technology that is unique to America. In a case like this, piracy is the only way to get the software.

Notes from the Underground…

Piracy Example

You run a company in Serbia that designs road signs for the government. You recently bought a new "RoadSign Painter 3000" and need a certain piece of software in order to interface with your new automatic painting machine. You contact an American-based software company that provides interfacing software for sign painters, get a quote for a license, and agree on the price. However, you are then told that because you live in a third-world nation and encryption cannot be legally exported to your country, the company cannot sell you the software.

Because of where you live, you were denied the right to buy the software. Persecuted by your geographical location and your country's economic status, obtaining a pirated copy of the software is now your only option.

PIRACY FACT…

In many cases, piracy groups in third-world nations act more as software distributors than as pirates. Focused on obtaining western software that cannot be sold in other countries, the groups first remove the copy protections and then mass-duplicate the often high-end, specialized software.

Drink Or Die (DOD) is a great example of this. This group was originally founded in Russia. The group focused mainly on CAD, CAM, and Computer Aided Engineering (CAE) software packages often worth tens of thousands of dollars each. Software companies were either not allowed to sell to Russia, or were unable to handle the foreign financial transaction. Russian companies either had to develop their own applications in-house, or live without.

DOD members found ways of obtaining American applications and then distributed them around Russia, giving many people the only chance they had of getting a particular piece of software.

Curiosity

Many people are naturally curious and Internet technologies open the possibility for obtaining strange digital media. From music to TV episodes, the Internet allows us to trade practically any information we want. One site that shows a good example of the amount of media pirated daily is *www.nforce.nl*, a Netherlands-based Web site that offers a searchable database of Info Files (NFOs). (See Figure B.2)

PIRACY FACT...

NFOs are text files that contain descriptions about the media. If the NFO is for software, you will probably find product installation notes such as CDKEYS or serial numbers, in this text file.

Figure B.2 A Visual Feast of Possible Avenues for Curious Minds

DATE	SECTION	RELEASE NAME	GROUP	SIZE	VOTE
2004-12-29	DVD-R	Cellular (2004) *NTSC*	CORRUPT	93x50 MB	5.3
2004-12-28	TV-Rips	King Of The Hill S03D03 *DVDR*	VDVA	92x50 MB	.
2004-12-28	XXX	Infirmieres A Lunettes French Prod (c) Lycy Video *DVDRiP* *XViD*	RECTAL	49x15 MB	.
2004-12-28	XviD	Trois The Escort (2004) *DVDRiP* *STV*	PROMISE	49x15 MB	.
2004-12-28	XviD	Cellular (2004) *DVDRiP* *REPACK*	KJS	49x15 MB	6.7
2004-12-28	VCD	Fat Albert (2004) *TS*	POT	63x15 MB	6.0
2004-12-28	XXX	Sperm Smiles (c) Platinum-X *DVDRiP* *VCD*	PORNOLATION	89x15 MB	.
2004-12-28	XviD	The Silver City (2004) *DVDRiP* *LIMITED*	ALLIANCE	98x15 MB	7.3
2004-12-28	XXX	Hot Latin Pussy Adventures 37 (c) TTB-Productions *DVDRiP* *DiVX*	PRONSTARS	98x15 MB	.
2004-12-28	PlayStation 2	Fullmetal Alchemist and the Broken Angel (c) Square Enix *NTSC* *FULLDVD*	MORRIGAN	32x50 MB	.
2004-12-28	PC App ISOs	ABSynth v3.0 VSTi DXi RTAS AU *ISO* (c) Native Instruments	SPIRIT	34x15 MB	.
2004-12-28	SVCD	Silver City 2004 *WS* *DVDRiP* *LIMITED*	XPD	162x15 MB	.
2004-12-28	XviD	Anything But Love (2002) *DVDRiP* *LIMITED* *REPACK*	FICO	50x15 MB	5.6
2004-12-28	XviD	Friday Night Lights (2004) *DVDSCREENER*	THEFLY	50x15 MB	6.6
2004-12-28	PC Game ISOs	American Chopper (c) Activision Value	VENGEANCE	206x15 MB	5.3
2004-12-28	XviD	Kinsey (2004) *DVDSCREENER* *LIMITED*	THEFLY	50x15 MB	8.5
2004-12-28	XviD	The Life Aquatic with Steve Zissou (2004) *DVDSCREENER* *LIMITED*	THEFLY	50x15 MB	8.4

Sometimes a gamer knows or suspects that a certain game is not worth $30.00. The last two games in the series were not up to his standards and he does not wish to spend money on the game. However, he is still curious about the game and would like to try it. There is no way to evaluate whether or not the game is worth buying because the company did not provide a demo. Publishers release demo versions of most games, but it can take months to produce, meaning gamers have to wait long periods.

Piracy Fact...

Gamers are some of the most prolific pirates on the Internet. A study released by Macrovision (developers of SafeDisc, an anti-piracy software toolkit) showed that 52 percent of gamers have admitted to downloading pirated games from the Internet, the highest amount of any Internet user demographic.

Out of the 52 percent who download games, 33 percent reported downloading International Organization for Standardization (ISO) images (full CD "clones") with the copy protection bypassed, often before the official retail date.

Gamers have to be careful when buying new PC games. In 2004, there were over 200 large PC games released. If a gamer bought 50 percent of the games released each year, he would be paying over $5,000. Ever-growing amounts of games are also of low quality, often lacking depth or plagued with bugs. Gamers have learned to be careful when choosing new video games and tend to be very cautious before handing over their cash. Large amounts of gamers prefer to download a pirated copy of a game first, play it for a few days, and then decide if they want it. If they do find some value in it, more often than not, they pay for it.

Pirates may get all the games for free, but pirated games often lack functionality. One common trick game publishers use is for each unique game to require a CDKEY to play online or in multi-player games. Without the unique CDKEY you are limited to a single player. The method of forcing those who enjoy the game to buy it seems to be highly effective, and many game companies have adopted the practice of online key authentication.

Another downfall of playing pirated PC games is the ability to update the game. Often, newly released games have "urgent" updates that fix critical problems. Each new update must have the copy protection removed before it will function without the retail CD. Because it requires extra effort to find an updated copy with the protection removed, it is often easier to buy it.

PIRACY FACT...

The most common phrase in any NFO file from a pirated game is "Support the software companies. If you play this game BUY it."

Pirates actively encourage fans of the games to buy the games. Sure, be curious and try the pirated copy, but if you enjoy it, BUY IT. Without the support of gamers, game companies will not continue to produce high-quality games.

Although piracy is often fueled by curiosity, the effect on the software industry is not all negative. I conducted a small research experiment with 50 people who admitted to regularly downloading pirated material. Out of the 50 people interviewed, 40 admitted to annually buying at least two products they had previously downloaded. When asked why they bought the product instead of continuing to use the pirated copy, the majority replied, "To support the company that made it" or "To get support and updates." The remaining 10 people use pirated products only and refuse to spend money on legitimate products. When these people were asked why they refused to buy digital products their replies ranged from "The cost is too great" to "piracy is my life, I mean, why spend money if I can have it for free?"

It is all too easy to blanket pirates as common thieves; however, in many cases a product is pirated only as a means of verifying a product's worth. When their curiosity is fulfilled and they are sure of the game, more often than not the product is purchased.

Corporate Piracy

Making the right decision can be harder than it sounds when money is involved. If a company buys a software license for one employee and installs it companywide, the terms of the license have been broken. Piracy is piracy; if you buy a single user license and install it on two computers, you are just as guilty of using pirated software as the teenager who downloads a copy from the Internet.

Many companies face the challenge of trying to control and educate their employees about piracy, thereby limiting possible license infringements. It is impossible to stop Fred from asking Joe if he can borrow the Microsoft .Net Studio CD the company just bought him. Many people never give a second thought to lending CDs to fellow employees because somehow it doesn't seem illegal or unethical.

PIRACY FACT...

A 2004 study undertaken by the BSA found that although 90 percent of corporations agreed that software piracy is a risk "no business can afford to take," 23 percent of corporations can name a piece of pirated software currently running on their network.

Intentions are not always innocent. Last year, I was contracted to write some software for a local Internet Service Provider (ISP). After meeting with the ISP it was decided that I would work on site and they would provide me a computer to use.

After working there for one day, I figured out that every piece of software used in the company was pirated. The technician in charge of desktop support told me that they save enough money through piracy to take the entire company on holiday every year. I was shocked. Not only was the company pirating software, they were outwardly boasting about it. Apparently, the only licensed software was Windows 95, but the technician was not sure that it was not pirated.

Another thing I found out was that no one in the company except the IT team and the Chief Executive Officer (CEO) knew about the piracy epidemic. All of the other employees honestly thought that the software was purchased. The ISP even used "Software Request" forms and made employees seek approval from their managers before software was "purchased."

Perhaps the most unethical form of piracy, by cutting simple financial corners and attempting to save money, this ISP has placed themselves in huge danger and face serious legal consequences if caught.

PIRACY TIP...

If you are concerned that a company you work for is using pirated software you can report their activity discreetly and anonymously to the BSA at *www.bsa.org/usa/report/Reporting-Form.cfm*.

Software piracy fines are huge and catching software pirates is becoming a booming business. Anti-piracy activists such as the BSA are funded almost entirely from the lawsuits they issue to corporations that infringe on license and intellectual property agreements. AutoDesk's (makers of commercial design software) anti-piracy activities have generated over 63 million dollars since they began in 1989, the majority of it stemming from out-of-court settlements from companies that abuse their product licenses.

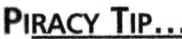

PIRACY TIP...

The fines for software piracy can cost up to $150,000 per offense; however, more often than not the company or IT manager is held directly responsible for the actions of all employees.

With the risks being so high, corporations are learning to play legally when it comes to obeying license restrictions, and the majority of piracy cases are often due to poor auditing rather than malicious intent.

Appendix C

Hazards, Solutions, and Tools

Solutions in this chapter:

- Cyber Pests
- Pornography
- Erroneous, Mislabeled, and Incomplete Files
- Product Defects
- System Recovery
- Language/Translation
- Disc Backups

Introduction

Software pirates face the same hazards as everyone else when surfing the Internet. However, they are at much greater risk if for no other reason than the sites they visit tend to harbor a disproportionately greater number of viruses and other threats. Though mainly interested in obtaining illicit software, pirates are typically sophisticated computer users. They anticipate unpleasant surprises and take the appropriate precautions.

This chapter discusses the ever-present dangers and what pirates do to protect their computers and their sanity.

Cyber Pests

There are all kinds of nasty pests in cyberspace, which are grouped under the "malicious software" (malware) heading. These pests are designed to annoy you, damage your computer, or both. Viruses, spyware, Trojans, worms, browser hijackers, scumware, and other cyber vermin are posed to attack, and can wreak havoc on your computer and your patience if you are not prepared. The risk of contracting malware goes way up, particularly when navigating to some of the "less savory" sites. However, there are specialized programs that can help prevent these attacks, and many of them are free.

The sites that cater to software piracy probably harbor the most viruses and spyware than other sites. Therefore, it is extremely important to have effective, up-to-date antivirus and spyware protection.

The following sections provide brief descriptions of some of the hazards that everyone (including pirates) encounters on the Internet.

Viruses

A virus is a harmful program or piece of code that is loaded onto your computer without your knowledge. Harmful effects range from crashing the computer, to altering data, to erasing the hard drive. Viruses can be contracted in many ways, but are most commonly picked up when installing downloaded code or opening e-mail attachments. Viruses often replicate themselves and are usually designed to spread from one machine to another.

As every online user knows, the number of computer viruses on the Internet has reached epic proportions. This isn't just something you hear about on the news; computer viruses are numerous and real.

Antivirus Programs

Fortunately, there are excellent antivirus programs from companies like Symantec, McAfee, and Grisoft, which guard against these threats. Some of these companies even offer free versions of their premium products, which are very effective. (See Figure C.1.) Among these, Grisoft's AVG software (*www.grisoft.com*) is arguably one of the best. The pay version has more bells and whistles, but it is hard to find fault with the free version. As with all such programs, virus definitions are updated frequently, therefore, it is important to keep everything current for maximum protection.

Figure C.1 Grisoft's Free Anti-virus Offer

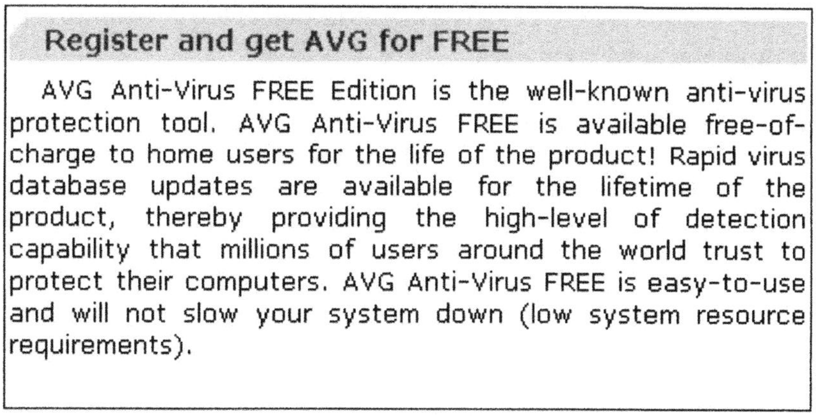

Register and get AVG for FREE

AVG Anti-Virus FREE Edition is the well-known anti-virus protection tool. AVG Anti-Virus FREE is available free-of-charge to home users for the life of the product! Rapid virus database updates are available for the lifetime of the product, thereby providing the high-level of detection capability that millions of users around the world trust to protect their computers. AVG Anti-Virus FREE is easy-to-use and will not slow your system down (low system resource requirements).

A free online virus scan can also be found at *www.mcafee.com*. (See Figure C.2.)

Figure C.2 McAfee Free Offer

FreeScan - Based on the Award-Winning McAfee VirusScan Engine
FreeScan is a FREE service that helps you detect thousands of viruses on your computer. Based on the award-winning McAfee VirusScan engine, FreeScan searches for viruses, including the latest known "in the wild" viruses, and displays a detailed list of any infected files. More

 SCAN NOW

Spyware

Sometimes called a "data miner," spyware is malicious software that gathers information about a user's surfing habits and Internet activities without their knowledge, and shares that information with interested parties. Running in the background, spyware can bog down your computer. At the very least it is an invasion of privacy. By nature, spyware is capable of collecting and transferring personal information such as e-mail addresses, usernames, passwords, and credit card numbers. Although often associated with adware, spyware can be contracted from nearly any type of Web site, and must be removed.

Anti-spyware Programs

Just as there are specialized programs for removing viruses, there are specialized programs for removing spyware. Different users swear by different programs, but unquestionably one of the most popular is Ad-Aware by Lavasoft (*www.lavasoftusa.com*). (See Figure C.3.) The free edition is worth having, but the pay version includes Ad-Watch. Running in the background, Ad-Watch is a real-time spyware detection program that prevents malware from being installed. Spyware definitions are updated frequently; therefore, it is very important to keep current.

Figure C.3 Ad-Adware Personal Anti-spyware Program

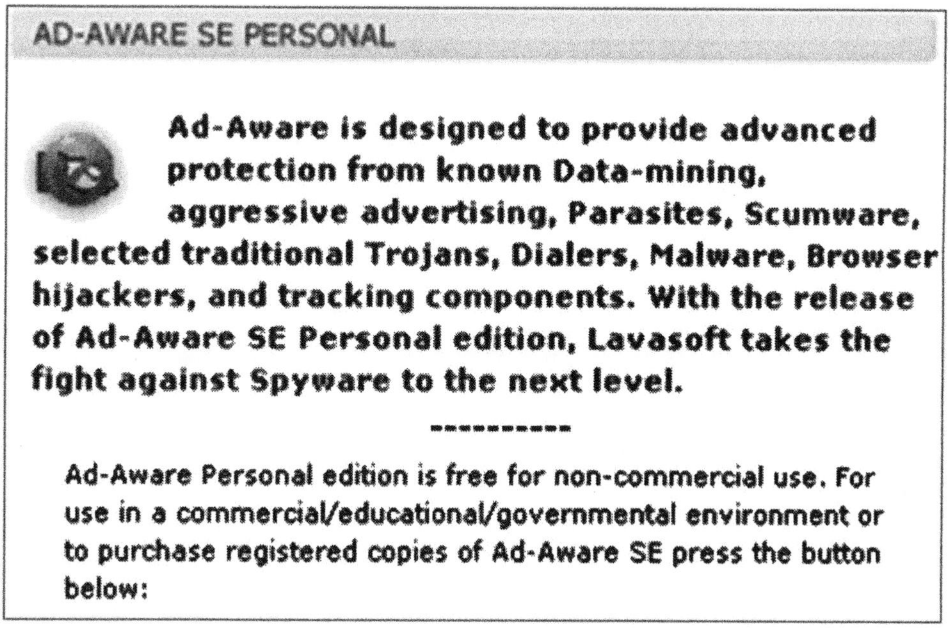

> ## AD-AWARE SE PERSONAL
>
> **Ad-Aware is designed to provide advanced protection from known Data-mining, aggressive advertising, Parasites, Scumware, selected traditional Trojans, Dialers, Malware, Browser hijackers, and tracking components. With the release of Ad-Aware SE Personal edition, Lavasoft takes the fight against Spyware to the next level.**
>
> ----------
>
> Ad-Aware Personal edition is free for non-commercial use. For use in a commercial/educational/governmental environment or to purchase registered copies of Ad-Aware SE press the button below:

Hackers

Just because they steal software doesn't mean that software pirates are any more immune from hackers than anyone else. To the contrary, the longer you are online the more you are at risk, and having a high-speed connection that is always on only exacerbates the problem. Being on the Internet is like being on a worldwide party line; your computer can communicate with everyone on the Internet, and everyone on the Internet can communicate with your computer, sometimes without you knowing about it. It is important to have a firewall to guard against intruders.

Firewalls

The basic function of a firewall is to control access between a computer or a computer network and the Internet. Essentially, it is a mini security system that grants access to the programs you choose, and restricts access to everything else. It inspects all incoming traffic before it is seen by any programs and blocks unsolicited data from getting through. It is always a good idea to employ a firewall to prevent hackers from gaining access, especially with an always on, high-speed connection,

The free version of ZoneAlarm from Zone Labs is an excellent program that can be downloaded from their Web site (*www.zonelabs.com*). There is a built-in firewall incorporated into Windows XP, but it does not have all the features of many third-party programs. (See Figure C.4.)

Figure C.4 Free ZoneAlarm Firewall Offer

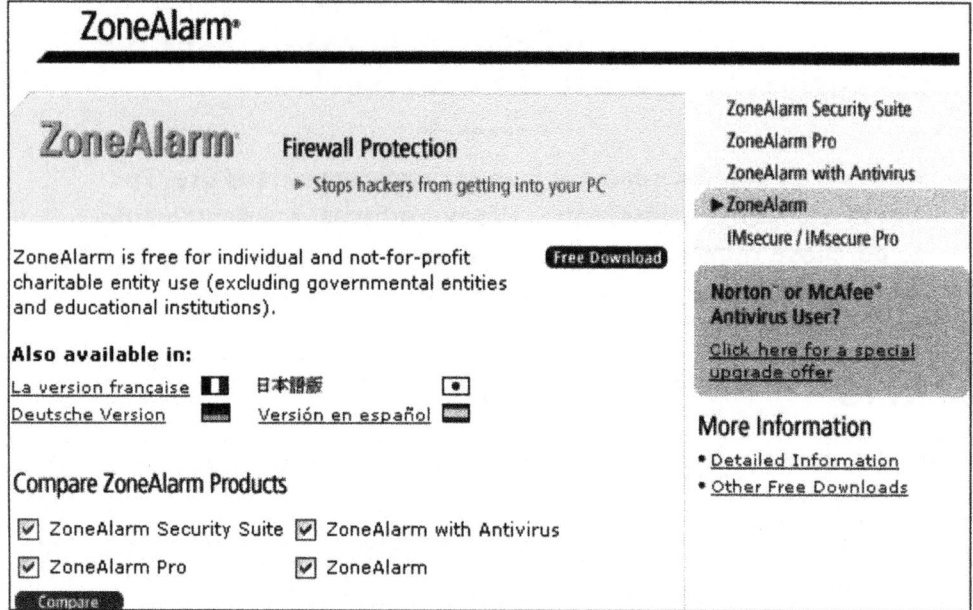

Although pay versions of antivirus, anti-spyware, and firewalls are well worth their price, the free versions will probably suffice for most users. There is no excuse for not having these essential programs running on your computer.

Browser Hijackers

As one of the more insidious forms of spyware, a browser hijacker (sometimes called a "browser parasite") can change a browser's start page, add new favorites or bookmarks, place new icons on the desktop, insert a new search bar, and even "brand" a new name onto the browser's title bar. Exploiting security holes, these programs can be particularly difficult to remove, and often return upon boot-up. Fortunately, antivirus and anti-spyware programs are usually successful in containing these pests.

Dialers

As destructive and insidious as viruses and spyware are, a dialer not only infests your computer, but also inflates your telephone bill. A dialer is an unwanted program that is loaded onto your computer (usually without your knowledge), which then proceeds to dial a number without your permission. Called *modem hijacking*, you can bet that it is not calling a local number. Dialers are often picked up from warez and pornography sites, or from being redirected from another site. Some dialers may cause your connection to be dropped while surfing, and then reconnect through a new number. Other dialers may connect when you are not even using the computer. You probably will not have a clue to what is going on until the phone bill arrives. Maybe you will get lucky and have the charges removed, but at best, it is bound to be a hassle.

Trying to remove the dialer along with any extra desktop icons and favorites it might have planted, may be a bigger pain than dealing with the phone company. Dialers are designed to be difficult to detect and remove, and their elimination is often beyond the ability of the typical computer user. There are specialized programs that can help, but no one should have to struggle to remove stuff that should never have been installed.

As a preventative measure, it is not a bad idea to physically disconnect the modem from the phone line when it is not being used, which also has the added benefit of protecting the computer from lightening-related damage. If you do not want to keep disconnecting and reconnecting the phone line and want additional protection, an Australian company called *stop-IT-now* (*www.stopitnow.com.au*) sells a software program for around $20.00 that prevents unauthorized numbers from being dialed. Antivirus and anti-spyware programs can usually remove this parasite. (See Figure C.5.)

Figure C.5 StopITNow

Pop-ups

We have all seen them, those aggravating pop-up screens that seem to appear out of nowhere. Compared to dialers, viruses, and spyware, pop-ups are child's play, but they are still very annoying. That is especially true if you land on a site that tries to open multiple pop-ups until the computer crashes. Rest assured, crack sites are no exception. Sites hosting pornography and pirated software seem to have many times the number of pop-ups than are encountered elsewhere. Eliminating pop-ups or reducing their number is something every computer user needs to do.

Fortunately, there are a couple of easy solutions for taming the pop-up problem. One solution is to install pop-up blocker software. There are several to choose from, but I recommend the highly effective and easy-to-use *Pop-Up Stopper* by Panicware (*www.panicware.com*). (See Figure C.6.)

Figure C.6 Panicware's Pop-Up Stopper

Other Browsers

Some users still surf the Internet using the programs that came installed on their computer, because they do not realize that there are alternatives. The following paragraphs look at some of these alternatives.

Internet Explorer-based Free Browsers

The following six browsers all use Internet Explorer as a core component and feature a tabbed operation, which permits faster and easier surfing. They all have numerous options to customize appearance and operation, and contain very effective built-in pop-up stoppers. The following three browsers (Figure C.7, C.8, and C.9) are all excellent and free.

Figure C.7 Avant Browser *www.avantbrowser.com*

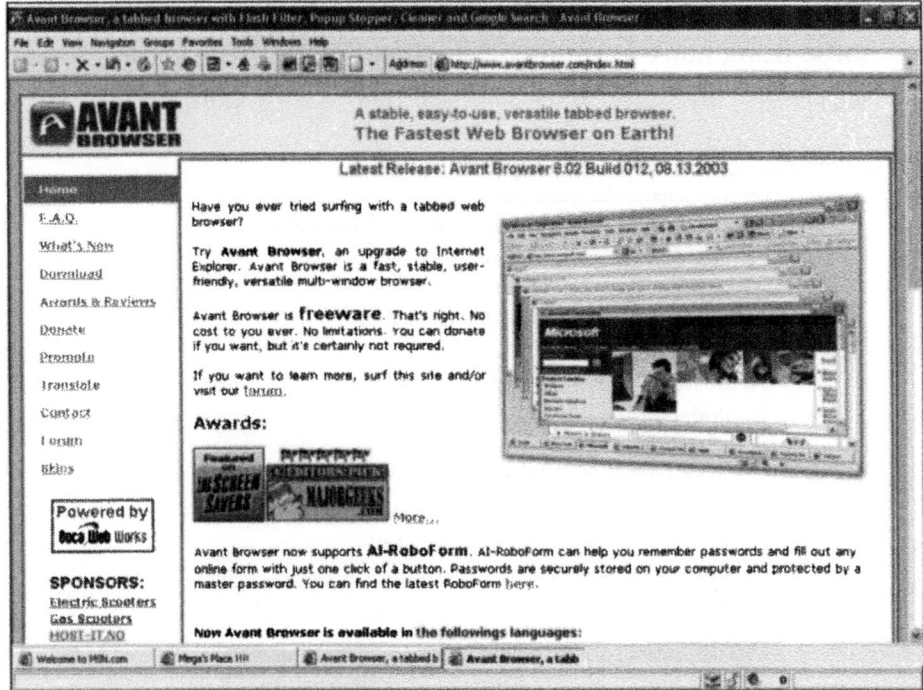

This browser is as good as the others and is constantly being improved.

Figure C.8 Maxthon *www.maxthon.com*

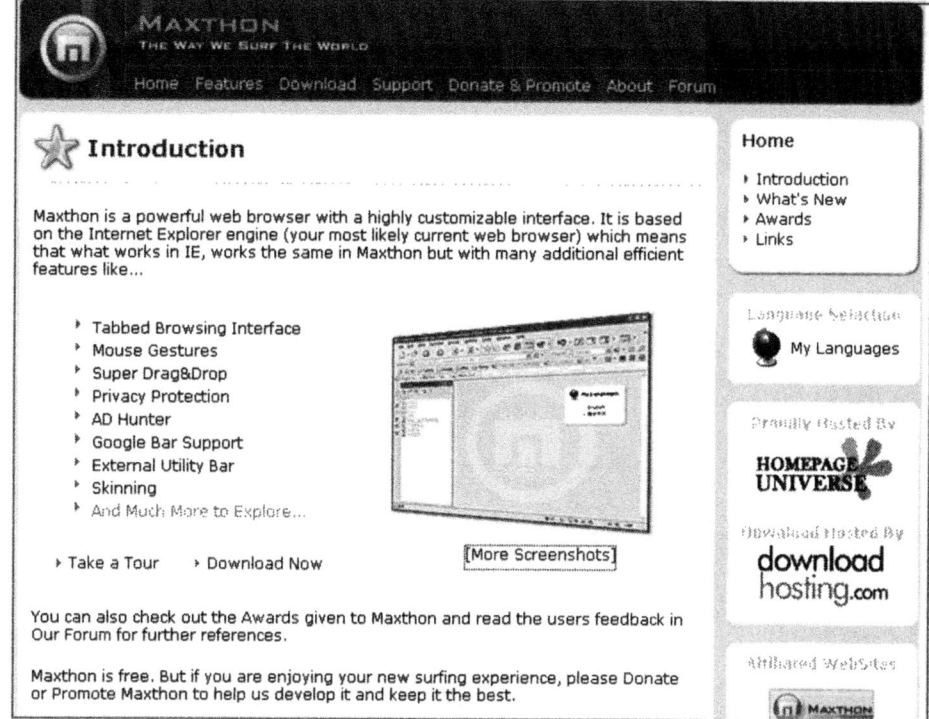

Formerly called MyIE2, this is another excellent free browser that is frequently updated.

Figure C.9 Crazy Browser *www.crazybrowser.com*

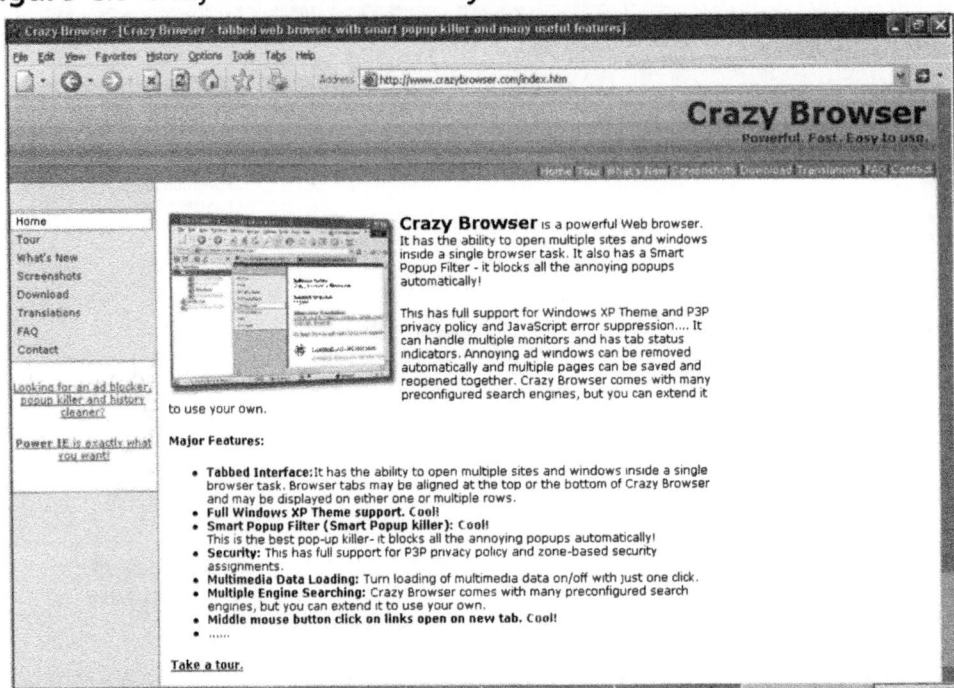

Internet Explorer-based Pay Browsers

There are several other browsers, such as NetCaptor, Fast Brower, and Smart Explorer, which offer features that are similar to the free browsers, but that sell for between $20.00 and $30.00. They all claim to be "faster" or "better" than the others.

Internet Explorer-based Pay Browsers

The following two browsers, Opera and Firefox, do not use Internet Explorer as their core component. For that reason alone, these browsers offer enhanced security against hackers. Because Internet Explorer is the most commonly used browser, it is also the number one target of those trying to exploit its weaknesses and disrupt its users. However, even if you do not select one of these as your default browser, it is a good idea to have one installed that will work if Internet Explorer becomes corrupted and will not function.

There are several other excellent browsers that are not listed here, so feel free to search further. Basically, all browsers do the same thing; it really comes down to personal preference.

Opera is free and comes with an ad banner. Paying a modest registration fee will remove the banner. (See Figure C.10.)

Figure C.10 Opera *www.opera.com*

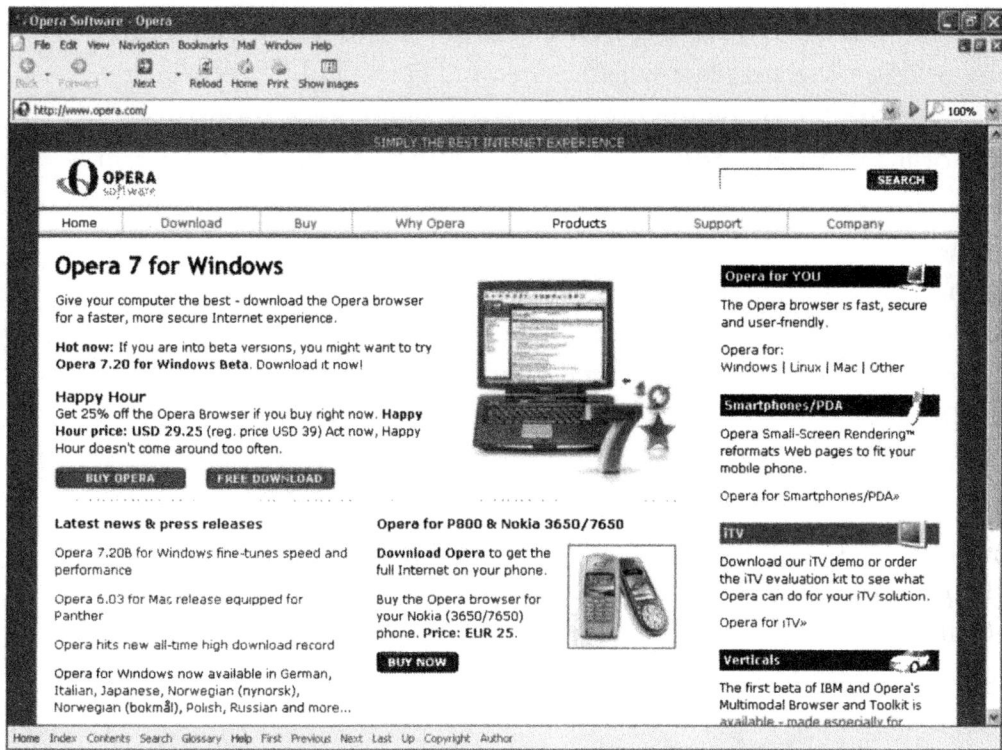

Pornography

Software pirates are more prone to encounter unwanted pornography than most people, because a lot of the sites that host pirated software contain pornographic advertisements.

Sites that are known to have pornographic advertisements are marked as such; however, hosting sites and advertisements can change without notice, and following unknown links can subject people to offensive material. Even if you have Net Nanny or another parent-friendly filtering software installed, there is no guarantee that sexually oriented material will not get through.

Erroneous, Mislabeled, and Incomplete Files

A pirate's life is full of risks and frustrations. Aside from the normal hazards, pirates frequently have to contend with downloading incomplete or nonworking programs. For whatever reason, crack and peer-to-peer (P2P) sites are full of erroneous information and corrupt downloads; some of it intentional. Some people believe that fooling, tricking, and screwing software pirates is their mission in life. In any case, it is not unusual for a pirate to spend considerable time searching and downloading a new program only to find that the download is corrupt and will not install, it is in a different language, it needs a password to unlock, it is an older version, or it is a totally different program.

After seeing all of the hazards and annoyances that confront pirates, I am amazed that anyone would go through all of it just to obtain a free program. However, as already discussed, a good deal of piracy isn't prompted by the desire to get something for nothing. They do not try to obtain the program because they want to use it. It is the challenge of "beating the system," it is their hobby, and as such, overcoming obstacles is part of the game.

Product Defects

Honest mistakes happen. Consequently, it pays to be cautious before rushing to install the "latest and greatest" programs and major upgrades.

We are all familiar when a manufacturer recalls cars, tires, toys, foods, medicines, and other products. Sometimes the flaws are minor and easily corrected, and sometimes they are more serious. Sometimes the recalls are voluntary, and sometimes they are mandated by a government agency. The computer/software industry is not immune from flaws either. Remember Intel's Pentium fiasco in December 1994? It was widely publicized that the newly introduced processor had a flaw that could generate erroneous results. And, although the problem went unnoticed by most, it was a big enough problem that Intel instituted a free replacement program.

Microsoft operating systems have a Windows Update feature built in because there have been dozens of "critical updates" ever since Windows XP was introduced in the fall of 2001. The majority of these updates are needed to patch security flaws. Not included are numerous so-called non-critical Windows and driver updates.

When the Nero Burning read-only (ROM) software came out with a major upgrade from 5.0 to 6.0, it was reported to contain a major bug that could cause a computer's hard drive to be reformatted. Fortunately, a new and improved update came out a week later.

A "bug infested" upgrade of Zone Alarm's firewall program from 4.5 to 5.0 caused major headaches for numerous customers before "repaired" versions were released. Some users complained that their computers went into a constant shutdown/reboot loop, while software conflicts prevented other programs from running altogether. Other users reported that program settings were not remembered. Worse yet, many users found it difficult or impossible to completely remove the upgrade (short of reformatting their hard drive) in order to reinstall an earlier version.

Sometimes less-than-wonderful upgrades are released, even from long-established companies with solid reputations. Therefore, it is best not to be too quick to upgrade. First, read what others say about the upgrade. Sometimes it doesn't pay to be the first in line.

Be cautious when downloading and installing a higher version of a program. It is not unusual for a new program or upgrade to appear on the Web days or weeks before it is officially released. It is suggested that you visit the manufacturer's Web page to check for the most current version before downloading. It is also good to take note of file sizes. Be suspicious if a full program is only a fraction of the size it should be. All of this applies to both pirated and legitimate software.

System Recovery

It's good to have a recovery plan prepared when things go wrong. Therefore, current backups of all programs, files, and data should always be maintained. It is only a matter of *when*, not *if*, that a hard drive will fail, which would result in all of the data being lost.

Restore Programs

First implemented in Windows ME and continued with XP operating systems, System Restore permits a computer's operating state to revert to the way it was at an earlier date. Manually creating a restore point prior to downloading and installing new software greatly reduces the risk of something going wrong. Therefore, it's good to remember to set a recent restore point *before* visiting questionable sites. It is even more important to set a restore point before installing questionable software. (See Figure C.11.)

Figure C.11 System Restore

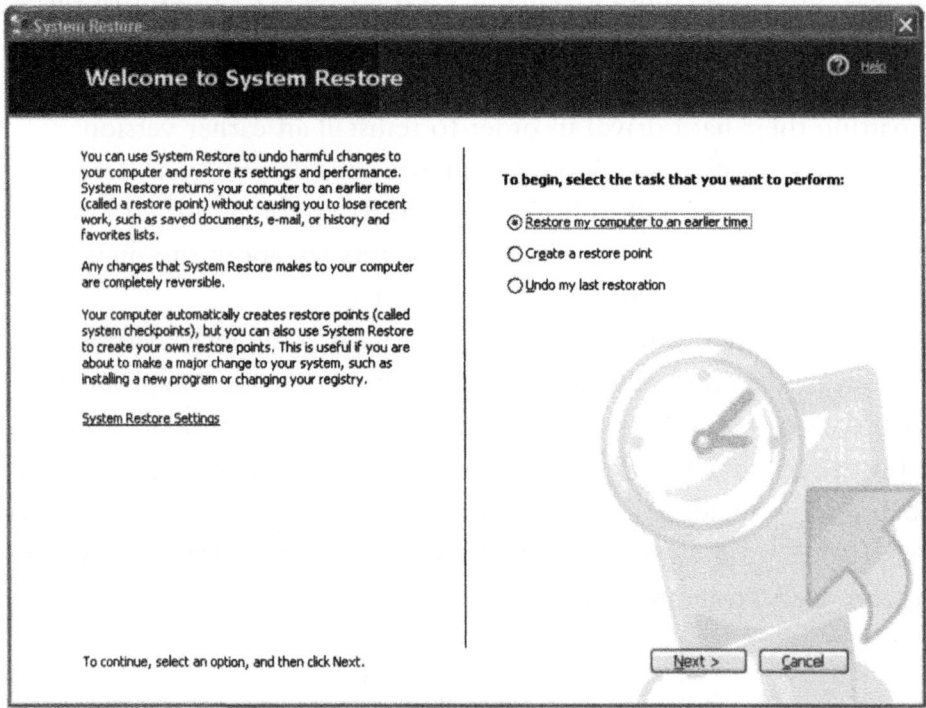

System Restore is a useful tool and very easy to use, however, it is not 100 percent reliable. A more complete tool is GoBack from Symantec (formally *GoBack* from Roxio). This rollback utility continually tracks all hard drive activity, thus permitting the computer to be restored to virtually any point in the recent past. (More complete information can be found at *www.symantec.com.*) This is a more reliable tool than System Restore, but there are disadvantages. Because every change is recorded, hard drive activity is dramatically increased, and some users think it slows things down. Depending on your surfing habits, using this or another restore or backup system might be prudent. SecurePC from FarStone (formally called RestoreIT) is another choice for a total backup utility. Complete information and a free trial may be downloaded from their Web site at *www.farstone.com.*

Keep in mind that recovery software will not do any good if the hard drive is down. Therefore, Web-based or CD backups are still necessary. There are several excellent "imaging" products available (e.g., Norton's Ghost and Drive Image) that can be used to make full backups.

Language/Translation

Because of the relaxed legal rules in other parts of the world, a lot of sources for cracked programs are located outside the U.S. Pirates do not exclude foreign sites because they are in a different language, particularly when searching for a hard-to-find program.

Although most software titles are in English (even if the site is in Russian, French, Spanish, or any other language), it is still confusing. Pirates usually don't have any idea how to download from these sites. Wading through the information to initiate a download is confusing even when you know the language; it is impossible if you don't. (See Figure C.12.)

Figure C.12 From a Chinese Site at *http://soft.ttdown.com*

The screenshot in Figure C.13 is from a Russian crack site. Figure C.14 shows what it looked like after going through Babel Fish.

Figure C.13 The Original Russian

```
ФБР ищет авторов вирусов Blaster и Sobig.F                    saint  CATEGORY: news

Американские спецслужбы активно разыскивают авторов компьютерных червей Blaster и Sobig.F, эпидемии
которых с небольшим интервалом поразили интернет в августе. Эпидемия червя Blaster сейчас несколько
спала, но зато потоки писем, заражённых Sobig.F, продолжают заваливать почтовые ящики пользователей
по всему миру. Учитывая большой ущерб, нанесенный вирусами простым пользователям и организациям, на
проведение связанных с ними расследований брошены значительные ресурсы ФБР и Министерства
внутренней безопасности США.

Что касается расследования в отношении создателей Blaster, то тут известно не слишком много
подробностей.
В случае же с Sobig.F ФБР удалось выйти на след преступников. Как оказалось, червь был запущен в
несколько порнографических конференций Usenet через сеть провайдера Easynews.com. Как удалось
установить, учетную запись у этого провайдера злоумышленники завели с использованием поддельной
кредитной карты. По словам директора ФБР Роберта Мюллера, сейчас делается все возможное, чтобы найти
преступников, инициировавших одну из самых мощных вирусных эпидемий в истории.

Впрочем, пока что правоохранительным органам редко удавалось поймать авторов распространенных
вирусов. В большинстве случаев их удавалось найти, выследив компьютер, с которого вирус был запущен
в Сеть. Именно так произошло с автором одного из первых почтовых червей Melissa Дэвидом Смитом. Автор
другого нашумевшего в свое время червя сам признался в содеянном.
Авторы же таких распространенных червей как Klez, Nimda, Tanatos и других остаются безнаказанными.

Комментировать? | Всего: 0)                                      Thursday, August 28 @
                                                                 09:43:02 EEST
```

Figure C.14 After Using Babel Fish

```
THE FBI searches for the authors of viruses Blaster and Sobig.F    saint  CATEGORY: news

American special services actively search for the authors of the computer worms Blaster and Sobig.F, whose
epidemics with the small interval struck the Internet during August. The epidemic of worm Blaster now
somewhat slept, but the flows of the letters, infected Sobig.F, they continue to fall the mailboxes of users 0 ON
throughout the world. Takeing into account the extensive damage, substituted by viruses to simple users and
organizations, to conducting of the investigations connected with them the significant resources OF THE FBI and
ministry of domestic security OF THE USA are.

As far as investigation in the attitude of creators Blaster is concerned, too not many details are here known.
However, in the case with Sobig.F OF THE FBI it was possible to leave to the track of criminals. As it proved to
be, worm was neglected into several pornographical conferences Usenet through the network of provider
Easynews.com. As it was possible to establish, criminals brought stock-taking record in this provider with the
use of a false credit map. According to Robert Mueller director FBI, now is done entire possible, so as to find
criminals, who initiated one of the most powerful virus epidemics in the history.

However, until which for the law-enforcement agencies rarely was possible to catch the authors of the extended
viruses. In the majority of their cases it was possible to find, after tracing the computer, from which the virus
was neglected into the network. Specifically, thus it occurred with author of one of the first mail worms Melissa
by David Smith. The author of another sensational in its time worm itself acknowledged in that effected.
However, the authors of such extended worms as Klez, Nimda, Tanatos and others remain unpunished.

to comment on? | in all: 0)                                     Thursday, August 28 @
                                                                09:43:02 eest
```

Disc Backups

One of the best ways to back up data is to burn it to a CD or a DVD and installing a CD or DVD burner is inexpensive and easy. Likewise, external drives are available that only have to be plugged in using their built-in Universal Serial Bus (USB) or FireWire interface. Recordable blank CDs are inexpensive, and the price of blank DVDs is decreasing. Also, name brand burning software is often included with the hardware.

Applicable laws, a program's specific licensing agreement, and the inclusion of any copyright protection software determine what can and cannot be legally copied. Many computer users may not be aware of the law or that making backups may be copyright infringement; however, users who know it's illegal make copies anyway. On the other hand, software pirates don't care about the law and have little difficulty getting around most copy protection software. Either way, burning content onto CDs or DVDs from the privacy of your home and with no Internet connection required is a pretty low risk activity.

CD/DVD Appearance

For easy organization, backup CDs and DVDs should be in cases with descriptive covers. (See CoverXP's printing software at *www.coverxp.com*.) (See Figure C.15.)

Figure C.15 CoverCD Details

created in partnership with **cdcovers.cc**, **coverxp** is a software that allows you to print your covers in seconds and in style...

cover printing has never been **so easy** or so complete, simply **drag your covers** inside the software directly from your browser and click the print icon. that's all there is to it - your new covers will be **printed in seconds**.

looking for more power? **coverxp** will let you do more, including customization or cover acquiring (with your scanner / webcam) and more). don't wait any longer - **download your free copy now**.

the free version is **unlimited** in time and uses it only displays adds while you prepare and print your covers...

Covers can be downloaded for almost all software titles and a wide variety of music CDs and video games. When covers are printed on photo-grade paper, even inexpensive Jewell cases can be made to closely resemble the original factory products.

Although CoverXP is adware, paying $20.00 more will add several features and remove the advertising banner. Another good source for downloading free case covers and disk labels can be found at *http://mega-search.net.*

One More Thing to Consider

There's one more hazard that all pirates face; namely the danger that a bootleg program will be detected by the manufacturer or a watchdog organization. Repercussions can range from benign pop-up warning messages, to the program being disabled, to receiving warning letters, and threats of lawsuits.

How someone feels about owning stolen property is a personal decision. Aside from the moral issues, the person must decide whether saving the cost of a computer program is worth going through a miniscule amount of extra anxiety.

Appendix D

Fighting Back

Solutions in this chapter:

- Blacklisting and Disguising Revisions
- Product Activation
- On-line Verification/Server Authentication
- Commercial Software Protection Systems
- Reporting Violators
- What Else Can Be Done?

Introduction

No company likes having their products stolen. Yet the reaction of some software companies makes you wonder if they care at all. Responses to piracy run the gamut from total neglect to out-and-out war. This chapter discusses the technical (non-legal) anti-piracy methods that various companies employ to fight back. Also included are some of the techniques that pirates use to circumvent a software company's countermeasures. As mentioned earlier, it's a continual cat and mouse game.

Some company security methods are rudimentary, some are overly complex, and some are just plain sneaky. Included in this chapter are some things that can be done to quickly improve the situation. However, as discussed in the following sections, such solutions entail far more than a strictly technical approach.

Blacklisting and Disguising Revisions

For programs that only require a username and password or serial number, it doesn't take long for the working registration code to be widely circulated. It also doesn't take long for the manufacturer to realize it. As a countermeasure, they sometimes blacklist a particular registration code(s) or change their password encryption scheme altogether. When that happens, the old crack no longer works with the "new" program.

If a program's code is modified in any way, it should have a new version number to distinguish it from previous versions. Sometimes revisions drastically alter a program's appearance and operation. Even if the change consists of nothing more significant than changing a comma to a semicolon in the program's help file, it's still theoretically a new version and should be indicated as such. It doesn't always happen, especially when a revision is made for the sole purpose of thwarting the pirates. Things can get very confusing when a pirated serial number that used to work with a certain version of a program no longer does.

A good illustration is Trojan Remover, a popular utility intended to detect and remove Trojan horses and Internet worms. Requiring only a serial number to remove the trial's 30-day limit, this program has been widely pirated. As with all antivirus and anti-spyware programs, periodic database updates are necessary to maintain the program's effectiveness. (The following figures illustrate old trial versions downloaded from the manufacturer's Web site at *www.simplysup.com.*) Starting with v.6.0.3, a pirated username and license key were posted on many of the crack sites. (See Figure D.1.)

Figure D.1 Pirated Username and License Key

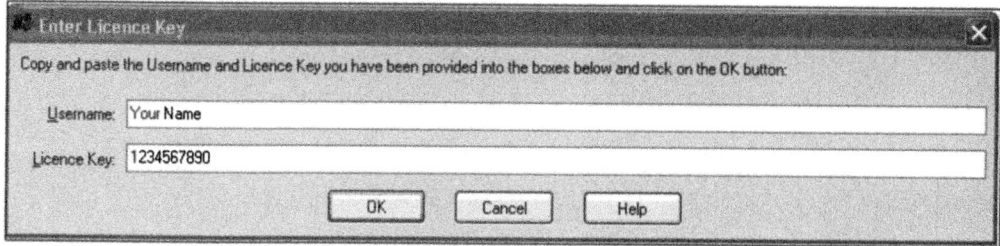

Once entered, the 30-day trial limit was removed, the program appeared to be legitimate, and database updates could be downloaded. The pirates were happy. (See Figure D.2.)

Figure D.2 Legitimized Program

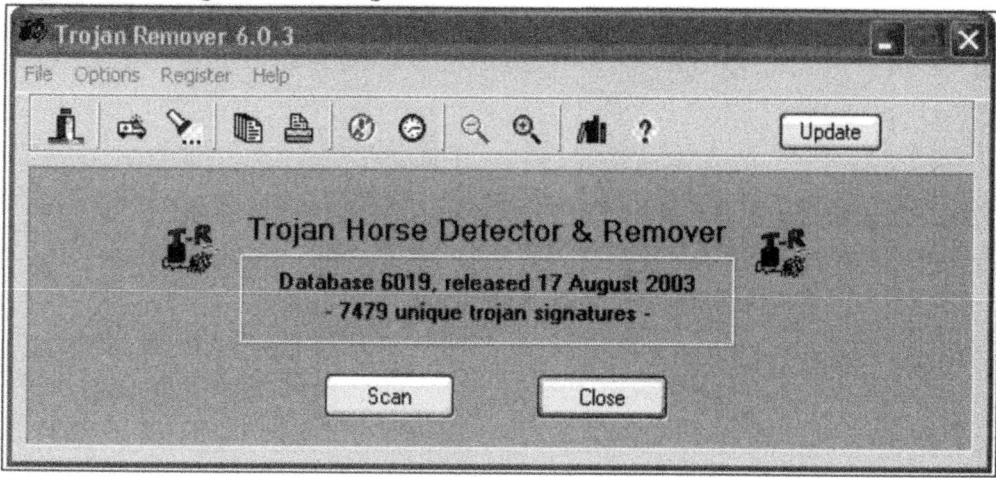

However, one day the same serial number would not work with the same downloadable trial. From numerous message board posts, it was apparent that more than a few pirates were baffled. As it turned out, the 6.0.3 code had been modified to "blacklist" the pirated serial number, while the program's version number remained the same. However, once word got around, the old v.6.0.3 began circulating and the program was again being cracked. When v.6.0.4 came out shortly thereafter, it was well publicized to download only database updates, because attempting to update the program to v.6.0.4 would cause it to revert back to a 30-day trial. The pirates were still ahead of the game. (See Figure D.3.)

Figure D.3 v.6.0.4 Update

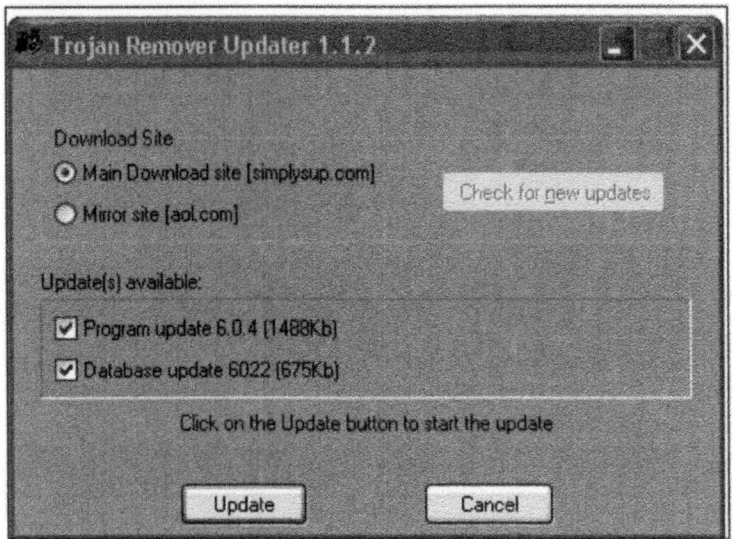

Not to be outdone, the manufacturer thwarted the pirates once again when they changed the database format to work only with v.6.0.4. When they attempted to download the database update they received the following pop-up message. (See Figure D.4.)

Figure D.4 Error Message

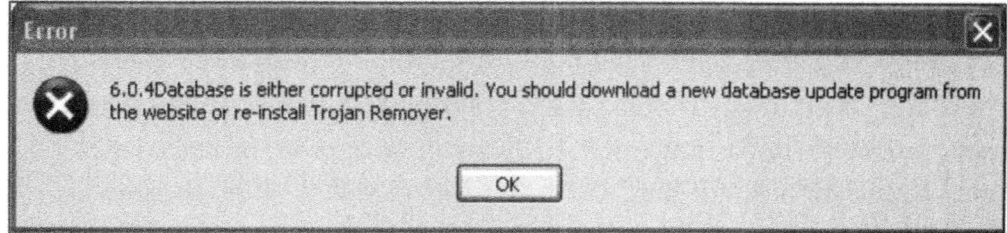

Without database updates, this program lost its effectiveness; the only recourse was to update the program to v.6.0.4. Once again, the pirates were stuck with a limited time trial. (See Figure D.5.)

Figure D.5 Unregistered Dialog Box

Crack requests for 6.0.4 immediately appeared on many of the message boards, but before a new crack appeared, a 6.0.5 version of the program was released. However, before a crack appeared, v.6.0.5 of the program was released. Whether or not that version had anything to do with security issues is unknown, but it demonstrates how the programmers were fighting back by changing data formats and blacklisting compromised serial numbers. Meanwhile, legitimate users only had to e-mail their name and address to the company to receive a new key code at no cost. There is a fine line between thwarting pirates and frustrating legitimate customers by requiring them to obtain new keys. Therefore, changes requiring new codes are done sparingly.

A few weeks later a new crack appeared for v.6.0.5. A week after that v.6.0.6 was released followed by v.6.0.7 several days later. Compromised serial numbers were again blacklisted, and the pirates found that keeping up was becoming more trouble than it was worth. So, they shifted their attention toward similar but easier-to-maintain programs, or paid the modest registration fee of $25.00. At the time of this writing, the program no longer appears to be a hot topic on the crack sites. Simply put, the creators of this program are on the ball, which illustrates how a smart company can successfully battle the pirates through determination and a minimal amount of vigilance.

Product Activation

In an attempt to reduce piracy, some manufactures have switched to a more robust form of security than just requiring a username and password, the most notorious being Microsoft's Windows Product Activation (WPA). In a nutshell, WPA is intended to restrict a program's installation to a single computer. While that requirement has always been part of Microsoft's End User Licensing Agreement (EULA), it has been largely ignored (e.g., Windows 98 and other programs could be installed on any number of machines by simply entering the identical product key code). Wholesale sharing was fast, easy, and widespread, and updates were available for free. WPA was intended to remedy that; and debuting with Windows XP, this anti-piracy technology was billed as unbeatable.

Technical Explanation

As part of WPA, an electronic data string (sometimes referred to as "hash") is generated based on the computer's unique hardware configuration that the software is installed on. That string is then used to generate an activation key that works only with that particular computer. Crosschecks are performed every time the computer is turned on. This means that if the hardware is significantly changed (e.g., adding a CD burner, extra memory, a new motherboard, and so forth), the software may cease to function. This situation would have to be explained to the software company before the program could be reactivated with a new key. Additionally, computer enthusiasts who assemble their own machines would have to obtain a new activation key if they wanted to install the operating system that they already own.

Activation, which is compulsory, should not be confused with registration, which is optional. Activation means entering the proper key before the grace period ends. If not activated, the software will stop functioning until the proper key is entered. Registration means supplying your name, address, phone number, and so forth so that the company can send information on special offers and updates.

Windows XP Pirated

As mentioned previously, no other software release was as widely anticipated as Windows XP. While both Home and Professional editions employed WPA, there was also a volume licensed version of XP Professional that did not require activation. Commonly referred to as "Corporate," and needing only a valid key code, this version was intended for companies and institutions with a large number of computers. This version became widely circulated even before XP hit the stores. Almost everyone used the same pirated key, the most infamous one beginning with "FCK." Those three letters are synonymous to software pirates.

Microsoft eventually clamped down by blacklisting the most widely used pirated keys, thus restricting upgrades and updates from their Windows Update page to legitimate users. Attempting to download a critical update (e.g., Service Pack 1 [SP-1]) to an unauthorized operating system would result in the following error message: (See Figure D.6.)

Figure D.6 Invalid Product Key Error Message

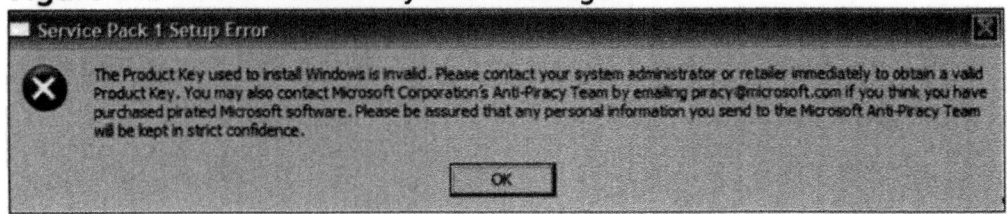

Needless to say, the struggle between Microsoft and the pirates did not end there. The pirates simply came up with methods of changing the product activation key. (See Figure D.7.)

Figure D.7 Changing a Volume Licensing Product Key

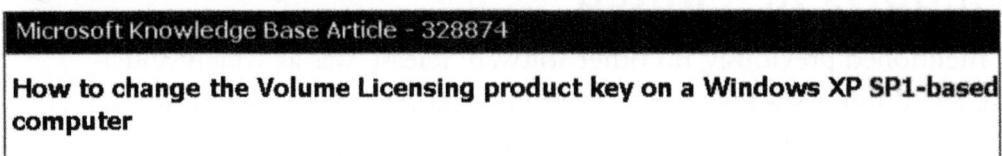

While not repeated here, Microsoft's step-by-step key-changing instructions involve a series of meticulous and risky registry changes. However, it didn't take long before several easy-to-use programs for viewing and changing product keys became widely circulated on the crack sites. New "working" keys were widely posted, and with no more than a click of the mouse, it became incredibly easy to view and change key codes. (See Figure D.8.)

Figure D.8 Changing Codes with Keyfinder

If locating valid keys wasn't good enough, a key generator soon appeared. Nicknamed the "Blue List Keygen," supposedly all one had to do was select the program's version, hit **PROCESS**, and come back later to "harvest" a crop of individualized key codes. From the chatter on the message boards, the keygen evidently worked, though many keys were reported as duds. Along with the keygen were detailed step-by-step instructions, complete with screenshots. Once the key had been success-fully changed, the operating system would appear as legitimate, and updates could once again be downloaded. (See Figure D.9.)

Figure D.9 Successful Key Change

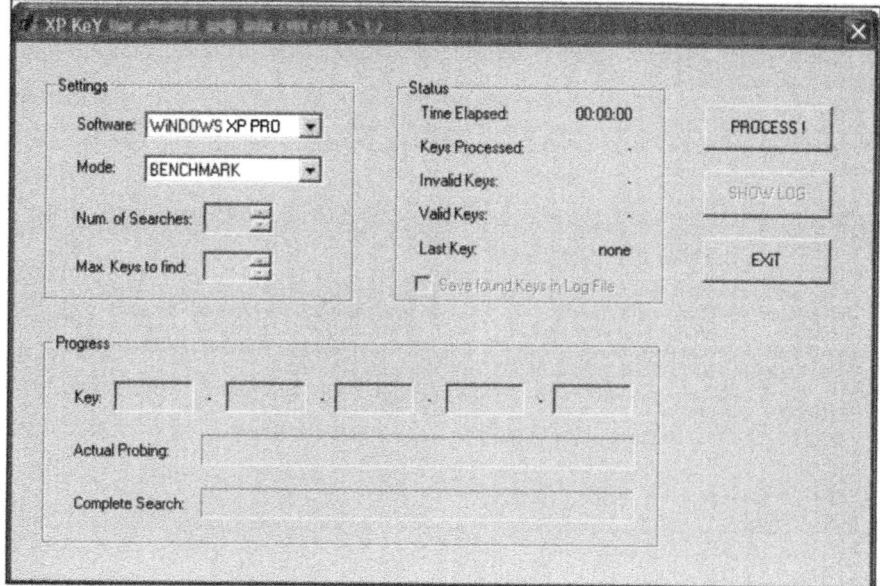

History Repeats Itself

Microsoft released its long awaited Service Pack 2 (SP-2) upgrade in August 2004. As before, it was rumored that illegitimate keys would be detected that would prevent the installation of SP-2 on pirated operating systems. Some crack sites actually alleged that illegal key detection was disabling the computers.

Whether Microsoft recognized the futility of battling the pirates or they truly wanted to improve Internet security is unimportant. The fact remains that in this instance, legitimate and non-legitimate users were treated equally. Still, as Microsoft verified, some of the more popular key codes were once again being blacklisted. What keys needed to be changed? Microsoft made it easy to find out just by visiting their Web site. (See Figure D.10.)

Figure D.10 Windows Validation

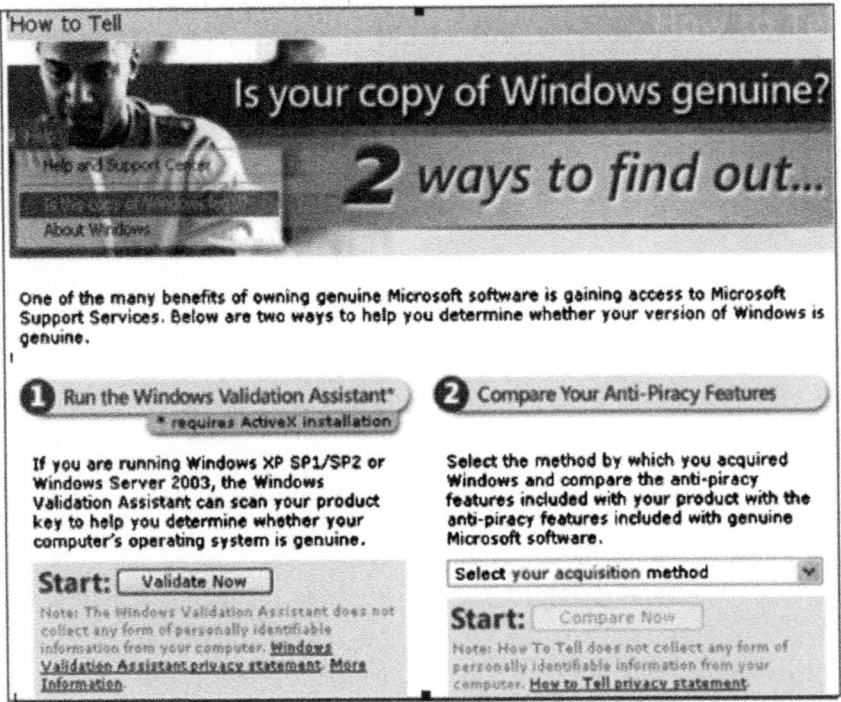

Hitting **Validate Now** with the "wrong" key brings up the following message: (See Figure D.11.)

Figure D.11 Invalid Software

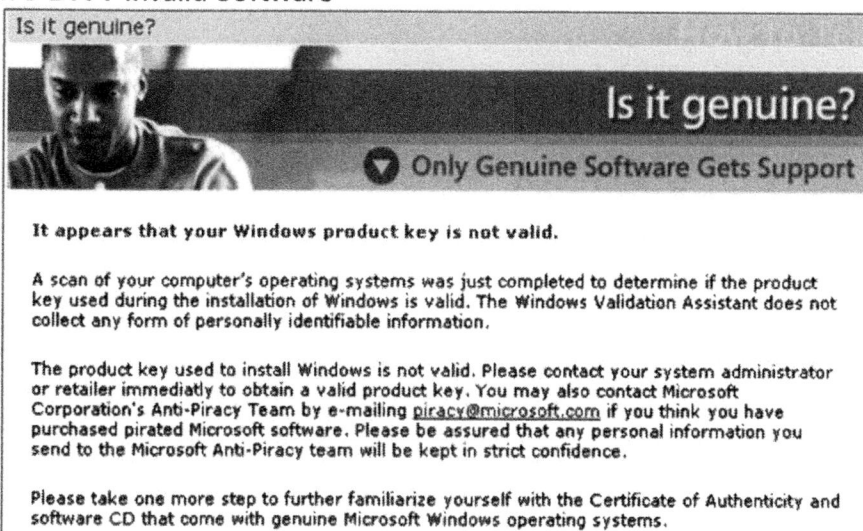

The "right" key is congratulated. (See Figure D.12.)

Figure D.12 Genuine Operating System

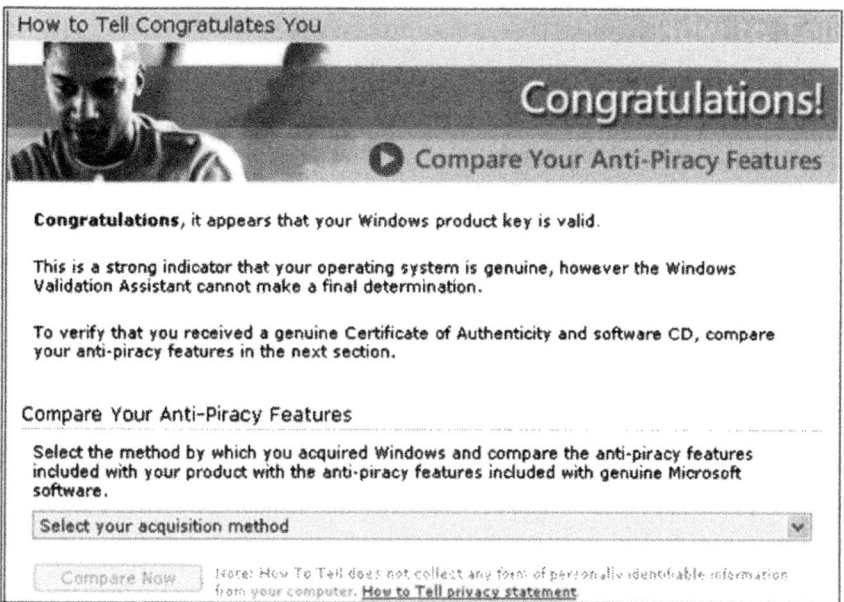

Although every company is entitled to protect its copyrighted software, even Microsoft admits that:

> "All intellectual property protection technologies will be cracked at some point—it's just a matter of time. The measure of success is not completely stopping software piracy, which is probably an unattainable goal. Success is more likely to be measured in increased awareness of the terms of the license agreement and increased license compliance."

Not all software piracy can be stopped, but there is a wide gap between 100 percent security and complete neglect. Reducing theft by making unauthorized use more difficult is a worthwhile and achievable goal. Other companies are experimenting with the same type of product activation to secure their software (e.g., Symantec's Norton Antivirus 2004).

Other Product Activation Examples

Pirated copies of Norton antivirus 2003 have been being widely circulated, including patches for extending the update subscription service. Not satisfied with this situation, Symantec went the Microsoft route with its 2004 antivirus release. As with Microsoft's WPA scheme, Norton's activation code is partially based on the computer's actual hardware components, thus making each installation one of a kind. Once installed, the software had to be activated within 15 days. For the pirates, the important thing, as always, is cracking the "latest and greatest" software. What the program actually does is almost irrelevant.

Almost as soon as the program was released, downloads appeared on many crack sites, complete with a Norton 2004 equivalent of the blue list key generator and detailed instructions. Program activation was cracked. Implementing the crack, however, takes a bit more work than previous versions, so there are bound to be fewer illegal installations. (See Figure D.14.)

Figure D.13 Activation Generator

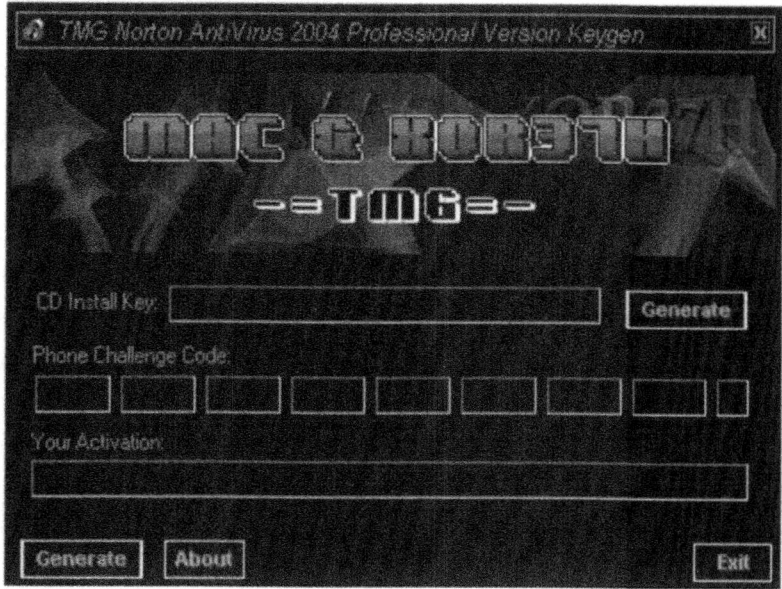

Another program that went the product activation route was ABBYY FIneReader v.7.0, an Optical Character Recognition (OCR) program. As with Microsoft and Symantec, they also claim " special protection technology is used to protect ABBYY products from illegal copying and distribution." Guess what? A pirated key and activation generator along with detailed instructions appeared within days of the new version's release.

Product Activation Bugs

It is clear that product activation, like most anti-piracy measures, has serious shortcomings. In fact, sometimes a company's effort to protect their software backfires. Symantec finally admitted that some of its legitimate customers were being asked to enter an activation code every time their computers were rebooted, and that eventually the software ceased to function.

In a similar vein, Intuit, the manufacturer of TurboTax, tried to implement a product activation scheme in their 2002 product line. The goal was to allow only one installation and to eliminate sharing. Customers could get an activation number from Intuit either by phone or over the

Internet, which would tie the program to their particular computer. It might have worked perfectly in theory, but many customers experienced installation difficulties. Even worse, product activation incorporated a registration/copy protection scheme called C-dilla. Many TurboTax users were incensed to have such an intrusive and insidious piece of spyware installed on their machine without their knowledge. Although Intuit tried to downplay its significance by claiming that C-dilla only checked for a valid license file and didn't gather or transmit any personal information, their arguments did little to appease angry users. Having no easy option to uninstall the program only added to the level of discontent, and word spread that this product was to be avoided at all costs. Intuit called it a "misunderstanding" and tried to debunk complaints on their Web site. Nonetheless, whatever the real facts were, the "battle" progressed, Intuit lost sales, and potential customers defected to other products. Eventually, Intuit stated that it would skip activation in 2003 versions, and is attempting to regain market share.

While creating hassles for legitimate customers, the so-called "crack proof" product activation scheme actually inspired pirates to defeat it. The same thing happened when the Motion Picture Association of American claimed that DVDs couldn't be pirated. Basically, any resident security system (i.e., one where the security resides solely in the product itself) is prone to being cracked. Nonetheless, it appears that the trend toward some type of product activation will continue.

On-line Verification/ Server Authentication

Another method of securing software is employing on-line (or server) authentication. Essentially, the program periodically connects to the manufacturer's Web site where the user's registration can be verified against an authorized user database. If the registration code isn't confirmed, the program can be disabled. To protect against a legitimate registration code being shared, simultaneous logons or repeated access attempts from a variety of different Internet Protocol (IP) addresses usually indicate that the code has been leaked. Compromised codes are generally blacklisted and are sometimes accompanied by an intimidating message such as "illegal software has been detected and your IP address has been recorded."

Needless to say, the pirates have also circumvented this type of security. Sometimes, setting a firewall to block access to the program's home server is all that it takes. Other methods involve patching the program to prevent it from trying to connect to a server. Most pirates have learned to assume that all programs will call their home server. Therefore, they either disconnect from the Internet or block the program with a firewall before opening it for the first time. However, there are some programs that are a lot more sophisticated. They not only try to connect with a server, but they "look" for a proper response.

This verification method only works where a program has to be online as part of its normal operation (e.g., browsers, newsreaders, download managers, or any program requiring an Internet connection). Word processors, graphic and video editors, games, diagnostic tools, and numerous other programs that can operate without a connection, are basically undetectable.

Booby Traps

It is inevitable that many cracks don't work. Sometimes, however, the detection of bogus code causes a program to trigger an attack. Some of the more minor annoyances include:

- Warning messages and labels
- Redirecting the browser to a "gotcha" page
- Appearing to register the program, while actually disabling it
- Reverting to a time-limited trial or demo program
- Refusing to accept an older working version and serial
- Uninstalling the program
- Making it (nearly) impossible to reinstall the program

Things can get worse. Some programs are "booby-trapped" to inflict nasty problems by:

- Rebooting the computer
- Rendering the computer unable to reboot
- Threatening to reformat the hard drive
- Reformatting the hard drive

It's not a bad idea to "investigate before you install." Because the following tips apply to any computer user, they bear repeating:

- Scan all downloads for viruses, Trojans, worms, and so on.
- Use a hardware and/or software firewall
- Read posts and reviews pertaining to a particular program before installing
- Use a system restore program
- Back up everything

Commercial Software Protection Systems

Creating software is a highly technical and specialized full-time job. So is protecting it from crackers. It's a tradeoff, because any effort that goes into protecting a program is effort that is taken away from working on the products themselves. And since there are third-party protection systems available to help secure copyrighted software, many companies don't waste time trying to develop their own; they leave that to the experts. This permits their developers to concentrate on developing and improving the product.

Software companies are mainly concerned about their evaluation (shareware) programs being used beyond their expiration dates or a cracker converting them into full operating versions. They certainly don't want cracked full versions distributed on the Internet. With names like

ASProtect and SoftwarePassport (Armadillo), these and a score of other third-party software protection systems help software developer's guard against copying and shareware misuse.

Among other things, these programs allow the software developer to set the number of times a trial or unregistered program will run or how certain features will operate before its license expires. Using proprietary compression algorithms, these programs also place "hidden" integrity checking keys in the operating system's registry, which are all but impossible for a typical user to locate, modify, or remove. Short of reformatting the hard drive, these entries prevent users from extending a trial program's operating time by altering the clock or reinstalling the program. In addition, these programs usually contain countermeasures against debugger and disassembly tools, thus making reverse engineering more difficult.

The Pirates Don't Give Up Easily

For the most part, these systems do an excellent job preventing the average computer user from bypassing shareware restrictions. However, they are a lot less effective against the sophisticated cracker. One of the downsides of using a commercial protection scheme is that its methodology becomes well known, which makes it easier to circumvent the protection, and sooner or later the product appears on the Internet for all to use.

As part of the pirate's arsenal, there is a specialized program circulating on the crack sites that reportedly locates and removes the registry entries written by these programs. (See Figure D.14.)

Figure D.14 Locating and Removing Registry Entries

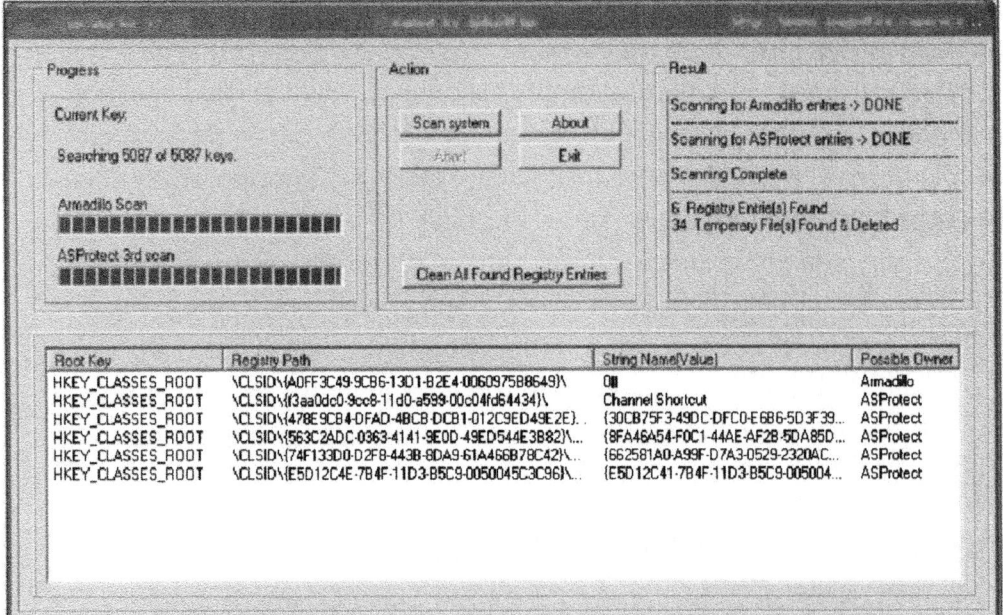

This tool is intended for removing entries that were installed with the program. However, a host of aboveboard registry monitoring programs can be used in its place. These programs can take a "snapshot" of the operating system's registry immediately before and after an application program has been installed. By comparing snapshots, any added entries will likely "belong" to the newly installed program. If the trial is later removed, and if a subsequent reinstallation is unsuccessful, the previously identified entries could be easily located and deleted.

It would be inaccurate to assume that the only reason to remove these entries is to "buy" additional trial operating time by reinstalling the program. Even if cheating is not contemplated, many computer users don't care to have unused remnants of programs remaining after a program has been uninstalled.

There are many programs that do not place hidden entries and that can be removed in their totality (e.g., some antivirus programs come with a one-year update subscription). If the program is removed and reinstalled, a full year's worth of updates will automatically result. It is not unusual to totally reformat a computer once or twice a , and start over with a clean install. Likewise, hard drives have a nasty habit of failing, taking all of their installed programs along with them. At that point, any trial program can be installed again and any program subscription will start anew.

Reporting Violators

More Web sites are including prominent references to piracy. Microsoft, Ahead Software (Nero), Symantec (Norton Antivirus), Adobe, Macromedia, and many others are devoting entire pages to piracy, including online reporting forms, e-mail addresses, and toll-free phone numbers. Reminiscent of "Big Brother," computer users are being encouraged to turn in anyone whom they suspect are "in violation." It is scary, especially considering the headaches that an innocent user might be subjected to if someone decides to report him.

The BSA, the Software & Information Industry Association (SIIA), and the Federation Against Software Theft (FAST) all have reporting sections on their Web sites. The SIIA even offers a reward of up to $50,000. These sites and many manufacturers' Web sites make pirating sound like the most heinous crime you could possibly commit. While most people know that obtaining unauthorized software is wrong, many are unaware of the harm piracy does and the likely consequences if caught. Educating computer users is a big part of the anti-piracy "plan."

What Else Can Be Done?

Besides integrating commercial protection software into their products or trying to come up with their own protection schemes, there are other common sense things software developers can do to make their products more secure. A program does not have to be totally crack proof; any amount of protection will help reduce piracy and enhance sales.

Reason for Shareware

One thing companies can do is to focus on what their shareware is intended to do. It should convince trial users that they want or need to buy the product. They need to convert potential customers into actual customers, but not "give away the farm" in the process. Most of the time, a trial program is identical to the full program, even if some of its features are restricted. Trial versions need to be different from full versions. If the code is not there in the first place, then even if a cracker succeeds in breaking the trial programs, they still will not be able to turn it into the full version.

Those users who are interested in evaluating the product with an eye toward purchasing it probably will not be turned off if the product is not fully functional. On the other hand, those users intent on stealing will probably not be nearly as interested with less than a full version. Deciding what the optimum amount of trial functionality should be is based on each program's unique function and its intended audience. Limiting a trial's functionality does not mean that a cracked full version will not eventually find its way onto the Web; however, there is no reason to make it any easier.

Identify the Customer

Companies should also consider what kind of customers they are targeting. For example, if they are marketing mainly to commercial customers, they can easily offer to send them full evaluation software. Most businesses are very aware of the possible consequences of using stolen software and are unlikely to do so. The company's name, address, and other personalized information could also be included in the splash screen, serial numbers, and printed on the disc, which would help minimize wholesale distribution because it would be instantly obvious that the software were stolen.

Security is more difficult if the software is being marketed to home users, as they are the ones most likely to use pirated software. That is where the limited trials come in. The companies should concentrate on marketing to those users most likely to buy their products. Likewise, companies and anti-piracy groups should concentrate their efforts on shutting down the most popular Web sites that host pirated software. In other words, go after the source. Even if only a few dozen sites were closed, it would put a big dent in the overall problem, and would make the operators of the other sites "sit up and take notice." Going after the thousands of individual computer users who dabble in using pirated software detracts from the real solutions.

Product IDs

Being able to remotely and positively identify each and every computer is probably the best way to mitigate software piracy. It would enable all of the installed software to be tied to a specific computer. Unfortunately, there is no standard method of uniquely identifying an individual computer (excluding the modem or network card, which transmits the computer's IP address). However, the industry came close to achieving such an ID reporting scheme several years ago. When Intel included an electronically readable Processor Serial Number (PSN) in its Pentium III processors, there was such a huge public outcry over privacy concerns that Intel dropped the PSN idea starting with its Pentium 4 processors in 2000.

A processor's PSN is not the only way to identify a computer, which is essentially what Product Activation is about. However, with the present activation scheme, no personally identifiable information is provided. The hash string that is generated from the computer's unique hardware configuration is anonymous, and it is from that string that the activation key is created. However, there is no technical reason that would prevent the same information that is gathered for creating the hash string from being transmitted intact to a company's Web site. That unique code could be stored in a database and forever associated with a software download. For that matter, all of the software on the computer could also be identified and tied to the computer.

Unfortunately, if the computer's hardware were changed sufficiently, new permissions would have to be obtained from all the vendors of the different programs. If the computer itself were replaced, new keys would have to be obtained from all of the program manufacturers in order to do a fresh installation. The trouble it takes to contact one company about obtaining a new key is compounded many times over when several different companies must be contacted. As product activation becomes more popular, that prospect is becoming more of a certainty.

In all fairness, some companies routinely permit a new activation without explanation after a "reasonable" period of time, such as during the initial installation. However, if you are unlucky enough to have a dead computer, you might also be unlucky enough not to fall into that grace period. Even from a non-technical viewpoint, product activation is far from perfect.

Index

Syngress: *The Definition of a Serious Security Library*

Syn·gress (sin-gres): *noun, sing.* Freedom from risk or danger; safety. See *security*.

Inside the SPAM Cartel
Spammer-X

Authored by a former spammer, this is a methodical, technically explicit expose of the inner workings of the SPAM economy. Readers will be shocked by the sophistication and sheer size of this underworld. "Inside the Spam Cartel" is a great read for people with even a casual interest in cyber-crime. In addition, it includes a level of technical detail that will clearly attract its core audience of technology junkies and security professionals.

ISBN: 1-93226-686-0

Price: $49.95 US $72.95 CAN

Phishing Exposed
Lance James, Secure Science Corporation, Dave Jevans (Foreword)

If you have ever received a phish, become a victim of a phish, or manage the security of a major e-commerce or financial site, then you need to read this book. The author of this book delivers the unconcealed techniques of phishers including their evolving patterns, and how to gain the upper hand against the ever-accelerating attacks they deploy. Filled with elaborate and unprecedented forensics, Phishing Exposed details techniques that system administrators, law enforcement, and fraud investigators can exercise and learn more about their attacker and their specific attack methods, enabling risk mitigation in many cases before the attack occurs.

ISBN: 1-59749-030-X

Price: $49.95 US $69.95 CAN

Google Hacking for Penetration Testers
Johnny Long, Foreword by Ed Skoudis

What many users don't realize is that the deceptively simple components that make Google so easy to use are the same features that generously unlock security flaws for the malicious hacker. Vulnerabilities in website security can be discovered through Google hacking, techniques applied to the search engine by computer criminals, identity thieves, and even terrorists to uncover secure information. This book beats Google hackers to the punch, equipping web administrators with penetration testing applications to ensure their site is invulnerable to a hacker's search.

ISBN: 1-93183-636-1

Price: $44.95 U.S. $65.95 CAN

SYNGRESS®

Printed and bound by CPI Group (UK) Ltd, Croydon, CR0 4YY

08/06/2025

01896868-0020